The Antimafia

The Antimafia

Italy's Fight against Organized Crime

Alison Jamieson

Foreword by

Luciano Violante
Speaker, Italian Chamber of Deputies
Chairman, Parliamentary Antimafia Commission, 1992–94

364.106
J32a

First published in Great Britain 2000 by
MACMILLAN PRESS LTD
Houndmills, Basingstoke, Hampshire RG21 6XS and London
Companies and representatives throughout the world

A catalogue record for this book is available from the British Library.

ISBN 0–333–71900–X hardcover
ISBN 0–333–80158–X paperback

First published in the United States of America 2000 by
ST. MARTIN'S PRESS, INC.,
Scholarly and Reference Division,
175 Fifth Avenue, New York, N.Y. 10010

ISBN 0–312–22911–9

Library of Congress Cataloging-in-Publication Data
Jamieson, Alison.
The antimafia : Italy's fight against organized crime / Alison Jamieson.
p.   cm.
Includes bibliographical references and index.
ISBN 0–312–22911–9 (cloth)
1. Mafia—Italy.   I. Title.
HV6453.I83M3536   1999
364.1'06'0945—dc21   99–39488
                                              CIP

This book is printed on paper suitable for recycling and made from fully managed and sustained forest sources.

10   9   8   7   6   5   4   3   2   1
09   08   07   06   05   04   03   02   01   00

Printed and bound in Great Britain by
Antony Rowe Ltd, Chippenham, Wiltshire

For Nigel

Contents

List of Tables

List of Plates

Plate 1. Judge Giovanni Falcone. (Adnkronos Photos)

Plate 2. The conference on 12 May 1992 in Rome at which Giovanni Falcone spoke in public for the last time. On the podium, left to right, are Giovanni Falcone, Daniele Ripeto (chair, adnkronos), Professor Francesco Bruno (criminologist), the author, Henry Marsden (Director, Office of Research, Office of National Drug Control Policy, Executive Office of the President, The White House). (Adnkronos Photos)

Plate 3. Giovanni Falcone, immediately after receiving an anonymous letter at the conference in Rome on 12 May 1992. (Adnkronos Photos)

Plate 4. The motorway at Capaci, with the bulletproof Fiat Croma in which Giovanni Falcone, his wife Francesca and bodyguard Giuseppe Costanzo were travelling when the bomb exploded. (*Polizia Scientifica*)

Plate 5. Via D'Amelio, Palermo, scene of the car bomb which killed Paolo Borsellino and bodyguards Agostino Catelano, Wlater Cusina, Vincenzo Li Muli, Claudio Traina and Emanuela Loi. (*Polizia Scientifica*)

Plate 6. Judge Paolo Borsellino. (Ansa Photos)

Plate 7. Mafia boss Salvatore (Totò) Riina photographed just after his arrest in Palermo on the morning of 15 January 1993. (Ansa Photos)

Plate 8. Father Luigi Ciotti with friends at a ceremony to commemorate victims of the Mafia. (Ansa Photos)

Plate 9. Document from American Consulate General. (Antimafia Commission 1976)

Foreword

Luciano Violante
Speaker of the Chamber of Deputies and
Chairman of Antimafia Commission 1992–94

When people describe the Mafia they often use terms such as 'octopus' or 'cancer'. Nothing could be further from the truth. The use of these expressions makes the Mafia seem mysterious, omnipotent, uncatchable – precisely the image that the *mafiosi* want people to have about their organization. As this book shows, the reality is rather different. The Mafia is composed of men, arms, money and political relationships. We need to arrest those men, destroy their arms, confiscate that money and break up those political relationships. The Italian experience shows that it *is* possible, but also teaches us that it will take more time, as well as an exceptional degree of international cooperation, before we can claim a final victory. When the Mafia goes through moments of crisis, it hides – *si ingrotta*, as they say in Palermo – and waits for better times to come. For this reason one should not misinterpret the Mafia's silence as its defeat. Nor should one have a 'national' vision of the Mafia-type organizations, since they exist and are active in most of the developed world as well as in developing countries.

In the past, countries like Japan, the United States, Italy and Turkey had their own Mafias which operated prevalently within national boundaries. This is no longer the case. The mafia groups have become transnational organizations, and therefore have an operational capacity which transcends national boundaries. This capacity derives from the intensification of the international movement of goods traditionally traded by organized crime such as drugs and arms. For arms as for drugs, the country of final destination is different from that of production. To reach the country of destination, consignments of drugs and arms must transit many other countries and cross their national boundaries. Trading arrangements involve the need to use the legal sector (banks, finance houses, customs formalities) and to maintain relationships with criminal groups of different countries. These commercial necessities have created solid international relations between all the most dangerous criminal organizations.

To the two traditional criminal markets of drugs and arms a third has now been added – that of people. The market is made up of refugees from war zones, of immigrants in search of work that they cannot find at home and of the international trade in prostitutes. Trafficking in people has become the new version of the old slave trade.

Like any legal multinational company, transnational crime groups are capable of establishing men, offices and activities in different countries depending on the profits to be made, the degree of impermeability to regulation and the possibilities of expansion. The origin of this phenomenon can be traced back to the change of geo-strategic conditions around the world. Since the collapse of the Soviet system and the consequent expansion of global markets, money, goods and people have circulated with a rapidity and facility which were once unthinkable. Civic values, honest citizens, business entrepreneurs, students, academics and those who work in the world of finance – all move freely. But criminal cultures also move freely, as do the members of the large criminal groups and the professionals – the lawyers, accountants and financiers – who are fully aware that by managing the affairs of the criminal organizations they are breaking all deontological and juridical rules.

One effect of transnationalization is the ability to move the centre of criminal activities to countries where conditions are more favourable and, conversely, to move away temporarily from countries where conditions are unfavourable. This analysis leads to three conclusions. The first is that we should not feel particularly reassured when the Mafia goes silent. It is possible that the organization has temporarily moved its business centre to another country. The second is that without major international cooperation the mafia organizations will never be defeated. Whereas serious crime is organized, our countries' response is still disorganized. The third conclusion is that a Mafia of such dimensions must have at its disposal large quantities of money; when organized crime has a mass of accumulated capital its principal weapon ceases to be murder and starts to be corruption. For groups with this type of economic means, corruption is a low-cost, low-risk instrument of great utility, both in the present and for the future. Whereas murder eliminates an obstacle, corruption creates an accomplice: the corrupted person inside the state system is a port of entry which is always open for the criminal organization. Those who have been corrupted once will be corruptible a second time, and in any event will always be vulnerable to blackmail.

In every country, organized crime tries to create an area of permanent complicity within the public sector by means of organized corruption. Corruption serves to eliminate competition in legal business such as public works projects and the management of public services, and to hinder investigation of illicit business such as drug trafficking or the management of prostitution rings. The corruption practised by organized crime aims not so much to obtain favours as to bind a public official to crime in a permanent way. Thus the main object of the exercise is not the favour itself, but the individual, in the form of a public functionary. Organized crime bosses know that sooner or later they are bound to need a policeman, a judge, a clerk in the Finance Ministry and so on, and therefore they seek out a relationship with that individual. In the language of the Sicilian Mafia, public officials are divided into those who are *non-approachable* and those who are *approachable*. The former are the honest ones. The latter move from being *approachable* to being *approached* and then, after a period of increasing efforts on the part of the Mafia, they become '*cosa nostra*', our thing, completely in the hands of the criminal group.

Corruption is more widespread than one would think. The many national frontiers that drugs, arms and people cross to reach the country of destination from that of provenance would not be so easily overcome were it not for the functioning of a well-oiled system of corruption within many of these countries. Similarly, money laundering would not have the colossal dimensions it has today without public connivance, which certainly does not come free of charge. The factors which facilitate corruption are a lack of attention on the part of public authorities, the inefficiencies of the state, confusing legislation, and a lack of sense of state within the population and in public officials.

Not only is Alison Jamieson's book exceptionally well documented, informing us as much about the history of the Mafia as it does about the history of the Antimafia, but it has the additional merit of describing the important transition now under way from a national strategy of antimafia fight to an international strategy. Big international organizations such as the United Nations, the World Bank, the International Monetary Fund and the G8 are all concerned with the fight against the Mafia and its methods, against corruption and the laundering of illicit assets, and view them as both problems of justice and as problems of democracy. The large mafia organizations have as their objective the construction of a form of *global criminal system* which in the next few decades could become the single greatest threat to our liberty. The most advanced nations are working together to prepare a system of prevention and global response. Whoever reaches their objective first will win.

Alison Jamieson's fine book makes no prophecies, but shows us that victory *is* possible, not only with the instruments of coercion, but also by utilizing the extraordinary instrument of education towards legality and good citizenship – as we in Italy are trying to do.

Luciano Violante, 12 July 1999

Acknowledgements

This book could not have been written without the extraordinary generosity of many overworked individuals who shared their time and experiences with me. In particular I would like to thank national antimafia prosecutor Pier Luigi Vigna; the chief prosecutor of Palermo Gian Carlo Caselli and assistant prosecutor Gioacchino Natoli; the chief prosecutor of Caltanissetta Giovanni Tinebra; the Juvenile Court prosecutors Maria Cristina Randazzo in Palermo and Piero Gaeta in Palmi.

I am grateful to the Questor of Palermo Antonio Manganelli; to the head of the Palermo Flying Squad Guido Marino; also to one of his officers, a fellow Briton, who gave me a memorable tour of Palermo.

I thank Leoluca Orlando, Mayor of Palermo, for his time and consideration.

Special thanks go to Umberto Santino and Anna Puglisi of the Sicilian Documentation Centre for their friendship and assistance over the years; likewise to journalists Franco Viviano and Alessandra Ziniti who helped me to understand what really goes on in Sicily.

A warm thank-you to Father Cosimo Scordato and to his assistants in the San Saverio Centre in Palermo for opening my eyes to what individual commitment can achieve.

I thank the Director of the Scientific Police in Rome, Dr Giuseppe Maddalena and his colleagues, in particular Dr Gianni Vadalà, for providing invaluable assistance and remarkable photographs.

I am particularly grateful to the family members of victims of the Mafia who shared what must have been acutely painful memories with me. They include Michele Costa, Maria Falcone, Rita Borsellino and my friend of many years, Giovanna Terranova. The women who have found their own ways of continuing the work of their murdered relatives were a direct inspiration to write this book. As were the founders of the association Palermo Year One.

I am grateful to Luciano Violante, Speaker of the Chamber of Deputies, for recalling his experiences as Chairman of the Antimafia Commission and to his assistants Antonella, Simona and Tiziana for their help over many years.

I thank Ottaviano Del Turco, current Chairman of the Parliamentary Antiamafia Commission; also Enzo Ciconte, consultant to the Commission, who was unstinting in his time and efforts to help me obtain documentation and who shared his encylopaedic knowledge of Calabria with me.

To Alfredo Nunzi, formerly with the UN Crime Division in Vienna and now Deputy Director of the International Institute of Higher Studies in Criminal Sciences in Siracusa, my warmest thanks for legal expertise and documentation.

I am indebted to Emanuele Marotta, Deputy Director of Europol, whose knowledge of Italian and international law-enforcement issues has been invaluable to me.

Thanks also to Peter Waterworth, First Secretary at the British Embassy in Rome, for advice on UK law.

I also want to thank several senior law-enforcement figures in the UK for helping to give an international perspective to an essentially Italian study – to Simon Goddard of the National Criminal Intelligence Service, to Joe Gorry, formerly Drugs and Organized Crime Liaison Officer in the British Embassy in Rome, and to Graham Saltmarsh of the National Crime Squad.

I would like to pay tribute to the memory of Richard Clutterbuck, whom I have greatly missed since his death in January 1998. He 'went out in harness' as he always hoped he would.

I thank my parents for all their love and support and remember in particular my mother, who died in April 1999.

Finally, I owe a huge debt of gratitude to my husband Nigel, who not only put up with my distractions and absences during the book's preparation but patiently read and commented on every chapter of the unedited draft – a real labour of love.

Introduction

On the morning of 12 May 1992, Sicilian judge Giovanni Falcone had just delivered a paper to a conference audience in Rome on the possible developments of international organized crime and the illegal drugs trade when he found a note beside his briefcase. Unsigned, it claimed that the Italian State was co-responsible with the Mafia for the expansion of drug consumption because it had allowed heroin use to spread among young people during the years of student rebellion, a convenient 'tool' for reducing levels of aggressiveness against state institutions. Implicit in the bizarre message was a warning – Falcone should beware of the duplicity of a state which pretended to fight the Mafia but in reality was colluding with it. From my adjacent seat on the podium I saw Falcone's face tighten with anger as he read the note, rose and strode out of the hall to confer with associates, returning an hour later. He refused to be drawn on the significance of the note at the time, but its contents and the security lapse that had permitted its delivery clearly disturbed him. Before he left for his office in the Justice Ministry, where for a year he had been Director of the Office of Criminal Affairs, we talked briefly, and he agreed to help me with an article on the use of state's witnesses in Mafia trials. The meeting never took place, for eleven days later he was dead.

Falcone was no stranger to threats and warnings, and had survived more than one attempt on his life by *Cosa Nostra*, the Sicilian Mafia.[a] He had learned to live with the round-the-clock protection of bodyguards and armoured vehicles, the impossibility of eating unobserved in a restaurant or of taking a stroll through the streets of his beloved Palermo, and with the knowledge that, however long he lived, his name would always be on *Cosa Nostra*'s hit list. What caused him greater anguish was the suspicion that he had enemies within the State, whose servant he was and in whose value he profoundly believed. Paradoxically, he seemed more secure in his dealings with *Cosa Nostra* than in his relationship with the political and professional classes around him. He once commented,

---

[a]   The word Mafia is used generically to mean Italian organized crime. Individual Mafia groups are referred to as *Cosa Nostra* (Sicily), the *Camorra* (Campania), the *'Ndrangheta* (Calabria) and the United Holy Crown (Apulia).

I believe in the State, and think it is precisely the lack of sense of State, of State as an inner value, that generates these distortions which are present in the Sicilian soul: the dualism between society and State, the falling back on the family, the group, the clan [...] What is the origin of the Mafia if not a mixture of *anomie* and primitive violence? Of that Mafia which, essentially, is nothing more than a need for order and therefore for State.[1]

Falcone's technical brilliance and prodigious memory, his instinctive understanding of *Cosa Nostra*'s language and symbolic gesture and his ability to perceive the international as well as the national consequences of *Cosa Nostra*'s operations brought him renown at home and abroad but also provoked jealousy among his peers. In the four years from 1987 to 1991 he was twice passed over for promotion, rejected in his candidature for the Superior Judicial Council, the judges' self-governing body, sidelined in his investigations by his chief, and was forced to watch as attempts to delegitimize his work were given credence. In February 1991 he accepted the position of Director of Criminal Affairs offered him by Justice Minister Claudio Martelli, and transferred to Rome. His friends made efforts to dissuade him, fearing that his political naïvety would make him vulnerable to manipulation by Martelli and his colleagues in the Socialist party, at that time under the leadership of Bettino Craxi. In truth, Falcone's career had reached an *impasse* in Sicily and his isolation from the judicial hierarchy had increased his concern for his own safety. In his interview-autobiography, published in 1991, he observed,

You are killed generally because you are alone or else because you have got into a game that is too big. You are often killed because you don't have the necessary alliances, because you are without support. In Sicily, the Mafia strikes the servants of the State that the State has not succeeded in protecting.[2]

If judge Falcone's move to Rome was initially seen as a personal defeat, a year later that perception had changed. The Office of Criminal Affairs, traditionally a moribund backwater of the Ministry, had become a powerhouse of innovation and strategic planning. Antimafia policies were being developed in a medium- and long-term perspective, taking into account the internationalization of organized crime and its activities. Falcone worked towards three main objectives – the increased professionalization of the investigative forces, the internationalization of criminal investigations and of legal norms to fight organized crime, and the means to identify, seize and confiscate illicit wealth wherever it might be concealed. At the same time he stimulated political momentum for the creation of a national antimafia prosecution office which would give impetus and coordination to organized crime investigations around the country and link up with international investigations as appropriate. Parliament voted approval for the *Direzione Nazionale Antimafia* in November 1991.

Falcone began to enjoy life in the capital, where he felt a greater liberty of movement. Occasionally he left his bodyguards behind when he went to the cinema or to a *trattoria* to eat with friends. He came to respect Claudio Martelli, in whom he perceived a genuine commitment to the antimafia fight, and under his guidance Martelli's criminal justice policies became more incisive. Although Falcone was Martelli's preferred candidate to head the new national antimafia prosecution office, his appointment depended on the approval of the Superior Judicial Council (*Consiglio Superiore della Magistratura*, CSM), whose members were divided over the choice of candidate. But in May 1992 the haggling was finally drawing to an end, and Falcone's appointment a virtual certainty.[3]

Falcone's 36-year-old wife Francesca was also a judge, attached to the Palermo Court of Assizes. She had requested a transfer to Rome on three occasions but had been turned down by the CSM on the grounds that she was too young to have priority on the waiting list for a transfer from Sicily. Falcone had vented his frustration at the bureaucratic obstacles to his wife's transfer during a dinner in Rome with friends on his birthday, 18 May, and had commented on how easy a target he had become, returning as he did to Palermo almost every weekend.

On the afternoon of Saturday 23 May Giovanni and Francesca Falcone flew from Rome to Palermo's Punta Raisi airport in a small aircraft provided by the domestic security service, SISDE. On their arrival an eight-man bodyguard squad took over responsibility for the half-hour journey by road to the couple's apartment in the city centre. Helicopter surveillance of Falcone's route along the motorway, the only main road between the airport and the city centre, had been discontinued some weeks before on economic grounds. As often happened, Falcone decided to take the wheel of the white bulletproof Fiat Croma, and drove with Francesca beside him and his driver, Giuseppe Costanzo, in the back seat. As the three-car convoy approached the exit for the town of Capaci a few minutes before 6 pm, a massive bomb exploded in a culvert under the motorway, gouging a crater 3 metres deep and 14 across. Costanzo's last memory before the explosion was of Falcone asking him to accompany Francesca into their apartment because he wanted to drive on with the rest of the squad, and of watching in alarm as Falcone withdrew his (Costanzo's) keys from the ignition and inserted his own while the car was in motion, reducing its speed abruptly to cruise for several seconds with the engine off. The sudden slowing of the convoy's speed caused the lead car to take the brunt of the explosion, which catapulted the vehicle into the air, over the opposite carriageway and into a field 60 metres away. The occupants, Antonio Montinaro, Rocco Di Cillo and Vito Schifani, were killed instantly. The second vehicle virtually imploded on the carriageway, causing Giovanni and Francesca Falcone severe internal injuries from which they died a short time later. Giuseppe Costanzo survived, albeit with permanent disabilities, while the four bodyguards in the third vehicle escaped with minor injuries.

The attack at Capaci sent Italy into a state of shock, all the greater because it had occurred in an institutional vacuum. President Francesco Cossiga had resigned immediately after the general election of 5 April to allow his successor to initiate negotiations on a future government, but after 15 ballots, Parliament had not yet voted a new president into office. Italy had no Head of State, Government or Prime Minister, and its largest political party, the Christian Democratic Party (DC), was leaderless. The new antimafia police force created by law six months previously was barely functional, while the national antimafia prosecution service which Falcone helped to create and had hoped to lead was stagnating in the wait for a chief prosecutor to be appointed.

After the funeral of his boyhood friend and colleague, judge Paolo Borsellino returned to his post as assistant chief prosecutor in Palermo. He found a form of serenity through his work, and kept telling his family that he had no time for outside activities, that there was not enough time for what he had to do. They thought he was referring to the burden of work, not realizing that he was counting the days left to him to live. He intensified his contacts with a number of newly 'turned' state's witnesses through whom he was piecing together the latest strategy and tactics of *Cosa Nostra;* at the same time he pursued his own enquiries into the Capaci attack, although the investigation had automatically passed to Caltanissetta, since a prosecution office cannot investigate crimes concerning its own judges. For this reason Borsellino himself requested a transfer to Caltanissetta, although he knew that he had little chance of its being approved as there was no vacant position at his level of seniority.

With Falcone dead, it was widely believed that Borsellino – the only antimafia judge comparable to him in experience and ability – would be appointed national antimafia prosecutor. But he had been opposed in principle to the establishment of the national prosecution office, fearing that under any direction but Falcone's it might become an instrument of political interference with the independence of the judiciary. Privately, he expressed doubts about his own suitability for the job, which he felt Falcone had created to his own specifications. He was also under pressure from his colleagues, who were convinced that without him antimafia investigations in Sicily would lose impetus, to remain in Palermo. His family was told later that a letter inviting him to apply for the post of national antimafia prosecutor had been sent, although it was never found. Others believe that he was considering the move and had selected one of his closest collaborators to accompany him.

Whether he went to Rome or stayed in Sicily, Borsellino was the greatest remaining threat to *Cosa Nostra*'s activities. Like Falcone, he was gifted with exceptional intuition and recall of detail, together with the capacity to inspire the trust of state's witnesses and to ensure that their testimonies were sufficiently corroborated to be usable in a court of law. For *Cosa Nostra*, to have killed Falcone without killing Borsellino would have been, in a sense, to leave business unfinished.

A review of Paolo Borsellino's security arrangements in the light of the Capaci attack was undertaken: a police report drawn up in early July noted 15 separate locations in Palermo to be kept under surveillance, including his mother's apartment in via D'Amelio, but no parking ban or special security measures were adopted there. In mid-July, Borsellino learned from an informant that the materials for the bomb intended to kill him had arrived in Palermo. He mentioned this to a priest friend but apparently did not insist on extra protection. Some years afterwards his sister Rita explained, 'Paolo always expected other people to do their duty in the way that he always did his.'[4]

Just before 5 pm on Sunday 19 July, 55 days after the Capaci attack, Borsellino's motorcade parked outside the apartment block in the quiet Palermo cul-de-sac where his elderly mother and his sister and family lived. The bodyguard squad was composed of Agostino Catalano, Walter Cusina, Vincenzo Li Muli, Claudio Traina and Emanuela Loi, a young Sardinian police inspectress who had joined the team a few days earlier. The bodyguards fanned out around the entrance as Borsellino walked the few yards from the gate to the main door of the building. He had just rung the doorbell when a Fiat 126 parked at the gateway exploded, blowing him and the five bodyguards literally apart.

For the many thousands of Italians who wept at the horrific scenes of destruction transmitted on television all that Sunday evening, Italy's last hope of winning the battle against the Mafia lay buried under the smoking piles of rubble in via D'Amelio. With the double killing of Falcone and Borsellino, it seemed as if *Cosa Nostra* had stepped into the institutional vacuum, bringing off its *coup d'état* with consummate ease. Indeed, few people would have contradicted judge Antonino Caponnetto, former chief and close friend of the two murdered judges, when he murmured, 'It's the end, it's all over ...' into a journalist's microphone as he arrived in Palermo for Borsellino's funeral.

As events turned out, it was not the end of the antimafia struggle, and Italy succeeded in pulling itself out of the abyss, thanks to an extraordinary mobilization by all sectors of society. Within 12 months, new legislation was in place in vital areas of witness protection and seizure of criminal profits; law-enforcement capabilities had been strengthened, the new investigative police and judicial services were functioning and 19 of the 30 most wanted criminal fugitives had been arrested, including the three highest ranking *Cosa Nostra* bosses, captured after decades on the run. Throughout the country, civic and community associations had sprung up which rejected decades of cohabitation with criminal behaviour, corruption and intimidation in favour of a commitment to legality and good citizenship. The all-party parliamentary Antimafia Commission had broken with precedent by publishing a report on the links between the Mafia and politics in Sicily, and had begun a critical reassessment of means to prevent and repress the phenomenon of organized crime.

Inevitably, the emotive surge which produced such dynamism in the months immediately following the Palermo atrocities could not continue at its initial pace. Successes were undermined by major setbacks. Seven years on, some still believe that the 1992 murders marked the beginning of the end for *Cosa Nostra* and a turning-point in the nation's consciousness. Others, more cynically, feel that the change of attitude was merely cosmetic and that the politicians took a firm stand when it was imperative to do so, salving their consciences with a package of harsh measures to obtain quick results, after which it became electorally inconvenient to maintain a rigorous stance. That, in other words, the hypocrisy of rhetoric rather than action to oppose the Mafia has prevailed. The truth probably lies somewhere between the two.

The aim of this book is to evaluate the successes – and the failures – of Italy's antimafia fight since 1992 and to analyse the impact of the antimafia movement upon the Mafia phenomenon. The different forms of Italy's response to the atrocities of 1992 are broken down into four principal types – political, law enforcement, civic or grassroots and international. All four are necessary for a comprehensive response, but political efforts predominate, since they are the engine of the antimafia movement: they provide the ideological context, legislative framework and resources within which law enforcement must operate; they are the principal stimulus for international cooperation and they serve as facilitators for social and community-based initiatives.

Both Falcone and Borsellino frequently stressed the *reactive* role of their work as magistrates exercising the criminal law in contrast to the *proactive* measures which were equally necessary to deal with a phenomenon as socially pervasive as the Mafia. Borsellino once remarked,

> The suggestion that bringing in more magistrates and police will solve the problem of the Mafia is totally inadequate. If the Mafia pays you, finds and keeps you in work, helps you win contracts, get promotion or run your business, then you won't reject it. The solution to the problem of the Mafia is to make the State work.[5]

The Mafia functions not as an anti-state but as a state-within-a-state, substituting itself for the State in functions such as the maintenance of public order, the use of force, economic regulation and the administration of justice wherever public institutions are weak or absent. According to Falcone, '*Cosa Nostra* has absolutely no interest in setting itself up against the State – but it does have an interest in using all the distortions, the malfunctions and the vacuums of power to insert itself into these vacuums.'[6] The parallel state of the Mafia exacts obedience by the threat or use of violence but it commands respect because it operates in a more efficient and timely way than its institutional counterpart. The Mafia, therefore, is not a product of economic underdevelopment but is a parasite that draws its strength from and aggravates the inadequacies of the parent body – in Borsellino's words, 'not the price of poverty, but the cost of distrust'.[7]

In a perceptive foreword to Blok's classic study of a Sicilian village,[8] Charles Tilly illustrates this concept:

> According to his [Blok's] analysis, *mafia* is in no sense a residue of the lawless past. It is an outgrowth of the particular form that the process of state-formation took in Italy. It grew up precisely because national systems of power expanded without obliterating local systems of power – and the connections between the two were few, fragile, and open to monopoly. [...] Although *mafia* could not have appeared without a measure of state-formation, *mafia* survives because of state formation's arrested development.

To undo the harms of arrested development and to make the State work is the real challenge that Italy's politicians and administrators face at the end of the twentieth century. It calls for good governance at national and local level; the orderly functioning of schools, hospitals, public services and courtrooms in the south as in the north; efficiency, integrity and accountability in public office-holders and transparency in their activities; freedom of competition, and from harassment, for all forms of legal business enterprise. Crucially, there must be an awareness on the part of young people that the Mafia is a suffocating force which retards development and not a dynamic vehicle bringing economic progress and social status. The series of antimafia efforts undertaken since 1992 must therefore be evaluated in terms of an overall contribution to the marginalization of the Mafia as a social, as well as a criminal, phenomenon. In sum, the Mafia must be seen as a factor which contributes to a dysfunctional state, not as the solution to it.

1
The Significance of 1992

Perceptions of domestic and international security risks have changed significantly over the last 15–20 years, in particular since the end of the Cold War. New forms of threat have developed and existing forms have mutated. In many cases the line which separates terrorism from organized crime has become blurred, in that both forms of criminality use violence or the threat of violence to achieve their ends, both sustain themselves financially through control of 'criminalized' resources such as drugs and arms, and both have a political strategy. Nonetheless, one can generally distinguish between the *ideological* content of political terrorism and the *pragmatic* goals of organized crime: whereas the primary aim of politically inspired violence is the pursuit of specific objectives involving the overthrow of a government and/or the status quo, the political agenda of an organized crime group is determined by the quest for power, impunity and profits. Organized criminals seek to penetrate and suborn the state and cohabit with it, using terrorist tactics to intimidate the State when their privileges are at risk, for example when a law on extradition is under discussion or when investigators come too close to certain vital interests. Another term sometimes applied to organized crime is *enterprise* crime because participants are usually engaged in the provision of illicit goods and services, or licit goods that have been acquired through illicit means such as theft or fraud. Yet 'enterprise crime' is inadequate in that it does not convey organized crime's inherent violence – a capital resource always available to it and the primary means by which contractual agreements within illicit business are enforced.

One of the principal characteristics that distinguish organized crime from other forms of criminality is its penetration of the legal economy and of institutional and public life. For this reason it is generally misleading to view organized crime – and certainly the Italian Mafia – as extraneous to society. *Cosa Nostra* is 'at the centre of a web of social relations founded on networks of association and on shared interests'.[1] And, as Giovanni Falcone observed, 'The men of honour are neither devils nor schizophrenic. They would not kill their mother and father for a few grammes of heroin. They are men like us. The tendency in the western world, and particularly in Europe, is to exorcize evil by projecting it on to ethnic groups and forms of behaviour which seem different from our own. But if we want to fight the Mafia effectively, we must not transform it into a monster or think of it as an octopus or a cancer. We must recognize that it resembles ourselves.'[2]

While clandestine trafficking in drugs, cigarettes and arms are held to be the 'typical' Mafia crimes and the most profitable, organized crime combines underworld operations with a wide range of less tangible activities such as extortion of businesses, corruption of public officials or law-enforcement agents and infiltration of lucrative public works contracts through privileged channels of access. The existence of a carefully managed interface between the legal and the illegal sectors hinders the identification and prosecution of organized criminal behaviour. The cover of a long-distance haulage company, an import–export business, an agricultural estate producing citrus fruit or olive oil, a real estate or construction company or a financial services brokerage firm may constitute a channel through which illicit goods or finances merge with those of the legal sector and, for the operators concerned, justifies active involvement in the economic life of a particular region. This might include access to public funding, European Community subsidies or credit facilities, participation in public works tenders or entry to business or commercial associations where contacts and partnerships are nurtured. For *Cosa Nostra*, the interweaving of covert political activism with economic and commercial entrepreneurialism from the postwar period onwards was a determining factor in the judicial impunity which it enjoyed uninterruptedly until the mid-1980s.

Although there were waves of arrests and Mafia trials in the course of the 1960s and 1970s, it was rare for *mafiosi* to pass more than a few years in prison, after which they would return to their former activities and position in the hierarchy with their financial investments substantially intact. The pattern began to change in 1982, when two murders prompted a national emergency and the passing of legislation which for months had lain dormant in Parliament – those of Pio La Torre, Sicilian regional secretary of the Italian Communist Party (PCI) in April, and of General

Carlo Alberto Dalla Chiesa, recently appointed Prefect of Palermo, in September. The passing of Law 646 of 13 September 1982, known as the *Rognoni–La Torre* Law after its two parliamentary sponsors, began the sequence of events within which the attacks of 1992 must be interpreted. Effective application of this legislation by a team or 'pool' of judges in Palermo headed by chief examining magistrate Rocco Chinnici culminated in the first 'maxi-trial' of 475 *Cosa Nostra* members which opened in Palermo in February 1986. A decisive contribution had been made by some 30 state's witnesses, despite the fact that there was no specific legislation in place to ensure their economic or physical protection or to offer a reduction in prison sentences. The most prominent among them were Tommaso Buscetta and Salvatore Contorno, whose evidence had led to the issue of 366 and 127 arrest warrants respectively.

The maxi-trial wound a long and tortuous course through the Italian judicial system from 1986 to the Supreme Court verdict of 1992. Numerous obstacles were placed in its path, some of which were clearly intended to derail it altogether. Prior to the trial's commencement, the defence challenged the President of the Court of Assizes, Alfonso Giordano (the trial judge in Anglo-Saxon terms). When the challenge was overruled and the trial was under way, the Mafia's defence lawyers requested that all the documents relating to the indictments – several hundreds of thousands of pages – be read out in court. The official reason for the request was to provide the members of the jury with a complete understanding of all the evidence that had led to the trial; in practice, apart from overwhelming the jury with a mass of indigestible legal detail, the principal result would have been that the maximum period of pre-trial detention would have expired for many of the 212 imprisoned defendants. The situation was overcome in February 1987 when, in an exceptional moment of cross-party consensus, Parliament passed a law which modified the rules concerning preventive detention and limited the obligation to produce court documentation whilst a trial was under way. It took effect immediately.

Outside the courtroom, *Cosa Nostra* tried to intimidate the state's witnesses into withdrawing their testimonies by carrying out attacks on their relatives – Salvatore Contorno had a total of 12 relatives murdered, Tommaso Buscetta 11, including two sons. Political pressure was also exerted through the ballot box. It would transpire that from the earliest stages of the legal proceedings *Cosa Nostra* had predicted the course of all three stages of the trial – that sentences would be heavy in the Court of Assizes, be modified on Appeal and then be considerably reduced or overturned in the Supreme Court, the court responsible for the verification of correct legal procedure. These expectations derived from a network of contacts in political and judicial circles whom the Mafia had been able to 'approach'. In Mafia parlance someone who is 'approachable' is someone in a position of authority such as a police officer, politician or magistrate who can be 'persuaded' to bring influence to bear in specific circumstances in exchange for protection, a package of votes, a cash bribe or a gift such as an apartment or luxury car. Such individuals were often contacted in the discreet surroundings of the numerous Masonic or similarly secretive fraternal associations which flourished in Sicily.

For years the principal *Cosa Nostra* 'families' had maintained ties with institutional figures in Sicily, through whom they were able in turn to influence national politicians. Because the Christian Democratic Party (DC) was the strongest political party both locally and nationally, it was natural that *Cosa Nostra* should gravitate around its Sicilian represent-atives. In the 1960s and 1970s its principal contacts were the Sicilian national deputies Giovanni Gioia, Giovanni Matta, Attilio Ruffini and Salvo Lima, while in Sicily the party's key figures were Vito Ciancimino and the cousins Ignazio and Nino Salvo, wealthy businessmen who ran a tax collection service. According to a state's witness, from 1968 onwards, when Salvo Lima entered national Parliament and in 1979 became Euro-MP for the Italian islands, he was the person to whom *Cosa Nostra* turned for 'all the matters that involved decisions to be taken in Rome'.[3] It was believed in *Cosa Nostra* circles that Lima was able to bring pressure on Supreme Court judge Corrado Carnevale through Giulio Andreotti, seven times prime minister and member of almost every postwar Italian government. Others said that the Sicilian born Carnevale had other more personal ties to *Cosa Nostra*.

Having delivered significant numbers of votes to Sicilian parliamen-tarians of all the government parties, but primarily the DC, *Cosa Nostra* had expected to call in some favours during the maxi-trial; thus the passing of the February 1987 law which prevented the reading of the indictments was a setback. During the run-up to the general election of June 1987, both the Socialist (PSI) and Radical parties were campaigning for a fairer justice system based on greater protection of defendants' rights. Apparently without approaching the candidates concerned, the *Cosa Nostra* bosses put out an order to transfer votes in Palermo from the DC to the Socialists and Radicals as a 'reminder' to the DC that it should exert itself more on *Cosa Nostra*'s behalf. The PSI did particularly well in the Mafia-dense areas of Palermo, where the party's percentage of the vote rose by an average of 10 per cent; in the district of Ciaculli, dominated by the Greco clan, the PSI went from 5.6 to 23.47 per cent, with a drop in the DC vote from 62.09 to 38.78 per cent.[4]

The maxi-trial ended in the Court of Assizes in December 1987 with 19 sentences of life imprisonment, 319 sentences ranging from 6 to 30 years and 114 acquittals. The Court accepted the prosecution's case that *Cosa Nostra* had a single, pyramid-type hierarchical structure at whose apex was a central decision-making body known as the *Interprovinciale* or 'Interprovincial Commission', each of whose members was individually responsible for the most important murders carried out by the organization. 'Provincial commissions' had authority over local activities.

Cosa Nostra – Organizational Structure[a]
The traditional structure of *Cosa Nostra* is that of a pyramid. At the base are the soldiers (*soldati, uomini d'onore*) or simple 'men of honour' each of whom belongs to a family or faction (*famiglia, cosca*). Families vary in size but range from an average of 50 up to 200 members. Groups of ten soldiers are a *decina*, and are coordinated by a *capodecina*. A family is governed by an elected head (*capo*), also known as a representative (*rappresentante*) who chooses his own deputy (*vice capo*). Another elected post is that of adviser (*consigliere*), who is selected on the basis of age and experience. If the *capo* is unable to rule or if an election cannot take place, authority is in the hands of one or more regent (*reggente*). Three families in a given geographical area comprise a *mandamento*, with a head (*capomandamento*) who is elected to the provincial commission (*commissione*) for a period of three years. There is a commission for the provinces of Agrigento, Caltanissetta, Catania, Palermo and Trapani but the Interprovincial Commission (*Interprovinciale*, or *Regione*), dominated by families in or around Palermo, is the ultimate decision-making body.

CAPO INTERPROVINCIALE (CAPO DEI CAPI)
INTERPROVINCIALE
CAPO COMMISSIONE/ COMMISSIONE (Commissions of
Agrigento, Caltanissetta, Catania, Palermo and Trapani)
CAPO MANDAMENTO/MANDAMENTO (three families)
CAPO FAMIGLIA/FAMIGLIA
vice Capo   Consiglieri   Reggente(i)
Capodecina
soldati

---

[a]   According to the collaborator Tommaso Buscetta, who described the structure to judge Falcone in 1984. Changes may have taken place since that time (see Chapter 7).

Attempts to sabotage the maxi-trial did not cease with the Court of Assizes verdict. In September 1988, judge Antonio Saetta, President of the Palermo Appeal Court, was murdered together with his handicapped son shortly before the date scheduled for the opening of the Appeal trial. *Cosa Nostra* had tried to 'approach' him in order to influence his judgement but he was killed because he had refused to be intimidated or corrupted. Under a new president, the Appeal Court terminated its deliberations on 10 December 1990, but issued verdicts which represented a substantial modification of those previously handed down. The Appeal Court did not accept the principle of responsibility through membership of the Interprovincial Commission as delineated by the prosecution in the Court of Assizes, but insisted on separate proof that each individual Commission member had been demonstrably in favour of the decision to commit a specific murder before issuing a guilty verdict. On Appeal the life sentences were reduced to 12; there were 86 new acquittals and 258 sentences ranging from 4 to 30 years. Several important bosses were acquitted altogether.

The Court of Appeal was compulsorily influenced by a ruling of November 1988 from the First Section of the Supreme Court on a question of territorial competence, after the prosecution office in Termini Imerese had transmitted an investigation into provincial Mafia activities to Palermo on the basis that the crimes concerned had been committed on the authority of the Interprovincial Commission. The Supreme Court decided otherwise and, against the view of Giovanni Falcone but in support of his chief in the Instruction Office, Antonino Meli, dispersed the investigation around 12 smaller courts, which had neither the resources nor the professional competence to conduct the complex enquiries. This ruling overturned a fundamental premise of the maxi-trial by stating that the family or *cosca* was the primary unit within *Cosa Nostra*, that each operated according to an autonomous structure and authority, and that the Interprovincial Commission had a coordinating function rather than one of command.

Subsequent decisions of the Supreme Court further undermined the evidentiary basis of the maxi-trial by disallowing some of the statements made by the collaborators on the grounds that the standard of independent corroboration had not been sufficiently rigorous. In February 1991, the First Section of the Supreme Court under judge Corrado Carnevale granted a request by defence lawyers for the release from prison of some 40 bosses who had been convicted in the maxi-trial, given that the maximum period of pre-trial detention had expired and the Supreme Court had not convened to reach a definitive verdict. However, a week later on 1 March, the Andreotti government passed a law decree which overturned the Supreme Court decision as a misinterpretation of the law, and the same bosses were rearrested and sent back to prison.

In August 1991 Supreme Court judge Antonio Scopelliti, nominated to represent the prosecution case in the Supreme Court hearing to conclude the third and last stage of the maxi-trial, was murdered near his summer home in Calabria. A judge of impeccable integrity, it was said that like Saetta he had refused to yield to Mafia intimidation. The Palermo prosecution office would later charge several members of the Interprovincial Commission with instigating the murder which, it was alleged, was carried out by killers from the Calabrian Mafia, the 'Ndrangheta, at the request of *Cosa Nostra*.

During the period of the maxi-trial, the word went around the bosses in prison that if they were patient all would turn out well in the Supreme Court thanks to 'guarantees' offered by Corrado Carnevale, whose practice of finding legal cavils, supported by a prodigious knowledge of the law, had overturned many verdicts in the past. It was believed within *Cosa Nostra* that he had been well remunerated for his efforts. The message was delivered by lawyers who cited political contacts 'close to the government', understood to be a reference to Salvo Lima.[5]

These assurances were not taken for granted since the parties of the government majority, including the DC, had begun to introduce a series of tough new measures against organized crime of which the March 1991 law decree was an important signal. The announcement in October 1991, confirmed in December, that judge Arnaldo Valente, not Corrado Carnevale, would be presiding over the First Section of the Supreme Court to evaluate the maxi-trial, was another indication to *Cosa Nostra* that things were going badly. Meetings of the Interprovincial Commission were held to decide on a course of action should the verdict be unfavourable.

The First Section of the Supreme Court convened in December 1991 to evaluate the maxi-trial without its usual members or its habitual president. The verdict, delivered on 30 January 1992, completely overturned the 1990 ruling of the Appeal Court and reverted to the original formulation of the Court of Assizes, namely that *Cosa Nostra* had a centralized structure with powers of hierarchical control, direction and authority, and that as a consequence, the series of political–institutional murders carried out in the 1980s was morally and judicially attributable to each member of the Commission. It also accepted the validity of the contribution of the state's witnesses and reversed previous decisions of the Supreme Court regarding independent corroboration.

With this ruling the Court vindicated the formulation set out by the antimafia pool in the instruction phase of the proceedings, turned earlier convictions for many Mafia bosses into definitive life sentences and necessitated a new appeal trial for some 20 murder cases according to the principles of joint responsibility, with the virtual certainty that new life sentences would be handed down.

The verdict laid down three precedents: it established *Cosa Nostra's* existence as an organization with a single, unified structure; it upheld the principle of joint responsibility within the Commission; and it confirmed the validity and the possibility of objective corroboration in a court of law of the testimonies of state's witnesses, thereby ensuring that legislation to protect and encourage future collaborators would follow.

Soon after the verdict, several *mafiosi* voluntarily gave themselves up to the police and judicial authorities, an event unprecedented in *Cosa Nostra* history. There were premonitions that something extremely serious and important was about to take place and that those who remained at liberty would find themselves caught up in it. Some, realizing this, preferred to avoid the risk. *Cosa Nostra's* immediate response to the Supreme Court defeat was to move onto the attack, punishing its erstwhile 'partners' and eliminating a number of powerful enemies. On 12 March 1992, Sicilian Euro-MP Salvo Lima was assassinated in the coastal resort of Mondello, near Palermo. He was murdered, according to the collaborator Gaspare Mutolo,

> [...] because he was considered the maximum symbol of that political faction which, having upheld a relationship of peaceful cohabitation and exchange of favours with *Cosa Nostra* for many years and having received in return the votes of the organization, no longer protected its interests at the precise moment of its most important trial, and on the contrary showed an inclination to pursue policies of an opposite tendency.[6]

Although Lima was killed for reneging on his assurances, the murder was also intended as a warning to Prime Minister Andreotti, Lima's friend and principal political contact in Rome, at a time when Andreotti was contemplating running for the presidency of the Republic.[7]

Both Giovanni Falcone and Paolo Borsellino had been sentenced to death by *Cosa Nostra* many years before, but as long as the rhythm of arrests, short prison sentences, releases and acquittals was maintained, it was not in the organization's interests to provoke a massive state reaction by killing such eminent figures. The Supreme Court verdict broke the pattern and the suspended sentences were carried out.

Cosa Nostra's last high-profile attack in 1992 in many aspects resembled the first: Ignazio Salvo, who had been convicted of Mafia association in the maxi-trial of 1986–87, was murdered on 17 September. Investigators concluded that, like Salvo Lima, he had been unable to use his political and judicial connections to mitigate the Supreme Court verdict. He was part of the old Mafia–institutional power axis whose collapse had forced *Cosa Nostra* to discard its old alliances and begin the search for new institutional interlocutors.

While the events described above constitute the catalyst for the tragic events of Palermo in 1992, it would be reductive to analyse Italian events of that period only in terms of the Mafia. In the early 1990s the repercussions of the end of the Cold War were just beginning to reverberate through a country which had been artificially maintained for years as a bulwark of resistance to communism. The political class that had governed Italy uninterruptedly since 1948 could not survive for long once the dust from the Berlin Wall had settled. With hindsight, it is clear that global bipolarity provided an alibi for the establishment and perpetuation of a bipolar national power structure based on exclusion in which the Mafia played a significant part. The permanence in power of the same coalition of parties, the same party leaders and the same supporting bureaucracies, cemented into place by virtue of their anti-Communist convictions, had encouraged complacency and a sense of superiority to the law that in 1992 were beginning to crumble. The predominance of the public over the private sector and the presence of the Mafia in the south precipitated the degeneration of political power in the *mezzogiorno*, but institutional decay was as deeply rooted in the north. The investigations of the Milan judiciary into extensive networks of corrupt dealings between political parties and their administrators, industrial companies and in some cases, criminal organizations, found echoes and connections in Sicily. The northern judges showed that in a post-Communist world it was possible to investigate and prosecute figureheads once considered untouchable, but discovered, as their Sicilian colleagues had done, that to disturb entrenched power structures was dangerous.

2
The Mafia–Antimafia Seesaw

Mafia in history

Scholars dispute the origins of the word *mafia* although it is generally thought to have entered the Italian language during the Arab occupation of Sicily in the ninth century AD. It may be derived from *ma afir*, the name of an Islamic tribe which dominated Palermo in the period. The word *mahias* meant 'arrogant' or 'insolent'; *mahà* signified stone cave, while *mafie* were caves of volcanic rock between Trapani and Marsala used by the Arabs in the eleventh century to flee from Norman oppression, hence an Arabic word for 'place of refuge'. In fifteenth-century Tuscany a *malfusso* meant a petty criminal, while *mafia* or *maffia* in Florentine dialect signified poverty and misery. In Sicilian dialect *mafiusu* or *marfusu* was widely used to mean an arrogant person, with overtones of manliness or bravado. The first documented appearance of the word as an organized band of delinquents was in 1863 when a play called *I mafiusi di la Vicaria di Palermo* – about the escapades of a criminal band in Palermo's Vicaria prison – opened to popular success in the city and was taken on a national tour to equal acclaim.[1] In 1865 the word made its first official appearance when a Sicilian police officer registered the arrest of a suspect on the charge of complicity in a Mafia crime, '*un delitto di mafia*'.[2] Those who belong to the organization do not in fact call themselves *Mafia* but *Cosa Nostra*, (our thing) and its members 'men of honour' or 'men of respect'.[3]

One of the earliest official accounts of delinquency in Sicily, published in 1876 and remarkably relevant more than a hundred years later, defines the Mafia as 'an industry of violence', a 'vast agglomeration of people of every station, of every profession and of every type who, without any apparent continuous or regular link between them, are always united in promoting their reciprocal interests, without any consideration for law, justice or public order'. It was quite impossible, the report concluded, for 'anyone with political ambitions to escape contact with persons who owe their existence to crime'.[4]

The three main Mafia organizations in Italy are *Cosa Nostra* in Sicily, the *Camorra*, centred on the city of Naples and the surrounding region of Campania, and the *'Ndrangheta* in Calabria, whose name derives from the Greek *andragathos* or 'courageous man'. All three emerged in the mid-nineteenth century but whereas *Cosa Nostra* and the *'Ndrangheta* were an outgrowth of a section of the middle class which had been licensed to use violence by the ruling classes of the day and were founded on codes of honour, secrecy and silence, the *Camorra* was an association of the poorest classes for whom crime was a means of survival, and was neither secretive nor elitist. The word is probably of Spanish origin meaning a garment worn by bandits. The fourth Mafia group, the *Sacra Corona Unita* or United Holy Crown in Apulia, has a shorter criminal history, and owes its expansion from the late 1970s onwards to a desire by the other three criminal groups, at different times and for different motives, to have a consolidated criminal base on Apulia's long south-eastern seaboard.

Sicily – a history of disembarkations

Sicily is the largest island in the Mediterranean Sea and lies almost at its centre. Its position as a bridge between Europe, Africa and the Middle East has made it a bitterly disputed prize throughout the centuries. First colonized by the Greeks in the eighth century BC, it was subsequently occupied by the Romans, and then by Arab colonizers from Tunis in the ninth century. The Normans invaded the island in 1061 and gradually extended their feudal monarchy until by the end of the eleventh century they were in control of most of southern Italy. In 1197 the Kingdom of Sicily passed to the German Hohenstaufen dynasty. Civilization flourished under the reign of Frederick II but on the death of his successor Manfredi, a long era of bitter conflict began. Sicily was ruled by the French house of Anjou for 20 years, then occupied by the Spanish Kingdom of Aragon while Naples and the rest of the South remained under Anjou reign. Naples and Sicily were united in 1442 for nearly three centuries under Spanish rule. In 1713 Sicily passed to the House of Savoy, was annexed seven years later by the Austrian Empire and was reoccupied by the Spanish Bourbons in 1734. The island was under British military occupation from 1806 to 1815, while the Kingdom of Naples was ruled by the French. After the Congress of Vienna of 1815 Sicily and Naples were reunited under the Bourbons, who reigned from Naples over the Kingdom of the Two Sicilies until Italian unification in 1860. On landing at Marsala in May of that year, Garibaldi proclaimed himself Dictator of Sicily in the name of King Vittorio Emanuele before leading the Expedition of the One Thousand to Calabria and thence to Naples.

During the centuries of foreign domination, the Italian south or *mezzogiorno* was administered by feudal barons on behalf of the King or, in Sicily, by a Viceroy. The land and its people were essentially seen as serving the needs of the occupying forces – as manpower to fight in the ruler's armies, as a source of taxes to pay for war efforts and as agricultural labour to work the land and make the barons richer. Feudal privileges were officially abolished in Sicily in 1812 but land distribution did not take place until many years later – in 1820, 80 per cent of the land was still in the form of large estates. When the estates were finally broken up many were simply distributed among the families of the existing landowners; others were leased out to farm managers and estate guards known as *gabellotti* and *campieri* who allocated work, food and housing, administered justice, provided credit for loans on exorbitant terms and kept the estate accounts. The nobility granted them the right to bear arms and, in some cases, to form small private armies to defend their estates against banditry. Whether working under licence from the latifondists or on their own behalf, the new middle class – from which the Mafia emerged – had every interest in keeping the peasants as backward and oppressed as they had always been. Far from being benevolent liberators of the repressed poor, as depicted in popular mythology, the early *mafiosi* exercised violence with impunity in the defence of privilege.

In the years after unification little was done to modernize or reform the land laws: instead, incentives for increased industrial production in the late nineteenth century served to accentuate the differences between the north and the south of Italy, where agricultural conditions remained antiquated and peasant farmers became steadily more marginalized. Nonetheless, under the influence of revolutionary thinkers such as Marx and especially Bakunin, who went to Italy in 1864, struggles for the expropriation of land gradually developed into organized peasant revolt in many parts of the south: an uprising in Palermo in 1866 was so well supported that an expeditionary force was required to quell it. Such events soldered the alliance between Mafia and aristocracy even more firmly.

Emanuele Notarbartolo

The first 'illustrious corpse' in the history of the Antimafia was Emanuele Notarbartolo, scion of one of the most eminent families of the Sicilian aristocracy. Notarbartolo had been mayor of Palermo from 1873 to 1876 and Director General of the Bank of Sicily from 1876 to 1890. During his tenure at the Bank, Notarbartolo had attempted to replace the political-clientilistic composition of the Board of Directors with banking professionals of his own choosing and had sought to terminate a series of corrupt credit practices linked to a senior Board member, Raffaele Palizzolo, a parliamentary deputy with numerous links to the Mafia.[5] In 1891–92 Notarbartolo acquired proof of these activities and reported them at ministerial level in Rome, but before the promised enquiry could take place he was murdered – stabbed 26 times on 1 February 1893 during a train journey from Termini Imerese to Palermo. Rumours immediately began to circulate that the assassination was linked to Palizzolo and his Mafia associates, although the only criminal charges brought initially were against two railway workers. The murder became an issue of such national importance that the trial was held in Milan on the grounds that there was a 'legitimate suspicion' that the defendants might not receive a fair trial in Sicily. Incriminating evidence emerged during the trial which linked Palizzolo to the murder. His parliamentary immunity from prosecution was waived and he was arrested in 1899. The next trial, held in Bologna, found Palizzolo guilty of murder and sentenced him to 30 years in prison but on appeal in Florence he was acquitted on grounds of insufficient proof, despite the 'irrefutable evidence of the relations that [Palizzolo] had maintained with known *mafiosi* in the Palermo area and of the numerous efforts that he had made on their behalf with public officials'.[6] A defence committee organized by supporters of Palizzolo called *Pro Sicilia* tried to blacken Notarbartolo's name, claiming he had dragged Sicily's reputation into the mud by his allegations of criminal dealings. At the same time the first ever antimafia committee was set up by the Prince of Camporeale to defend Notarbartolo's integrity; it sponsored the erection of a bronze bust in his memory. Not until much later was there official acknowledgement of Palizzolo's connections to the Mafia and of the extent of the cover-up of the murder trail by public officials under his influence. Notarbartolo's courage, commemorated in the name of a once elegant, now traffic-congested street in central Palermo, was tragically linked in 1992 with that of Giovanni Falcone, when the magnolia tree outside Falcone's apartment in via Notarbartolo became the rallying point for a new antimafia movement.

Fascism, and re-emergence, 1922–63

After the takeover of power by Benito Mussolini's Fascist party in 1922, all forms of political opposition were banned and the monopoly of the use of force by central government was asserted for the first time in southern Italy. Mussolini recognized the power of the Mafia and sent 'Iron Prefect' Cesare Mori to demonstrate the Fascist State's military and administrative superiority. Mori organized public and humiliating arrests of hundreds of Mafia *picciotti* or footsoldiers whom he frequently had tortured and shot, but in general the most important bosses – who by then were often eminently respectable doctors, lawyers and landowners – were left in peace if they paid lip service to Fascism and to the rule of law. By treating the Mafia as if it were an ordinary criminal band Mori took out of circulation the most visible evidence of its presence – the threat to public order – while leaving the subversive elements relatively undisturbed. *Carabinieri* reports of the time reveal that the Mafia had already become a secret organization, structured in the form of clans or *cosche* and divided by sector of activity and geographical area. Only a few exemplary cases showed that the official tolerance and the collusion with public power to which the Mafia had become accustomed had been interrupted: legendary Mafia boss Vito Cascio Ferro, accused of 69 major crimes including 20 murders of which he had been regularly acquitted, was found guilty for the first time in 1926.

During the Second World War *Cosa Nostra* reacted to the public humiliations and loss of privileges inflicted by Fascism by supporting the Separatist Movement, the only organized resistance movement in Sicily. The Mafia's pro-US and anti-Fascist sympathies were exploited by the Allied occupation forces – amongst whom were Italo-American *mafiosi* released from prison to provide intelligence and to liaise with Sicilian counterparts – which landed on the west coast of Sicily in 1943. The Allied advance across the island was swift and almost bloodless. In recompense, *mafiosi* were appointed as administrators and mayors throughout western Sicily; they were the only Italians permitted to hold gun licences and, as such, were entrusted with subduing banditry and lawlessness. Moreover their privileged contacts with the occupying forces provided access to supplies of cigarettes, grain, olive oil and pasta on which a lucrative black market was founded. A parliamentary commission would later conclude,

It is indisputable that [..] the conduct of the Allies, before and after the occupation, constituted a factor of primary importance for the re-emergence of Mafia activities on the island and that the separatist political movement, which the Allied military government initially supported, represented both a convenient cover for unprincipled Mafia infiltration and the instrument used by the dominant class for the defence of its interests.[7]

Letters written by the American Consul General to the US Secretary of State in 1944 (see plate 9) confirm US support for the separatist cause and the high regard in which the *Maffia* was held by the occupying forces:

I have the honour to report that on November 18, 1944 General Giuseppe Castellano, together with *Maffia* leaders including Calogero Vizzini conferred with Virgilio Nasi, head of the well-known Nasi family in Trapani and asked him to take over the leadership of a *Maffia*-backed movement for Sicilian autonomy [...]. General Castellano [...] has developed close contacts with the *Maffia* leaders and has met them on frequent occasions. [..] prominent members of the *Maffia* met in Palermo and one of the results of this conference was the decision to ask Virgilio Nasi of Trapani to head up this movement with the ultimate intention of his becoming High Commissioner. The Nasi family have been well known in the Province of Trapani for at least two genera-tions and are highly respected by all classes.[8]

Support for Sicilian separatism continued after the war ended, although Allied interest in promoting the cause fell away for fear of provoking a civil war after Italy had been liberated. The new government in Rome also recognized the risk and defused the independentist cause by granting regional autonomy to Sicily in 1946. Under a special statute, a regional government for Sicily took over responsibility for the local economy, banking, finance, tax collection, transport, building and public works. Private industry was virtually ignored such that in economic terms Sicily remained predominantly agricultural, with farming methods still based on the *mezzadria* or share-cropping system. Peasant farmers and trade unionists who encouraged land occupation and organized struggle were opposed by an alliance of Mafia with local banditry, operating on occasions under police protection. The most notorious band, that led by Salvatore Giuliano, was responsible for some 430 murders, including those of 11 picnickers celebrating May Day 1947 on a hillside at Portella della Ginestra. In 1944, 245 murders were committed in the province of Palermo alone, while 31 trade unionists were murdered between 1945 and 1958.

The 'bourgeois' Mafia expanded, became more wealthy and began to develop interests in urban property, land speculation, public sector construction, commercial transportation and the wholesale fruit, vegetable, meat and fish markets that served the burgeoning city of Palermo, whose population rose by 100 000 between 1951 and 1961. The seat of Sicilian power moved from the countryside to the cities and in particular to the regional capital, Palermo, and from private hands to public administration. The Christian Democratic Party (DC), the largest national political party and strongest advocate of regional autonomy, became the major political force on the island. As such it was courted by those who sought power, including the Mafia. A new relationship developed between the Mafia and the dominant political class with the former no longer mediating between two sectors of society, but bargaining on its own behalf. In a position to guarantee substantial electoral support for those who favoured it, *Cosa Nostra* began to penetrate the administrative and political heart of the region.

Competition between rival Mafia clans for control over lucrative new activities led to a spate of murders and woundings in what is described as the first 'Mafia war'of 1961–63. It culminated on 30 June 1963 when a car bomb, originally intended for members of the Greco clan led by Michele 'the Pope' Greco, exploded in the Ciaculli district of Palermo, killing seven police and bomb disposal experts who had been summoned to the spot by an anonymous phone call.

The Ciaculli car bomb prompted the first series of concerted antimafia efforts enacted in postwar Italy. Within a period of ten weeks, the police forces had arrested 1200 suspected *mafiosi*, many of whom would be kept out of circulation for five to six years. The Commission or governing council of *Cosa Nostra* was dissolved and, of those who had escaped arrest, a significant number went to the USA, Canada, Argentina, Brazil and Venezuela, where networks of Sicilians were already established and where bases for heroin and cocaine trafficking were created or consolidated. Finally, the atrocity galvanized Parliament into implementing a law passed in December 1962 for the constitution of an all-party Antimafia Commission which met for the first time on 6 July 1963.

The Antimafia Commission 1963–76

The designated task of the Antimafia Commission was to 'examine the origins and characteristics of the Mafia phenomenon in Sicily, to propose measures to repress it and to eliminate the causes'.[9] Only a month after its inauguration the Commission presented its first report together with a series of recommendations:[10]

- the criminal law should be modified to incorporate provisions against the Mafia;
- all institutional agencies should be coordinated to combat the Mafia;
- all the vacant posts in the Sicilian judiciary should be filled;
- the selection of public officials in Sicily for regional and national responsibilities should be made with particular care;
- the collaboration of all three police forces, namely the State Police, *Carabinieri* and Finance Police, should be ensured;
- controls over public works contracts and wholesale markets should be improved.

As a blue-print for action it was a practical starting point.

By the summer of 1963 Italy had the means at its disposal to rid Sicily of the Mafia, perhaps for good. *Cosa Nostra*'s leadership had fled or was in prison; public opinion – although it saw *Cosa Nostra* as a primitive and uniquely Sicilian phenomenon and therefore not a danger to national security – was in favour of decisive action; and political attention through the Antimafia Commission was focused on causes and solutions.

On 19 September 1963 the Commission presented a draft law, passed by Parliament on 31 May 1965 as Law 575 entitled 'Dispositions against the Mafia', the first time the word Mafia had been used in legislation. The law extended 1956 legislation concerning individuals considered to be 'socially dangerous' to those 'suspected of belonging to associations of a Mafia type, to the *Camorra* or to other associations whatever their local name, which pursue objectives or act with methods corresponding to those of Mafia associations'. The measures included special surveillance, the possibility of ordering a suspect to reside in a designated place outside his home area and the suspension of publicly issued licences, grants or authorizations. The law gave powers to a public prosecutor or questor (chief of police) to identify and trace the assets of anyone suspected of involvement in a Mafia-type association. In order to do so the authorities could demand information concerning the provenance of income and the tax situation of the suspect from any public administration office or any public or private credit institution with regard to the suspect, his spouse, children, anyone with whom he had lived in the previous five years or any physical or juridical person over whose assets the suspect had partial or total control. Assets could be seized preventively if, after the application of surveillance and other measures, there was sufficient evidence – such as a notable discrepancy between a suspect's lifestyle and his apparent or declared income – to indicate that the assets were the product of illicit activity. If it could be shown that the seized assets in whole or in part represented the proceeds of criminal activity in the context of a Mafia-type association, or if the suspect was unable to prove their legitimate source, the seized assets were confiscated.

The efficacy of the new law was severely limited on two counts, firstly because there was no legal definition of a Mafia association, and secondly because the obligation for *mafiosi* to reside in areas outside Sicily, instead of limiting their operational capacity, actually opened up new opportunities to develop illicit activities in the cities of northern and central Italy.

From 1963 until the end of the decade *Cosa Nostra* remained quiet, and levels of violence in Sicily fell sharply: murders in Palermo dropped to a historic minimum of 16 in 1968. The trials for the crimes committed during the late 1950s and early 1960s, including the Ciaculli car bomb, were held in Catanzaro (Calabria) and Bari (Apulia) in 1968 and 1969 on the grounds – as with the Notarbartolo murder trial – of 'legitimate suspicion' that a fair trial would not be possible in Sicily. On both occasions nearly all the defendants were acquitted or given short sentences. Of 113 *mafiosi* on trial, only 10 were convicted at Catanzaro. Corleone boss Luciano Leggio was acquitted in Bari of nine murders, the only restriction on his liberty being to reside at his home. Leggio ignored the court order and left Corleone, first for a private health clinic in Rome and then for Milan, where he set up and ran a profitable kidnap ring in collaboration with the Calabrian *'Ndrangheta* until his rearrest in 1974. Judge Pietro Scaglione, the prosecutor general of Palermo who had been responsible for Leggio's restriction order and, in the opinion of some, for not enforcing it, became in May 1971 the first institutional figure murdered in Sicily after Emanuele Notarbartolo. Initially it was thought that Scaglione had been in collusion with *Cosa Nostra*, given the assumption at that time that the Mafia 'only murdered its own', but with hindsight the murder was considered to be one of the first attempts by the Mafia to intimidate the State.[11]

The acquittals that resulted from the trials at Catanzaro and Bari reversed the antimafia momentum that had begun in 1963, restored *Cosa Nostra*'s sense of impunity and permitted the 'old guard' released from prison to resume illicit activities in Sicily. This in turn unleashed a new wave of conflict between the old bosses who expected to take up their former responsibilities and those who had assumed leadership in the intervening period. Colonel Carlo Alberto Dalla Chiesa, commander of the *Carabinieri* in Sicily at the time, gave an account of the situation to the Antimafia Commission in November 1970. He observed that public faith in the police and judicial organs had decreased in the years 1969–70, and with justification:

> these gentlemen have the feeling that they can get off scot free. You have to get inside their minds [...] They are acquitted of the charge (that is, of [Mafia] association, which can be hard to understand outside Sicily) and then when they come back out they find us unprepared to receive them as we should because we do not have the necessary procedural tools with which to complete the investigation. We have no fingernails, that is the problem of dealing with these people – compared to an ordinary investigation of common crime which we can deal with and achieve significant results, with regard to the *mafioso* it is hard for us to get the proof inasmuch as he operates in a very specific context.[12]

The work of the Antimafia Commission continued from 1963 to 1976 through different parliaments and under different chairmen, who were always of government parties. The analyses generated by the Commission were subsequently published in their entirety and constitute a valuable archive for today's scholars. The final report of 1976 was passed by all the party delegations that composed the Commission, with the exception of the neo-fascist Italian Social Movement party (MSI). It retraced the origins, nature and development of *Cosa Nostra* from pre-unification onwards and contained some perceptive observations:

> Organized crime's goal of wealth accumulation is achieved by forms of mediation, by parasitic infiltration, by the systematic use of violence and above all by contact with public power; [.....] notwithstanding the distinctions between the various clans that divide up territory and responsibilities, there exists a tacit agreement, a criminal structure which, in putting up an impenetrable wall to non-compromised authorities, operates for the support and protection of Mafia criminal activities: a criminal structure which is not destroyed even by the cruel and ruthless struggles between the clans.

Referring to the period from unification to Fascism, the Commissioners concluded that one of the Mafia's striking characteristics had been impunity, due to 'the intimidation of juries, laxity and negligence on the part of the judiciary, the *omertà* or bond of silence and its capacity to contaminate evidence'.[13] Some 78 per cent of crimes in Sicily had been committed by unknown persons and even where there were defendants, many had been acquitted. Living with the need for some form of protection had been seen as a necessity, a fact of life in a region where the State had been absent:

> The distance and weakness of the State may have been sufficient for the Mafia to substitute its own force for [the State's] absence, but this was also the principal factor of illicit collusion precisely because it could induce state officials and politicians to search out the first contacts and relations with the Mafia, or to submit to its persuasive presence.[14]

An expert contribution in the form of an annex to the final report was provided by sociologist Franco Ferrarotti, who described the Mafia as

> a typical example of informal power, characterized by the existence of an organization, by its extension to all spheres of public life, by the capacity to interfere in the private lives of persons and by the acceptance of Mafia power within the average conscience of the social groups in which it operates, which [together] have determined its relative institutionalization.

The Commission documented the extent of Mafia infiltration of public administration in Sicily after the granting of regional autonomy in 1946 and revealed that, between 1946 and 1963, over 90 per cent of all those recruited to regional government had been taken on without any qualitative selection but for reasons of favouritism and friendship, and that they included convicted criminals, relations of Mafia members and persons believed to be Mafia members. Mafia-dominated western Sicily had accounted for 73 per cent of all those taken on by the Sicilian region compared to 16 per cent from eastern Sicily, although population numbers were similar.

Two names that were referred to many times throughout the final report were those of the influential DC politicians Vito Ciancimino and Salvo Lima. The period 1958–64, when Lima was mayor of Palermo and Ciancimino was assessor for public works in Palermo City Council, was later referred to as the 'sack of Palermo' for the extent of building land speculation that took place. Of 4000 building licences awarded during the period, more than half were granted to three old-age pensioners who had no connection with the construction industry whatsoever, but were merely front men for unauthorized building work. The Commission noted,

> It was in Palermo in particular that the phenomenon [of illegal construction] took on dimensions such as not to leave any doubts about the insidious penetration by the Mafia of public administration. The administrative management of Palermo City Council reached unprecedented heights of deliberate non-observation of the law around 1960.[15]

Lima' s friendship with the La Barbera clan of *mafiosi* when mayor of Palermo was also criticized.

> The undeniable contacts of the La Barbera *mafiosi* with the individual who was Palermo's First Citizen, as well as with persons who were socially respectable or who pretended to be so, constitute a confirmation of what has been previously stated about the infiltration of the Mafia in various sectors of public life.

The final report recommended that a series of actions be taken:

- revision of the regional statute to break up the centralized structure;
- introduction of measures to revitalize the economy, increase productivity and stimulate employment;
- measures to modernize agriculture, to reduce discretionality in the management of agricultural property and to bring water supplies under public control;
- restructuring of the wholesale markets and of the system for granting licences;
- democratic oversight of public banks, credit institutions and building licence authorities to be guaranteed through the representation on boards of directors of both governing and opposition parties.

The generic attributions of political weakness and of vulnerability to Mafia intimidation on the part of the postwar political class as depicted in the Commission's final report of 1976 did not satisfy the Communist Party and Independent Left commissioners, who supported much of its contents but objected to the omission of all but a handful of names of collusive politicians and to the exoneration from specific blame of the political administrators of the government parties, responsible in their view for gross negligence. They argued that the interpenetration of criminal and political power was not a result of weakness or intimidation but was consensual, and that rather than shunning and censuring such behaviour, the majority parties were continuing to appoint men of dubious ethical standards to positions of government responsibility.

A key member of the Commission between 1972 and 1976 was Sicilian judge Cesare Terranova, elected to Parliament as an Independent Left candidate under the auspices of the PCI. Terranova had been responsible for drawing up the indictments of some of the most important Mafia criminals in the 1960s, and was one of the first to investigate the financial operations of *Cosa Nostra*. He had also perceived its links with institutional circles by, for example, identifying in Palermo City Council an important centre of interests which favoured Mafia property speculation. Intervening during discussion of the Commission's final report, Terranova called on his colleagues to live up to their responsibilities after 13 years of investigation, and to

> give a response to the country's expectations by a clear and unequivocal indication as to the infected centres of the structures contaminated by the Mafia phenomenon, thereby permitting the profound process of renovation that is required for re-establishing the citizen's faith in the State and consequently the formation of a widespread antimafia consciousness. That is the indispensable premise for tackling the Mafia at its roots, destroying the halo of untouchability that surrounds those who protect it, those who collude with it and those who derive from it benefits and advantages of all kinds.[16]

The refusal of the delegations representing the government in the Commission, chaired by Christian Democrat Luigi Carraro, to incorporate the requested modifications led to the drafting of a minority report, written by commissioners Terranova and PCI deputy Pio La Torre, which was intended to complement the final report of the government majority parties. It pointed to past links between the Mafia and certain influential politicians, such as the support given to Corleone boss Luciano Leggio by DC regional deputy Canzoneri and the close contacts between an MSI candidate in the 1972 election, Pino Mandalari, and several notorious *mafiosi* including Totò Riina, Leggio's right-hand man in Corleone. The minority report claimed that a recent increase of Mafia activity in the Palermo hinterland was proof of

> the persistence of connivance between Mafia power, local administrators, public functionaries and politicians. [...] This is why it would

be a grave error on the part of the Commission to accept the theory that the Mafia–political link has been eliminated. Even today the behaviour of the ruling DC group in the running of the City and Provincial Councils offers the most favourable terrain for the perpetuation of the system of Mafia power.[17]

Prior to voting on the majority and minority reports in January 1976 Terranova intervened again:

If we wish to attribute a concrete and serious significance to the fight against the Mafia it is vital first of all to regain the faith of the citizen in our institutions, starting with the removal from all positions of power of all those who [...] rightly or wrongly, have been in some way compromised or involved with the Mafia. And this is true not only for politicians but for all those who, in whatever role, have been occupying public office of considerable responsibility.[18]

His words were essentially disregarded and the documentation of the Antimafia Commission was left to gather dust in parliamentary archives. One by one, the opportunities opened up in the mid-1960s to defeat the Mafia had collapsed. Seventeen years would pass before Parliament would seriously tackle the Mafia–political nexus. Cesare Terranova would talk of the 'thirteen wasted years' of the Antimafia Commission, and returned to the judiciary in June 1979. In the same year Salvo Lima was elected to the European Parliament for the Christian Democratic Party and remained in office until his murder in 1992, despite the presentation in Strasbourg in 1984 of a dossier containing the criticisms made by the Antimafia Commission of his alleged Mafia connections.[a] When Leoluca Orlando refused to appear with Lima on the list of DC candidates for the Italian Islands in the European elections in 1989, the national party management preferred to drop Orlando rather than Lima.

The 'heroin Mafia'

The 1970s were the decade of maximum growth and tranquillity for *Cosa Nostra,* for three principal reasons. Firstly, the main narcotics cultivation–refining–trafficking axis had relocated. Under pressure from the US government, (a) Turkey had phased out its opium poppy cultivation,

---

[a] The dossier was compiled by the Sicilian Documentation Centre in Palermo whose work is discussed in Chapter 5.

causing heroin producers to look to Southeast Asia for the raw materials, and (b) the French–Corsican heroin refining and trafficking network based in Marseilles had been broken up. This opened up the market to new entrants, in particular to the Sicilians who used the well-established networks for contraband cigarette smuggling set up by the *Camorra* to expand their own heroin activities. By the end of the 1970s, five heroin refineries working full time in Sicily were satisfying around 30 per cent of all the North American heroin demand. Contacts at source in Thailand, the collaboration of morphine base producers and trafficking groups in Turkey, their own refining capacities in Sicily and distribution networks of Sicilian clan representatives in the USA and Canada gave *Cosa Nostra* substantial control over the entire opium–heroin chain. Between 1976 and August 1980 when the first laboratories were discovered, the principal exporting consortium – that of the Spatola–Inzerillo–Bontate families – is thought to have refined and exported an average of four to five metric tons of pure heroin annually, making $US600 million of profits per annum.[19]

Massive capital accumulation dictated the second factor of change for *Cosa Nostra*, namely the beginning of its penetration of international financial markets on- and off-shore. Using the cover of anonymous companies notionally set up to provide import–export or financial services and of banks such as Michele Sindona's *Banca Privata Italiana* and Roberto Calvi's *Banco Ambrosiano*, Mafia assets were laundered and invested in havens safe from the reach of the law.

A third and final factor has attracted little attention, and yet merits examination. The period of the 1970s, during which the 'heroin Mafia' was entering its maximum phase of expansion, was precisely the time when the anti-terrorist fight absorbed the cream of Italy's criminal investigators and commanded a massive share of national resources in the form of political and institutional attention, law-enforcement outlays and protection of targets. Moreover this wave of violence was almost entirely concentrated in the north and centre of Italy: of all the 2712 acts of politically-motivated violence against persons or things between 1969 and 1982 for which responsibility was claimed, 35 per cent took place in north-west Italy (in particular the cities of Turin, Milan and Genoa); 17 per cent in north-east Italy; 38 per cent in the centre (31 per cent in Rome alone) and only 10 per cent in the south and islands (4 per cent in Naples alone).[20] Terrorism dominated political parties and the work of Parliament, the business community, public opinion and large sections of all the daily newspapers nearly every day. Yet during a 13-year span only a small share of that activity occurred south of Naples. It should hardly be a matter of surprise, therefore, that *Cosa Nostra* was able to run its business activities with a minimum of hindrance. Prison governors positively welcomed *mafiosi* inmates as – in accordance with *Cosa Nostra* rules – they behaved impeccably and kept order over the more troublesome political prisoners who planned escapes, organized revolts and hunger strikes and tried to indoctrinate their fellow inmates. *Mafiosi* were also given considerable privileges – Tommaso Buscetta, held in Palermo's Ucciardone prison from 1973 to 1977, spent his entire imprisonment in the hospital wing where he was able to receive friends, family and lawyers and telephone all over the world. They could send out for luxury food, wine and champagne and prepare meals for themselves in their cells at the hours that suited them.

Cosa Nostra evolved rapidly during this period. The colossal profits from drugs made its leaders more arrogant with political interlocutors and impatient to resolve issues with immediate action. Many public figures and politicians succumbed to corruption or intimidation, and those who refused or made clear that cohabitation was unacceptable were eliminated. In the four years between 1979 and 1982 *Cosa Nostra* systematically assassinated the most committed political, institutional and judicial representatives of state power in Sicily – two judges, three politicians, two police officers and the Prefect, the principal government representative on the island. There were two common denominators – each had made a key discovery in the Mafia's operations and, possessing the courage to act on that knowledge, would have imperilled those operations; and each experienced a strong sense of isolation.

DC provincial secretary Michele Reina was attempting to bring more accountability to the allocation of public works contracts and was murdered in March 1979 shortly after proposing the freezing of a large sum destined for construction projects in Palermo's old city centre. Piersanti Mattarella, DC President of the Sicilian region, had likewise taken a stand against corruption and collusion within his party and was killed in January 1980 after daring to challenge a tradition which had been accepted by his own father, Bernardo, also a prominent local DC politician. Boris Giuliano, chief of the Palermo Flying Squad, had begun to investigate the international financial channels used by *Cosa Nostra* to launder heroin profits and was shot dead in July 1979, while *carabiniere* Captain Emanuele Basile, who was leading the search for Mafia fugitives, was murdered in May the following year. On 25 September 1979, when his nomination as chief examining magistrate of Palermo was imminent, Cesare Terranova was murdered with his police driver Lenin Mancuso as he left his Palermo apartment. The combination of his political experience in Rome with his investigative skills in Sicily had made him a more formidable enemy than before. Gaetano Costa, chief prosecutor of Palermo, was murdered in August 1980, three months after signing 55 arrest warrants for the principal Palermo heroin trafficking families. His signature stood alone on the warrants, his colleagues in the prosecution office having refused to add their own.

In April 1982 the PCI regional secretary Pio La Torre, co-sponsor in March 1980 of a draft law which defined an 'association of a Mafia type' for the first time, thereby ensuring that the freezing and confiscation of Mafia assets could be effectively pursued, was murdered with his driver. The murder of La Torre in an attempt to block the law's progress was a sign of the harm it would inflict on the organization. A state's witness would later say, '*Cosa Nostra* had to deal the first blow to the one who had presented the draft law. And they did.'[21] La Torre had also campaigned strenuously against the installation of Cruise missiles at the Sicilian NATO base of Comiso on the grounds that it would offer opportunities for Mafia infiltration and enrichment.

Early in 1982, General Carlo Alberto Dalla Chiesa was offered the post of Prefect of Palermo. His successful strategies while in charge of the anti-terrorist fight during the 1970s and early 1980s had won him national admiration, and he wanted equally firm powers to deal with the Mafia. Before he could fully argue his case for these the La Torre murder prompted his departure for Palermo. Dalla Chiesa did not receive the political support or the powers of investigation and coordination he requested, and in an interview given a month before his death he stated,

> I think I understand the new rules of the game: the powerful man is killed when a fatal combination occurs – he becomes too dangerous, but he can be killed because he is isolated. Costa became too dangerous when, against the majority in the prosecution office, he decided to incriminate the Inzerillos and Spatolas. But he was isolated, therefore he could be killed, cancelled out like a foreign body.[22]

On 3 September 1982 Dalla Chiesa was murdered with his young wife and bodyguard while driving through central Palermo.

The *Rognoni–La Torre* Law

The murders of Pio La Torre and of General Dalla Chiesa marked a new initiative in the antimafia fight. Parliament created the office of High Commissioner for the Mafia Fight, endowing it with many of the

Murders of State Representatives by *Cosa Nostra*, 1963–98

Date	Victim(s)
30 June 1963	seven *carabinieri* and bomb disposal experts
5 May 1971	Pietro Scaglione, prosecutor general of Palermo, and driver Antonino Lo Russo
20 July 1977	*Carabiniere* Colonel Giuseppe Russo
9 March 1979	Michele Reina, Provincial Secretary of Palermo DC
21 July 1979	Boris Giuliano, head of Palermo Flying Squad
25 September 1979	Judge Cesare Terranova, with driver Lenin Mancuso
6 January 1980	Piersanti Mattarella, DC President of the Sicilian Region
3 May 1980	*Carabiniere* Captain Emanuele Basile
6 August 1980	Gaetano Costa, chief prosecutor, Palermo
30 April 1982	Pio La Torre, Regional Secretary, PCI
3 September 1982	General Carlo Alberto Dalla Chiesa, wife Emanuela and bodyguard Domenico Russo
14 November 1982	Calogero Zucchetto, officer of Palermo Flying Squad
25 January 1983	Giacomo 'Ciaccio' Montalto, assistant chief prosecutor, Trapani
13 June 1983	*Carabiniere* Captain Mario D'Aleo, Corporal Giuseppe Bommarito and *carabiniere* Pietro Morici
29 July 1983	Rocco Chinnici, chief examining magistrate, Palermo, bodyguards Mario Trapassi, Salvatore Bartolotta and the janitor of his apartment building, Stefano Li Sacchi
28 July 1985	Giuseppe Montana, head of 'capture of fugitives' section of Palermo Flying Squad
6 August 1985	Antonino Cassarà, deputy head of Palermo Flying Squad, bodyguard Roberto Antiochia
14 January 1988	Police officer Natale Mondo
25 September 1988	Antonio Saetta, President of Palermo Court of Appeal, and son Stefano
21 September 1990	Rosario Livatino, public prosecutor, Agrigento
9 August 1991	Antonio Scopelliti, Supreme Court judge
4 April 1992	*Carabiniere* Marshal Giuliano Guazzelli, colleague of judge Livatino
12 March 1992	Salvo Lima, Euro-MP
23 May 1992	Judge Giovanni Falcone, Judge Francesca Morvillo Falcone, bodyguards Rocco Di Cillo, Vito Schifani, Antonio Montinaro
19 July 1992	Judge Paolo Borsellino, bodyguards Agostino Catalano, Walter Cusina, Vincenzo Li Muli, Emanuela Loi, Claudio Traina

coordinating functions previously requested by Dalla Chiesa, and passed Law 646 on 13 September 1982, known as the *Rognoni–La Torre* Law (after the amalgamation of La Torre's proposals with a draft law presented in 1981 by DC Interior Minister Virginio Rognoni). The law made two important innovations – it modified article 416 of the criminal code by creating the crime of 'association of a Mafia type' and it extended existing powers – passed in legislation of 1956 and 1965 – to limit the freedom of movement and carry out surveillance of suspected criminals. It also incorporated the asset-tracing, freezing and confiscation powers of the 1965 law. According to the new article 416 *bis* of the criminal code, an association was 'of a Mafia type' when it consisted of three or more members and

> when those who belong to it make use of the power of intimidation afforded by the associative bond and the state of subjugation and criminal silence which derives from it to commit crimes, to acquire directly or indirectly the management or control of economic activities, concessions, authorizations or public contracts and services, either to gain unjust profits or advantages for themselves or for others.

The penalty for ordinary membership of such an association was three to six years of imprisonment, while that for promoting, leading or organizing it was between four and nine years. Aggravating factors included the use or availability of arms, and the use of criminally derived profits to gain or maintain control of the economic activities concerned. If the Mafia association were proven, neither the guilty party nor their spouse, children or cohabitant could be included on accredited professional lists, be recipients of public funding or be granted a licence to provide public services. Persons convicted for Mafia association were obliged to communicate to the tax police any variations in the value of their assets over 20 million lire (around $13 000). Whoever omitted to do so was given an additional prison sentence and the assets not reported were ordered to be confiscated. For those convicted, the confiscation of the instruments or means used to commit the crime, and of any direct or indirect proceeds of it became obligatory. Assets could also be confiscated from third persons who had at their disposal the proceeds or assets deriving from criminal activities which had been made available to them by the convicted person.

Over and above the ordinary criminal association, the Mafia-type association has three qualities deriving specifically from its methods of operation – intimidatory force, the power to subjugate and the imposition of *omertà* or criminal silence. Whereas an ordinary criminal association has the sole objective of committing crimes, the Mafia association may be focused on other aims such as gaining unjust advantages or monopoly-type privileges. The commission of ordinary crimes may be part of this larger project.[23]

An investigation based on Mafia association can be triggered by an apparent discrepancy between a suspect's nominal income and his extravagant spending habits, and therefore 'upstream' from the usual investigative starting-point of a specific crime. It may begin by looking at the flow and transparency of business transactions, from there to possible links between economic activity and criminal association and only then to a specific crime. Thus instead of having to prove the crime and then the Mafia association, since 1982 investigators have been able to pursue crime by means of the association.[24]

The fusion of public-order concerns with economic controls and socio-criminological theory made the law unique in Italian legislative history. Investigations were no longer concentrated on 'the crimes of the Mafia' but on 'the Mafia as a form of criminality', a dynamic organization engaged in a wide variety of legal and illegal activities. It was the conceptualization of wisdom expressed by the Antimafia Commission in 1965 and never realized – 'We do not mean that the magistrate should fix all his attention on the wood alone and neglect to study the individual trees, but rather we draw to his attention the necessity that when examining each individual tree one should never forget that it stands in the midst of that particular wood.'[25]

Although some of the provisions of the *Rognoni–La Torre* law had existed on paper since 1965, investigations had ground to a halt because of the difficulties of pursuing the specificity of the Mafia-type association within the parameters of laws against common crime, as the then Colonel Dalla Chiesa had noted in 1970. Equally importantly for the efficacy of the law, there were judges who were competent to apply it, such as Rocco Chinnici, appointed chief examining magistrate in Palermo after the Terranova murder and the founder of Palermo's antimafia 'pool' or team of judges in which Falcone and Borsellino worked. The pool system had originally been set up in the 1970s by anti-terrorism judges in northern Italy, and was a methodological approach particularly appropriate for those whose lives were constantly at risk. It was based on teamwork and the sharing of all vital information such that the assassination of one magistrate would not eliminate a unique repository of knowledge.

Luciano Violante, Chairman of the Antimafia Commission from 1992 to 1994, summed up the strategic importance of the moment:

Until Falcone there was no antimafia fight; individual crimes like murder, extortion and dynamite attacks were pursued but the organization itself was untouched. Falcone and his chief Rocco Chinnici realized it wasn't enough just to look for the authors of individual crimes and that in any case they would never even be arrested unless Mafia association was understood and pursued as a crime in itself. This reform, allied with the particular professional skill of Falcone, produced an explosive mixture for *Cosa Nostra* precisely because Falcone was ready and waiting to apply it.[26]

The wave of attacks on institutional figures coincided with a second 'Mafia war' which reached a peak in 1981–82, and caused around one thousand deaths among *Cosa Nostra* affiliates and their families. It grew out of rivalry between the Corleone faction, led by Totò Riina, and the Inzerillo–Bontate clans in Palermo, but unlike the first war of 1961–63 which saw entire families lined up against opposing families, the *Corleonesi* skilfully manipulated their opponents, drawing in individuals from the opposing faction and using them to trap and then eliminate their own relatives.[27] The surviving losers, the majority of whom belonged to the Inzerillo–Bontate clans, fled abroad, leaving the *Corleonesi* and their allies the Greco, Calò and Marchese clans in Palermo to dominate the scene in the years to come.

Diligent police work together with the new legislative powers brought impressive results: some 15 000 individuals were reported for Mafia association between 1982 and 1986 and over 20 000 asset-tracing investigations were carried out.[28] Several heroin refineries were discovered, leading to the arrest of a number of drug and money couriers. By the end of 1982 a police investigation known as the 'Report of the 162 (Michele Greco + 161)' provided judge Chinnici and his colleagues with a 'map' of the winners in the Mafia war on which the foundations of the first maxi-trial were laid.

Chinnici did not live to see the results of his work however: he was blown up in July 1983 by a car bomb together with two bodyguards and the janitor of his apartment block. It was the first occasion on which *Cosa Nostra* used the plastic explosive Semtex, which all the Palermo clans had obtained from a Lebanese arms and drug trafficker, Bou Chebel Ghassam. Semtex was used in 1992 and again in 1993. Chinnici had kept a diary in which he wrote frequently of his sense of isolation, and noted his suspicions of several colleagues and their links with business and political figures close to the Mafia, one of whom had suggested that Chinnici should avoid giving delicate investigations to Giovanni Falcone.

After Chinnici's murder, judge Antonino Caponnetto was appointed as chief examining magistrate.

The punishment of over-zealous public servants was relentless. Giacomo 'Ciaccio' Montalto, assistant chief prosecutor of Trapani, was shot dead in January 1983. He had prosecuted numerous members of the powerful Minore clan in a period when a colleague, prosecutor Antonio Costa, was in collusion with the same clan; Costa was later sent to prison for having accepted bribes and for illegal detention of arms. Captain Mario D'Aleo was assassinated with two *carabinieri* officers in June 1983, and police commissioner Giuseppe Montana in July 1985. Less than two weeks later Ninni Cassarà, author of the '162 report' and deputy head of the Palermo Flying Squad, was murdered with one of his two bodyguards, Roberto Antiochia. (The other, Natale Mondo, survived but was assassinated in 1988). During the tense period that followed Cassarà's death Falcone and Borsellino were finalizing the indictments for the maxi-trial. For their own safety they were advised to complete the work in a more secure location and were flown to the island of Asinara, off Sardinia, where one of Italy's top security prisons was located. On their return each received a bill for his board and lodging. The sums were duly paid.[29]

The period of four years between the passing of the *Rognoni–La Torre* law and the maxi-trial in one respect mirrored the state of affairs between 1963 and the Catanzaro and Bari trials of 1968–69: many *mafiosi* went abroad, especially those linked to the losers in the Mafia war. A new factor was that of collaboration. The betrayals and deception perpetrated by the *Corleonesi* had caused a number of imprisoned *mafiosi* such as Tommaso Buscetta, seven of whose relatives were killed at the end of 1982, to take their revenge by revealing the secrets of the organization. According to Giovanni Falcone,

> Buscetta gave us innumerable confirmations of the structure, the recruitment techniques, the functions of *Cosa Nostra*. But most of all he gave us a broad global vision, the whole spectrum of the phenomenon. He gave us an essential key to reading and under-standing, a language and a code to decipher it [...] Buscetta gave me the coordinates that permitted me to devise a working method.[30]

The reputation of the antimafia pool stirred up jealousy among colleagues of judges Falcone and Borsellino and criticisms were also voiced by a number of Italian intellectuals: writing in Italy's leading daily paper *Corriere della Sera* on 10 January 1997, the respected Sicilian writer Leonardo Sciascia suggested that certain individuals, including the then mayor of Palermo, Leoluca Orlando, were constructing their careers on the status of 'antimafia professionals' and criticized the promotion of Paolo Borsellino to chief prosecutor of Marsala over the heads of more senior colleagues on the sole grounds of his Mafia expertise. The comments caused a storm of controversy.

In January 1988 Antonino Caponnetto retired as chief examining magistrate, expecting that Giovanni Falcone would be appointed his successor. However this time the Superior Judicial Council (CSM) decided on the basis of seniority to nominate Antonino Meli, whose experience of Mafia investigations was negligible compared to Falcone's, and whose working methods ran directly contrary to Falcone's own. Within a few months of taking up his post Meli had appropriated most of Falcone's cases and the antimafia pool was virtually extinct. Caponnetto would repeat many times after Falcone's death that he had 'begun to die' in January 1988 as a result of progressive isolation. It was as if, the maxi-trial having concluded the previous December, there was a frantic haste to shelve the problem of the Mafia, to remove it psychologically from the public consciousness and return to 'normality'. This was certainly the prevalent attitude among senior institutional figures: in April 1988 Interior Minister Amintore Fanfani stated categorically that the Mafia was not one of his priorities; in July his successor Antonio Gava and Chief of Police Vincenzo Parisi promised that there was 'nothing to worry about' and that all was 'under control'.

In July 1988 Paolo Borsellino gave interviews to two national newspapers in which he criticized the dismantling of the antimafia pool and the paralysis of Mafia investigations in Sicily. At the end of the month Giovanni Falcone asked to be transferred to another post because of the impossible working conditions in Palermo and the 'infamous slander and denigratory campaign of exceptional baseness' directed against him.[31] Public alarm prompted President Cossiga to request a full investigation by the CSM, in the course of which Falcone expressed his conviction that the campaign emanated from judicial circles.

After the murder of judge Saetta and his son in September 1988 (see Chapter 1) the office of High Commissioner for the Mafia Fight which had been created after the Dalla Chiesa murder was restructured with more extensive powers. Falcone applied for the job but again he was passed over, this time in favour of Domenico Sica, a judge with long experience of terrorism in Rome but none of the Mafia in Sicily. In November Falcone and Meli made peace and the request for a transfer was withdrawn.

The gradual erosion of the accusatory principles on which the maxi-trial had rested – caused by successive verdicts of the Appeal and Supreme courts – began to be evident in early 1989, when only 60 of the 342 defendants convicted at the maxi-trial were still in prison. In June of that year Falcone was pursuing enquiries into *Cosa Nostra*'s financial activities in Switzerland with the assistance of Swiss judges Carla del Ponte and Claudio Lehmann, who came to Palermo to confer with him. On the 19th, Falcone invited his Swiss colleagues to relax during the following day's lunch break at the seaside villa he rented near Palermo, but the work took longer than envisaged and only he returned to the villa for a brief rest. In the early hours of 21 June, a bodyguard noticed a sports bag lying on the beach below the villa, left there the day before. It contained 58 sticks of dynamite with a remote control detonating device. In fact, the bomb as found could not have exploded – either it had been incorrectly assembled or it was intended as a warning.

Falcone initially offered journalists two possible motives for the attack – the money-laundering investigations he was conducting with his Swiss colleagues, or an attempt by one faction of *Cosa Nostra* to hegemonize the other by eliminating a common enemy. He was convinced that an insider had passed on the information about his likely movements. Strange rumours went around during the following weeks: some claimed that the bomb had been a fake because *Cosa Nostra* 'never missed' its key objectives; it was even said that Falcone had organized it himself in order to win sympathy for his application to become assistant chief prosecutor of Palermo. Investigations into the bomb were sluggish and were overshadowed throughout the summer by the circulation of five anonymous letters relating to the surprise arrest in Sicily in May of Salvatore Contorno, an important state's witness in the maxi-trial, who had been discovered in a hideout full of arms and in the company of *mafioso* cousins with whom he was apparently about to carry out a series of attacks. The anonymous letters, which were written on Interior Ministry notepaper and were obviously penned by someone thoroughly familiar with judicial procedures in Palermo, were circulated in parliamentary and media circles. They accused Falcone, Domenico Sica and other senior law-enforcement officials of having secretly lured Contorno back to Palermo in order to wage war on the *Corleonese* faction of *Cosa Nostra*, a conflict which would culminate with the death or arrest of *capo dei capi* Totò Riina. The investigation into the anonymous letter-writer collapsed in farce after a clumsy effort by High Commissioner Sica to take the fingerprints of the Palermo judge who had fallen under suspicion. This event served to confirm the growing impression that the High Commission for the Mafia Fight was an ill-conceived institution with an imprecise role. It had been envisaged as a means of providing coordination and efficiency to organized crime investigations throughout Italy, but in practice it had created a service in which judicial, police and intelligence functions were confusingly blurred. Technically a Prefect and therefore under the authority of the Interior Ministry, High Commissioner Domenico Sica had not resigned from the judiciary but combined the role of 'superjudge' with intelligence and police powers which made his position largely unaccountable.

The summer of 1989 was the bleakest time of Giovanni Falcone's career, when he realized that an irrevocable decision to eliminate him had been taken and that his enemies were not confined to the ranks of *Cosa Nostra*.[32] In early July, perhaps to protect himself, he uncharacteristically speculated on the background to the attack on his life during a press interview. It had been organized by

> extremely sophisticated minds who are trying to direct certain actions of the Mafia. Perhaps there exist points of contact between the top level of *Cosa Nostra* and occult centres of power that have other interests. I have the impression that this is the most likely scenario if we want to understand the real reasons for someone wanting to assassinate me. [..] I'm undergoing exactly the same process as that which led to the elimination of General Dalla Chiesa. That's the script. All you need is eyes to see.[33]

Not until December 1997 were arrest warrants for the attempt on Falcone's life issued for Totò Riina and several other imprisoned *Cosa Nostra* bosses. The investigating magistrate commented, 'The hypothesis that there were *eminences grises* external to *Cosa Nostra* in the planning and decision-making for the attack on Giovanni Falcone's life was until recently a possibility, whereas now it appears a probability.'[34]

The attempts to discredit his work did not prevent Falcone's appointment as assistant chief prosecutor of Palermo, which was announced in July after the other applicants had withdrawn in his favour. During the second half of 1989 the focus of organized crime violence moved from Sicily to Calabria, where a full-scale war was being waged between rival factions of the *'Ndrangheta*. Northern Italy also registered a high percentage of Mafia-related violence, with increasing signs that Milan had become an international crossroads of money laundering and narcotics distribution.

In 1990 elections were held for the Superior Judicial Council, whose membership was composed two-thirds of 'robed' judges and one-third of lay political party appointees. Falcone put his name forward for the four-year assignment on the basis of a series of proposals, including a national antimafia prosecution service which would streamline and coordinate the work of the existing prosecution offices around the country, channelling information and experiences as appropriate. His decision not to run a campaign and to let his proposals speak for him was taken as arrogance, and he was not elected.

Heroes and martyrs

In September 1990 *Cosa Nostra* murdered a young judge from Agrigento, Rosario Livatino. An eyewitness saw him being shot at by two men on a motorcycle while driving along the highway between Canicattì and Agrigento. He had tried to escape by running down an escarpment and through an adjacent field, but tripped and was shot through the head at point-blank range. The 37-year-old Livatino had been investigating the activities of *Cosa Nostra* in the Agrigento area and had ordered asset-tracing investigations to be carried out of prominent local *mafiosi*. The murder shocked public opinion and provoked a flood of criticism that 'youngster judges' should be exposed to such dangers.

When Antonino Meli retired in 1990 Falcone supported the appointment of his colleague, the more senior assistant chief prosecutor Pietro Giammanco, on the understanding that Giammanco would let him handle all the Mafia investigations. But this did not happen, and Giammanco deliberately undermined his work, excluding him from politically sensitive investigations and preventing him from acquiring the information he needed. 'I am like a bear in a cage', he told his friend and former boss Antonino Caponnetto.[35] From a sense of duty that dictated he should not 'rock the boat' too much, Falcone put his signature to the La Torre murder indictment even though he considered its conclusions to be peremptory. This was the last compromise he made before accepting the position of Director of Criminal Affairs in the Ministry of Justice in February 1991.

In August 1991 *Cosa Nostra* murdered a Palermo businessman who for several months had used the print and television media to denounce continuing attempts to extort his business and to lament the lack of support given him by the local business community. Proprietor of a men's clothing factory, 67-year-old Libero Grassi had received the first 'requests' for money in 1984. When he refused he was given several warnings to pay up, was robbed of precisely the sum demanded of him by the extortionists, had his dog nearly killed and was threatened by telephone and to his face. After the publication in January 1991 of an open letter written by Grassi to his extortionist in Sicily's main daily newspaper, he was provided with protection for himself and his family, but this became increasingly sporadic. He succeeded in identifying his extortionists, who were arrested in March, but was punished a few weeks later by an arson attack on his factory.

In early April 1991, Catania judge Luigi Russo acquitted several prominent businessmen of collusion with the Mafia on the grounds that, although they had tolerated and even paid the Mafia, they had been obliged to do so in order to work without harassment. Libero Grassi attacked the decision bitterly:

It is the juridical legitimization of the relationship of cohabitation–connivance between entrepreneur and *mafioso*. Judge Russo has in practice admitted that if the Catania [businessmen] had not had links with the Mafia they could not have done their jobs. This translates into a kind of collective impunity, a general amnesty which justifies past, present and future. Worst of all: it's an indicator of how to behave in the face of *Cosa Nostra*'s offers.[36]

Far from receiving solidarity from business colleagues, Grassi was criticized and progressively isolated, accused of demolishing the image of the Palermo business world.

My colleagues have begun to attack me, saying that one should not wash dirty clothes in public. But in the meantime they continue to put up with it: because I know that they all pay. In my opinion, being intimidated and being collusive is the same thing. Some confess to giving in out of fear, others boast about having important strings to pull. These are very common attitudes; but I think that if everyone was ready to collaborate with the police and *carabinieri*, to report and to name names, this racketeering would not last long. I myself have had eight people arrested. If 200 businessmen talked, 1600 *mafiosi* would be in handcuffs. Don't you think we would have won?[37]

Grassi's frequent television appearances had made him a popular public figure, and outrage following his murder accelerated momentum for the new national antimafia police and prosecution services which were created by law in the following three months, together with a package of measures which provided more protection to victims of extortion and closed the loophole that had led in February to the release of convicted Mafia killers.

Between March 1988 and the end of the legislative period in February 1992 a new Antimafia Commission under the chairmanship of PCI Senator Gherardo Chiaromonte worked intensively, with the support of Interior Minister Vincenzo Scotti and Justice Minister Claudio Martelli. The Commission studied the connections between the four Mafia organizations, and subversive links between the Mafia and secret Masonic lodges dating back to 1970. It carried out detailed studies of specific sectors of Mafia activity and lobbied for the introduction of new legislation, some of which was passed in the legislative period. Among the laws introduced were: a reform of the *Rognoni–La Torre* law, whereby asset seizure and confiscation provisions were applicable to other forms of criminal association including drug trafficking, to persons whose income was derived from specific crimes such as extortion, usury, kidnapping, money laundering, smuggling or prostitution and to persons whose activities favoured those crimes (Law 55 of March 1990) ; anti-money-laundering legislation (Laws 55 of March 1990 and 197 of July 1991); legislation on state's witnesses (Law 82 of March 1991) and a law empowering the Interior Minster to dissolve municipal councils on grounds of infiltration by organized crime (Law 221 of July 1991). According to Law 55 of 1990, no one who had been charged with crimes typical of Mafia-type association, or who had preventive measures applied against them, could stand as a candidate for office in a regional, provincial or town council or become a councillor or assessor, health service or any other public sector administrator. The appointment or election of such individuals was annulled automatically if it had already taken place. By a further law in June 1990 local administrators were removed from office when they committed 'acts contrary to the Constitution or for serious and persistent violations of the law or for serious reasons of public order'. The laws proved an effective tool: between November 1990 and the end of 1993, 185 local administrators were removed from office.[38] By the end of 1997, as Table 2.1 shows, a total of 98 municipal councils had been dissolved for Mafia infiltration.[39]

Looking ahead to the general election of 5 April 1992, in February of that year the Antimafia Commission urged political parties to apply a code of self-regulation when presenting candidates, a measure intended to mirror the legislative provisions for public-office holders passed in 1990: no one should stand for election who had been committed for trial, was a fugitive from the law, was serving a criminal sentence, was subject to preventive measures or was convicted, even though not definitively, for crimes of corruption, Mafia association, murder, kidnap, violence, robbery, money laundering, fraud, drugs or arms-related offences; crimes against public administration, falsification or perjury. The Commission promised to monitor adherence to the code by all the parties and to denounce failures to observe it.[40] To judge from past records, the political parties were in need of the warning: the Commission noted that in the 1990 local elections 13 candidates in Reggio Calabria had been reported for Mafia association, 8 of whom were elected, while another 106, 59 of whom were elected, had been reported for crimes against public administration. In Naples, 53 candidates had been 'contiguous with' *Camorra* groups. It was estimated that in the previous general election of 1987, 10 per cent of all votes cast in the southern regions had been 'directly controlled' by the Mafia and 25 per cent had been Mafia-influenced.[41]

Table 2.1   Municipal councils dissolved on grounds of Mafia infiltration (by Law 221/91), total at 31 December 1997

Sicily	27
Campania	44
Calabria	18
Apulia	7
Basilicata	1
Piedmont	1
Other regions	0
total	98

Source: Interior Ministry, 1998.

A week before the election, the Antimafia Commission reported that on the basis of information received from two-thirds of the prefectures in the country, 33 candidates standing in the forthcoming elections were 'non presentable' according to the code of self-regulation. All the 33 had either been committed for trial or had been convicted of charges ranging from membership of an armed band and subversion to fraud, extortion, corruption, robbery and murder.[42]

By early 1992 it had become clear that a stronger political leadership in the antimafia fight, together with Falcone's tenure in the Rome 'desk job', was becoming an encumbrance not only for the Mafia but also for those who were accustomed to the customary bureaucratic immobility of the Justice Ministry. On his first Sunday as Director of Criminal Affairs, Falcone had drafted a questionnaire to send to all the Prosecutors General in Italy to seek their views and suggestions for improving coordination of the activities of the prosecution offices. Without exception, the first responses he received ignored his request and asked whether he had the authority to take such an initiative. Only after strenuous diplomatic efforts on the part of Justice Minister Martelli was the rift healed.[43]

The antimafia struggle in Italy which began over one hundred years ago with Emanuele Notarbartolo has been characterized by long periods of inertia and compromise punctuated by knee-jerk reaction and frenzied activity. The result has been a Mafia–Antimafia seesaw, swinging between alternate highs and lows with long periods of equilibrium. The balance was upset when isolated individuals – the heroes of the Antimafia, endowed with unusual intuition and courage – dared to violate the truce of reciprocal tolerance. But these individuals were easily identifiable and could be eliminated, after which, following a period of reaction and reorganization on the part of the State, the balance was re-established.

The pattern emerges in two consecutive sequences of action>reaction>restoration of status quo: the car bomb at Ciaculli which prompted a law-enforcement offensive and the setting up of the first Antimafia Commission, followed by the acquittals at Catanzaro and Bari; and the series of attacks on institutional figures between 1979 and 1982 which led to the passing of the *Rognoni–La Torre* Law and the maxi-trial. The third part of this sequence is exemplified by successive verdicts in the Palermo Appeal Court and in the Supreme Court (until 1992), certain decisions taken by the CSM and, possibly, collusive arrangements between Mafia and non-Mafia individuals to pervert the course of justice (see Chapter 7). The continuity was only broken when a combination of national and international circumstances prevented the habitual swing back towards the 'normalization' of relations. With the Supreme Court verdict of January 1992 the Mafia end of the seesaw hit the ground. By then the Antimafia had gained momentum and instead of being halted by the murders of the last remaining heroes, it was accelerated by them. If the Antimafia ultimately triumphs – and the question remained open in 1999 – then it will be because society as a whole wills the defeat of the Mafia, not just the few who step out of line. To paraphrase Brecht, blessed is the land that has no need of heroes ...

3
The Political Response

Of national democratic institutions with public order responsibilities, Parliament alone, unlike the police, judiciary or military forces, is directly accountable to the population. In a situation of national emergency caused by criminal action it must therefore act and be seen to act immediately. It has three principal tasks: (a) to intervene to restore calm and guarantee public order; (b) to evaluate the appropriateness of existing anti-crime measures and introduce modifications or new legislation where necessary; (c) to ensure that these are implemented, and that all persons with relevant institutional responsibilities are fulfilling their duties.

When the Italians looked to their elected representatives for an immediate response after the murder of Giovanni Falcone, his wife and three bodyguards, they found an institutional vacuum – no president, a newly installed parliament with no Speaker for either the Chamber of Deputies or Senate and a caretaker government expecting to handle no more than the daily oversight of routine business. Moreover the ritual post-election horse-trading for state office was expected to be particularly prolonged and complex on this occasion: the general election of 5 April had fragmented the vote and weakened the power base of the two habitual government allies, the Christian Democratic Party (DC) and the Socialist Party (PSI) as allegations of political corruption began to spread. The traditional parties had all suffered losses – in the Chamber of Deputies the DC had dropped almost five percentage points to 29.7 per cent, the PSI to 13.6 from 14.3 per cent and the former Communist Party, making its general election debut as the Democratic Left (PDS) and split off from its extreme left wing, had taken 16 per cent of the former party's 26.6 per cent[1] – whereas the smaller but statistically significant opposition protest parties such as the Northern League (*Lega Nord*), the Refounded Communists (*Rifondazione Comunista*) and the Sicilian-based Net – (*La Rete*) led by former mayor of Palermo Leoluca Orlando – had made impressive gains. The so-called 'CAF' alliance of PSI secretary Bettino Craxi, DC Prime Minister Giulio Andreotti and DC secretary Arnaldo Forlani had been weakened by the murder of Salvo Lima in March, widely interpreted as a warning to Andreotti not to run for President at the expiry of Cossiga's seven-year mandate in July. Cossiga's surprise resignation two weeks after the election and the evidence of illicit party funding of the PSI emerging from the Milan 'Bribesville' investigations effectively ended Craxi's chances of becoming Prime Minister. Cossiga explained his decision to resign on the grounds that the vote had given an unequivocal sign of a need for change, for strong government and for a head of state at the height of his powers rather than one who was concluding his mandate. The national emergency caused by the Falcone attack concentrated parliamentary attention and on 25 May, after 15 unsuccessful ballots to elect a new president (in whose remit lay the invitation to form a government), the first impasse was overcome, with the election of Oscar Luigi Scalfaro, a former judge, member of the Constituent Assembly of 1946 and a seasoned DC politician with a reputation for moral rectitude. In his inaugural address as President on 28 May Scalfaro took a strong stance over corruption, with an implicit encouragement to the judiciary to continue their work. 'The abuse of public money is an extremely serious occurrence which defrauds and robs the citizen who faithfully pays his taxes [..] There is no greater danger for democracy than the murky interweaving of politics and business.'[2] It was an important signal, given that the Italian President is also the chairman of the Superior Judicial Council (CSM), the judges' self-governing body.

Scalfaro invited Giuliano Amato, a long-time economic adviser to Craxi but untainted by the corruption scandal, to form a government. The process was not completed until late June when Amato retained PSI deputy Claudio Martelli as Justice Minister but appointed DC Nicola Mancino to replace Vincenzo Scotti at the Interior.

In the meantime on 8 June, 16 days after the massacre at Capaci, the outgoing Andreotti administration passed a law decree which went into effect immediately. (In Italy a government law decree is a temporary measure which can be enacted only on criteria of urgency. It automatically lapses after 60 days unless it is either reiterated or is ratified by Parliament, thereby becoming law.) Law Decree 306 of 8 June, containing modifications added after the Borsellino attack of 19 July, was converted into Law 356 on 7 August. The most important provisions included investigative procedures for serious crime, measures to encourage state's witnesses or collaborators, asset confiscation provisions, and prison regulations for Mafia leaders.[3] Subsequent legislation is described in the Annex to this chapter.

Law Decree 306/8 June

Investigation of serious crime

The maximum period permitted for the preliminary investigation of specific serious crimes – that is, the period within which investigations can be carried out in secrecy – was extended for the more serious types of crime (aggravated robbery or extortion, terrorism, detention of arms and of large quantities of drugs) from 6 to 12 months. This period could in certain circumstances be extended to 18 months and, in the case of Mafia-type crimes, to two years. Officials of the *Direzione Investigativa Antimafia* (DIA), the interagency antimafia police force, could be delegated by a public prosecutor to hold 'investigative conversations' with prison inmates with the aim of preventing or investigating Mafia-type crimes. In urgent cases the authority of the Chief of Police was sufficient. The head of the national antimafia prosecution service, the DNA *(Direzione Nazionale Antimafia),* (see Chapter 4) could decide to hold 'investigative conversations' on his own initiative. For those caught *in flagrante* participating in crimes relating to Mafia association, arrest ceased to be optional and became obligatory.

Article 416 *bis* of the criminal code concerning the crime of Mafia association was extended by a third clause to include a reference to Mafia pressure on electoral candidates. An association was thus 'of a Mafia type' when it consisted of three or more members, and,

> when those who belong to it make use of the power of intimidation afforded by the associative bond and the state of subjugation and criminal silence which derives from it to commit crimes, to acquire directly or indirectly the management or control of economic activities, concessions, authorizations or public contracts and services, either to gain unjust profits or advantages for themselves or for others, *or with the aim of preventing or obstructing the free exercise of the vote, or of procuring votes for themselves or for others at a time of electoral consultation.*

A subsequent addition created the offence of obtaining the promise of votes in exchange for financial reward. In practice, this was both relatively rare and almost impossible to prove; an alternative proposal from the Democratic Left (PDS), which would have criminalized 'the promise to favour the granting of concessions, authorizations, public works contracts, contributions, public financing or the realization of illicit profits in whatever way', was overruled by the DC and PSI.[4]

Penalties for the crime of kidnap for ransom were increased. Immunity could be granted to officers of the DIA and of other specialized police units if, in the course of an investigation, they infiltrated criminal groups and became involved in simulated arms deals or in money-laundering operations in order to acquire evidence. A prosecutor had to be informed about the presence of infiltrators, as in the past they had been placed at risk and even arrested because their role was not known about.

Since 1982 a public prosecutor could authorize the interception of telephone conversations of persons considered 'socially dangerous' and suspected of Mafia association who were subject to preventive measures such as asset restraint and special surveillance. Legislation passed in 1991 permitted the authorization of interception when the procedure was considered 'necessary' for the investigation of crimes relating to organized criminality (without specifying precise crimes) and when there was 'sufficient evidence' to justify suspicion of the individual or individuals concerned. The permitted duration for this procedure was 40 days, with a possible extension of up to 20 days. Decree 306 stated that, in the interests of *preventing*, or of obtaining information about, specific crimes such as Mafia association, kidnap for ransom, crimes committed in the context of Mafia association or of an association to traffic in drugs, the Interior Minister or, on his behalf, the Chief of Police, the Director of the DIA or other heads of special police units, could ask a judge or public prosecutor to authorize telephone interception. Preventive interception could be authorized on private property only if there was reason to believe that a crime had been perpetrated there. If the purpose of the interception was directed at the pursuit of a specific criminal or the investigation of a specific Mafia crime, it could be authorized with regard to private property even without such indication. Transcriptions of preventive interceptions could be used for intelligence purposes only, whereas those carried out after the commission of a crime were allowable as evidence in court.

Protection of state's witnesses

Legislation to encourage state witnesses or collaborators, sometimes known as *pentiti*, had been passed in 1991. The collaborator was defined as one who

> dissociating himself from others, acts in such a way as to prevent criminal activities from having further consequences, at the same time giving concrete assistance to the police or to the judicial authorities in the gathering of evidence which is decisive for the reconstruction of facts and for the identification or the capture of those responsible for committing crimes.

(The term *pentito* is inexact as it has overtones of moral repentance which is rarely the case and has no bearing on the individual's legal status.) For those who actively collaborated, terms of life imprisonment could be replaced by sentences ranging from 12 to 20 years and other sentences were reduced by from a third to a half. In addition to reductions in sentence, increased resources were made available for their physical and economic protection which automatically lapsed if they broke the terms of their agreement. The law stated that admission to a special protection programme and the evaluation of a collaborator's contribution should be made by a Central Committee composed of an under-secretary of State, a judge and five members of the police forces with particular expertise in the area. In practice, delays in setting up the Committee, a lack of provision in the law for standards by which the aspiring collaborator's contribution could be evaluated, a shortage of resources and an imprecise definition of the Committee's functions prevented satisfactory coordination between administration and operation, and between the Committee and the police units responsible for physical protection.[5] The already imperfect legislation came under considerable strain from the rapid increase in collaborators from 1992 onwards, as will be seen in Chapter 4, and in mid-1999 was urgently awaiting modification by Parliament.

The June 1992 law decree made provision for state's witnesses to be heard in court trials by video testimony wherever these facilities existed. The intention was to avoid the costly and potentially dangerous transfer of state's witnesses to prisons adjacent to courtrooms where their proximity to other, non-collaborating prisoners could put their lives at risk. There were clear advantages to this system from the prosecution's point of view, but it was seen as the erosion of a defendant's right to attend court trials or, in cases when a collaborator accused a former companion, of a defendant's right to have his accuser cross-examined in open court. Consequently video testimony was rare until January 1998, when state's witnesses and prisoners subject to maximum security restrictions could be obliged by law to testify at a distance.

From June 1992, defendants who had given evidence as state's witnesses either in a previous trial or in pre-court hearings before an investigating magistrate for the trial in progress could be absolved from repeating the same statements in open court and, even if they retracted or refused to repeat their earlier statements, these were still allowable as evidence and did not require further corroboration. The provision was introduced on the grounds that collaborators or their families might be intimidated into withdrawing their evidence. This provision was modified in 1997 and again in 1998 (see Chapter 4).

Asset confiscation

Law Decree 306 provided that for those charged with specific Mafia-related crimes and who had assets which were out of proportion to their declared income or to their stated economic activities and whose legitimate source they were unable to justify, confiscation of the share of assets representing the unjustified source of income was *obligatory*. In February 1994 this measure was judged to be invalid by the Italian Constitutional Court because the confiscation concerned persons who were accused rather than convicted; the law was modified in June of that year to take account of the verdict, and henceforth would apply to those who had been *convicted of or who had plea- bargained* on charges of Mafia-type crimes and could not prove the legitimate source of their assets.

Prison regime and regulations

Benefits granted to prisoners on grounds of good behaviour which enabled them to take up work outside the prison, leave the prison on parole or spend short periods at home with their families were abolished for those convicted of serious crimes unless the individuals concerned were actively collaborating with the authorities.

Article 41 *bis* of Law 354 of 1975 had been introduced as an emergency measure to deal with prison unrest and revolts during the years of terrorism. It authorized the Interior and/or Justice Minister to suspend certain prison regulations, especially those concerning the socialization and re-educative elements of the prison regime, and to impose exceptional security measures until such time as order could be re-established, or for as long as the suspension of such regulations was felt to be necessary to the smooth running of the prison. It was modified in June 1992 to exclude mention of 'revolts or other serious emergency situations' and to exclude reference to the re-establishment of order. The new article stated that when there was 'serious concern over the maintenance of order and security', the Interior and/or Justice Minister could suspend prison regulations for certain categories of prisoner within the maximum security level, including those detained for Mafia-type crimes. The application of article 41 *bis* restricted visits to one per month, and exclusively to close family members. Prisoners could only communicate with visitors by intercom through thick glass, mail was subject to censorship, telephone calls were recorded and no outgoing calls were allowed. Prisoners could not take part in organized sporting or cultural activities and were allowed one hour of exercise each morning and afternoon. The aim of article 41 *bis* was to prevent association, and therefore the exchange of messages, between Mafia prisoners and to break the chain of command between Mafia bosses and their subordinates, whereby the *capi* preserved their prestige and authority in prison through actions committed by henchmen outside. In July 1993 article 41 *bis* was extended for a further year, and in February 1995 it was prorogued until 31 December 1999.

In the days following the Borsellino attack, 400 imprisoned Mafia bosses were transferred by helicopter and military transport aircraft from Palermo's Ucciardone prison to top security prisons on the mainland at Ascoli Piceno and Cuneo, and to the island prisons of Pianosa, seven miles beyond the coast of Elba, and Asinara, off Sardinia, where the severity of the article 41 *bis* regime was accentuated by geographical remoteness.

Other measures contained in Law Decree 306

- Restrictions were placed on the quantity of munitions that a private individual could purchase.
- Arms and munitions vendors were required to communicate to the authorities lists of arms and explosives sold.
- In order to search a specific area for arms or in the hunt for fugitives, agents of the judicial police – police acting on the orders of a public prosecutor – could search entire buildings or blocks of buildings, notifying a public prosecutor immediately and at the latest within 12 hours of doing so.
- To profit from conditions of economic difficulty of another by charging usury rates became a criminal offence.

- Penalties for perjury were increased, as were those for falsification of documents produced for court proceedings such as medical certificates.
- The office of the High Commissioner for the Mafia Fight, created in September 1982, was to be absorbed by the new antimafia police, the DIA, by the end of 1992.
- The Parliamentary Antimafia Commission was reconvened.
- The position of national antimafia prosecutor was reopened to applicants of suitable experience.
- The number of prison warders was increased by 2000.

The provisions of Law Decree 306 were debated throughout the summer. While there was general agreement that the introduction of tighter laws was necessary, a significant current of opinion held that the measures were an unbalanced response, and that they overturned the cardinal principles of the 1989 code of criminal procedure which had aimed to establish greater parity between prosecution and defence. The most controversial areas were those concerning the abolition of concessions to prisoners other than state's witnesses, the interception of communications, the admissibility of accomplice evidence (the testimonies of state's witnesses), and the extended period of secret investigations.

Professor Guido Neppi Modona, a leading criminologist who had contributed to the drafting of the 1989 code of criminal procedure, was one of the decree's sharpest critics. He saw its provisions as a sign that Italy was still not ready for a democratic application of the criminal law, and said its conversion into law would be 'a black day for the Italian legal system'. The two-year period within which suspects could be investigated without their knowledge, the powers given to the judicial police to question prisoners without specific controls imposed by the prosecution and the new rules governing the acquisition of evidence were 'characteristics of a totalitarian regime'.[6] Neppi Modona was convinced that Falcone himself, in whose name these new powers had been invoked, would have opposed the decree.

The majority of Falcone's former colleagues in the Palermo courthouse welcomed Law Decree 306 since, according to judge Gioacchino Natoli, it incorporated measures which they had been requesting for three years. Existing laws – for example that on state's witnesses – were 'unworkable', either due to inherent deficiencies or because the mechanisms for implementing them had not been created. The decree was drafted in a record ten days precisely because its provisions were part of a package of requests that had already been drawn up.[7] Many were bitter about the sacrifice that had been the premise for its introduction: Palermo prosecutor Roberto Scarpinato called it 'scandalous' that measures which had been awaiting parliamentary approval for years had been introduced with a decree that was 'dripping with blood'. Mario Cicala, President of the National Association of Magistrates, regretted that the measures had been imposed as an emergency package instead of going through the usual parliamentary process.[8]

The fact that many key *Cosa Nostra* bosses had evaded Italian justice for more than a decade was a source of particular alarm, and this was emphasized in early July 1992 when Nino Fileccia, a defence lawyer representing the interests of *Cosa Nostra* boss Totò Riina, on the run for 23 years, told journalists that he had regular meetings with his client, and always in Sicily. Given that Fileccia would never have made such a declaration without Riina's permission, the message was clear – Riina was using his lawyer as a mouthpiece to affirm his leadership over *Cosa Nostra* and its actions, and to ridicule the State's efforts to assert its authority.

The assassination of judge Paolo Borsellino and his five bodyguards less than eight weeks after the Falcone attack made a mockery of Italy's professed crackdown on organized crime. The judiciary and police forces were incensed that despite the rhetoric nothing had been done in concrete terms to improve the security of those most at risk. After Falcone, Borsellino was the most obvious target for assassination by the Mafia yet no comprehensive security plan had been implemented for the locations he regularly frequented. Many believed that the murderers must have been protected by corrupted members of the security services or the police, with privileged information about the judges' precise movements on the days they were killed. A newspaper editorial summed up the prevalent mood:

No one stopped them and they killed Borsellino too. They are there, in Palermo [..] trying to prove that the territory is theirs and that in this wretched country they can do what they like because no one can or wants to stop them. But we must not give up, even if the Government seems not to exist, even if an entire political class has lost credibility, even if people simply cannot take it any more and do not know which saint to pray to. [..] The blow has been too hard, the grief too strong, the fear too much, not only for today but for tomorrow. Fear, yes: that we won't be in time to pull our country back from the precipice.[9]

In a speech to the Senate on 23 July, Justice Minister Martelli vowed *Cosa Nostra* would rue the day it had decided to kill Falcone and Borsellino:

> We will capture the fugitives, we will punish the colluders and the corrupted; we will protect those who come forward to give evidence, we will reward the state's witnesses, and keep the unrepentant ones in tough prisons with no early release. We will leave nothing but desertion, flight and surrender to the Mafia army for as long as it takes for them to go down on their knees, confess their crimes and beg forgiveness of their victims.[10]

On 25 July Interior Minister Mancino held a meeting of the National Committee for Security and Public Order, comprising the most senior law-enforcement, military and intelligence officials. The Committee's recommendations, once approved by the government, became effective immediately. Among them was to reduce to a minimum the number of bodyguards employed on the mainland, using strict criteria of need rather than status. The decision was taken in response to a formal protest from the police union, SIULP, about the working conditions of the VIP protection units and also to the public outcry when it was learned that former Interior Minister Antonio Gava had a round-the-clock team of 83 bodyguards to protect himself, his family and five residences. At the time, a total of 3445 members of the three police forces were assigned to protect a total of 732 individuals – 212 politicians, 280 judges and 240 others (businessmen, and others) – of whom 22 politicians, 47 judges and 16 others were in Sicily.[11]

Prime Minister Giuliano Amato also convened a government meeting on 25 July to approve Law Decree 349 (converted into Law 386 on 23 September) by which 7000 army troops were sent to Sicily. Dubbed 'Operation Sicilian Vespers', the mission's aim was to deploy soldiers in surveillance and general public order functions in support of the police forces, thereby freeing police and *carabineri* units for investigative duties. The military were granted temporary police status and had the power to stop and search vehicles or individuals when circumstances were of an exceptional and urgent nature. (For a full description and the effects of this measure see Chapter 4.)

A sense of instability permeated the country. A leading weekly magazine talked of the 'Lebanonization' of Italy and aired rumours of a possible *coup d'état*, which, although not given wide credence, were also not considered pure fantasy in a country which had run the risk some three times in its 46-year republican history. Numerous public figures received threats to their lives and had their protection reinforced, such as President Scalfaro, Justice Minister Martelli, Leoluca Orlando and the anti-corruption judge Antonio Di Pietro. Security was increased for passengers and baggage at the airports of Milan and Bergamo after an intercepted telephone conversation between two *mafiosi* indicated *Cosa Nostra* might pursue its terror campaign in the north. The intelligence services intensified border controls in the north-east, fearing a link-up of terrorists and organized crime after the discovery of a flourishing arms traffic between Italy and Croatia.

In the final vote on 4 August to convert Law Decree 306 into law, the Independents, the Greens and the Radicals in the Chamber of Deputies, and the Greens and Refounded Communists in the Senate voted against the decree, while the deputies and senators of the Net and the PDS deputies abstained, all the other groups being in favour. Although the PDS and the Net supported many of the provisions in principle and were convinced of the necessity of a strong response to Mafia aggression, they objected to the abolition of benefits for non-collaborating prisoners (an amendment to restore concessions to those who were not in a position to collaborate was defeated). Above all, their abstention reflected doubts as to the Government's genuine commitment to a comprehensive antimafia strategy – a scepticism motivated by the refusal of the PSI and DC to accept the amendment to the *Rognoni–La Torre* law that would have criminalized the promise to favour the granting of licences, authorizations and other benefits in exchange for votes.

Politically, the autumn and winter of 1992 were dominated by the 'Bribesville' or *Tangentopoli* scandal which had spread rapidly since the first arrests in February. Local elections in December were a disaster for the Christian Democrats and for the Socialists, who lost further ground. On 16 December former Prime Minister and PSI Secretary Bettino Craxi received notice that the Milan prosecution office was investigating his alleged receipt of bribes totalling 36 billion lire (US$21 million) and a request to proceed against him was sent to Parliament in January 1993. To the fury of the general public, the request was refused. Craxi's party colleague Claudio Martelli became implicated in the organization of illicit party funding through a secret bank account in Switzerland, and resigned as Justice Minister in February. His successor Giovanni Conso, a non-politically aligned appointee, presented a law decree in March which would have transformed the illegal financing of political parties from a crime into a lesser offence involving the admission of personal responsibility, repayment of sums due and a ban on public office for a number of years. Public opinion was outraged and Amato offered his immediate resignation, but was persuaded to remain until a series of referendums had taken place on 18 April. In a referendum on electoral reform, the Italians voted overwhelmingly to move from a purely proportional system to a first-past-the-post system for all but a 25 per cent share of the vote. Amato left office on 22 April. In the course of his short premiership, five party secretaries had been forced to resign because of their association with corrupt activities, while two men once considered 'untouchable' – seven-times Prime Minister Giulio Andreotti and former Interior Minister Antonio Gava – had fallen under formal suspicion of collusion with the Mafia.

Throughout the spring of 1993 senior political and law-enforcement figures warned that a Mafia offensive was imminent. Their deductions were based partly on intelligence sources and partly on information from collaborators who knew or guessed how the Mafia would react to the law-enforcement offensive of the previous months. An anonymous letter sent to Milan police headquarters claimed that *Cosa Nostra* was trying to make contact with the Italian intelligence services to find a compromise over the recent legislation, but that if the attempt proved unsuccessful, the Mafia would ally with Croatian criminals to carry out attacks on the Italian border with Slovenia.

On 14 May a car bomb exploded in the fashionable Parioli district of Rome just as the popular chat show host Maurizio Costanzo was leaving the theatre where his show had been recorded. It was followed over the next ten weeks by four other car bomb attacks in which 10 died and 90 were injured. In the absence of any responsibility claims the bombs were generically attributed to the Mafia, but there was widespread speculation that other destabilizing forces were at work. The 1993 mainland bombings are analysed fully in Chapter 7.

Political life in Sicily became very muted after the murders of Falcone and Borsellino. Those thought to be at risk were advised to leave Sicily for a period and either abandoned political life altogether or buried themselves in low-profile party work in Rome. Others, like former Palermo prosecutor Giuseppe Ayala – who had left the judiciary in April 1992 to enter Parliament for the Republican Party (PRI) – and Net leader Leoluca Orlando, refused, in Orlando's words, to 'let the spotlight go out' on Palermo. As national deputies representing Sicily, both men were convinced that Parliament had the primary responsibility for burying the old corrupt political system and for bringing about ethical and political reform – an indispensable premise for the cessation of Mafia violence.

When Giuliano Amato resigned, rather than call a general election less than a year from the last, President Scalfaro called on a former chairman of the Bank of Italy, Carlo Azeglio Ciampi, to form a government. In Ciampi's favour was his distinguished international reputation and, above all, his independence from discredited party politics. He took over from Amato on 26 April on a programme of radical economic and political reform. On 13 May 1993 the Chamber of Deputies voted to abolish the parliamentary privilege which prevented parliamentarians from being investigated without prior authorization from Parliament. Once the law came into force in October, the judiciary were required to request authorization only for the arrest or search of sitting parliamentarians, for interception of their communications or to carry out a search of their houses or offices.

With the most critical stage of the emergency overcome, Parliament's task was to study in detail the existing structures and institutions for dealing with the Mafia threat and to evaluate their appropriateness for the task. This responsibility was devolved to the all-party Parliamentary Antimafia Commission.

The Antimafia Commission 1992–94

Italy's first Parliamentary Antimafia Commission had been created in 1963 and continued working until 1976 (see Chapter 2). The Commission was reconstituted by parliamentary vote in 1982 for a three-year period, and then again in 1986, 1988, 1992, 1994 and 1996. In 1994 its period of operation was set as the duration of the parliamentary legislature. The Commission is composed of 25 senators and 25 deputies in proportion to parliamentary seats. The Chairman is nominated jointly by the Speakers of the Senate and the Chamber of Deputies after consultation with party leaders. Its task is to study the phenomenon of organized crime in all its permutations and to measure the appropriateness of existing measures, legislatively and administratively, against results. The Commission has judicial powers in that it may instruct the judicial police to carry out investigations, it can ask for copies of court proceedings and is entitled to ask for any form of collaboration which it deems necessary. Those who provide testimony to the Commission are obliged to tell the truth. The Commission can report to Parliament as often as desired, but at least on an annual basis.

On 23 September 1992 PDS deputy Luciano Violante was appointed Chairman of the Commission. Violante, a 51-year-old former magistrate from Turin, had gained extensive knowledge of the Mafia as a member of the Justice and Antimafia Commissions of the Chamber of Deputies and was considered one of the country's principal experts on organized criminality in its various forms. Setting his objectives for the Commission, Violante pointed out that in the ten years from 1982, Parliament had passed 113 laws on public order of which around 40 had dealt specifically with the Mafia, and that the Commission was more likely to seek modification or improved application of existing laws than propose new measures. His priorities included:

(a)   the international context. It was necessary to extend the axis of international cooperation, in particular with regard to the investigation of criminal finances.

(b)   the socio-economic context. Economic conditions, such as the fact that interest rates on loans were higher in the southern regions than in the north of Italy, were a factor in the cycle of extortion/usury/money laundering.

(c)   law enforcement. The new police and judicial services had to be made to work; interagency rivalry had to be overcome within the police forces.

(d)   arrest and punishment. It was necessary to destroy the myth of impunity surrounding the Mafia.[12]

Under Violante's chairmanship, the Commission worked for 17 months until the dissolution of Parliament in February 1994, and passed 13 reports covering some of the most important aspects of organized crime in Italy. These were:

(1)   Report on a forum held with the National Antimafia Directorate, the District Antimafia Directorates and the Working Group of the Superior Judicial Council (approved 9 March 1993)

(2)   Report on the municipal councils dissolved in Campania, Apulia and Calabria (30 March 1993)

(3)   Report on the links between Mafia and politics (6 April 1993)

(4)   Report on the Commission's visit to Gela [Sicily] on 12 November 1992 (25 June 1993)

(5)   Report on the Commission's visit to Barcellona Pozzo di Gotto [Sicily], (20 July 1993)

(6)   Recommendations for a crime-free economy (20 July 1993)

(7)   Report on the state of school building in Palermo (4 August 1993)

(8)   Report on the situation of organized crime in Apulia (5 October 1993)

(9)   Report on the situation of criminality in Calabria (12 October 1993)
(10) First Annual Report (19 October 1993)
(11) Report on the *Camorra* (21 December 1993)
(12) Report on the settlement and infiltration of organized criminality in non-traditional areas (12 January 1994)
(13) Final Report (18 February 1994)

The report on Mafia–political links of April 1993 was the defining achievement of Violante's chairmanship. The subject had been touched upon during the work of previous Commissions, notably in the 1972–76 session and again in 1988–92, but primarily in reports of the non-governmental parties and never as a central theme. In the course of its work the Commission heard testimonies from politicians, police officers and magistrates and summoned state's witnesses from each of the four Mafia organizations. The documentation and previously unpublished material from the work of previous Commissions were re-examined and integrated where appropriate.

The intention of the Mafia–Politics report, written entirely by Violante himself, was

> not simply to demonstrate the pure and simple existence of these links. The aim is rather to understand the characteristics of these links, the conditions that favoured them, the way in which they diversified in the course of different political periods and the factors that made them so incisive at certain moments of national and Sicilian political life.[13]

Several dominant themes emerged in the report: firstly, there was a vital distinction to be made between criminal and political responsibilities.

> Criminal responsibilities are ascertained by the judiciary through the formal rules of the trial and are sanctioned with established juridical measures. Political responsibility is characterized by a judgement of incompatibility – reached on the basis of determined facts, rigorously verified – between a person who occupies a political position and that position. They may not necessarily constitute a crime but nonetheless are held sufficiently valid to incur the judgement of incompatibility.[14]

A second premise was the role of the Mafia as political actor.

> *Cosa Nostra* has its own political strategy. The occupation and government of territory in competition with the legitimate author-

ities, the possession of considerable financial resources, the availability of a clandestine and well-equipped army, a programme of limitless expansion, all these characteristics make of it an organization which moves according to a logic of power and utility without any rules except those of its own protection and its own development. The political strategy of *Cosa Nostra* is not borrowed from others but imposed on others by corruption and violence.[15]

The interpenetration between the Mafia and the legitimate sector was not limited to politics, but included corruption of the police and judiciary and of the business and professional classes. The situation in Palermo between 1959 and 1964, when Salvo Lima was mayor of Palermo, was emblematic.

Many links were created between *mafiosi,* businessmen and individual politicians which caused the utter degradation of public office, the destruction of the market place and the ridicule of administrative legality. That peculiarly Palermo phenomenon of 'vertical alliances' grew up between *mafiosi*, businessmen, bureaucrats, the professional classes and politicians, each one set against the other. The politicians who counted each had their own entrepreneurs, their own professionals and their own Mafia boss. Thus a sort of integrated system of competences, functions, and powers was created which had its centre of gravity in *Cosa Nostra* and which succeeded in conditioning matters of public spending, political equilibrium and the balance of power within the various groups of *Cosa Nostra*. The political struggle became the terrain for the extension or restriction of the market shares of the contenders and *Cosa Nostra* intervened frequently with threats or with physical elimination, even in political matters, because it was on them that the fate of the business class, the earnings of the Mafia and the weight of individual men of honour depended.[16]

The report warned against criminalizing entire political sectors or parties; relationships were constructed between individuals, and almost always on a basis of reciprocity.

The rapport between *Cosa Nostra* and politicians is one of dominance of the former over the latter; the availability of coercive means confers on *Cosa Nostra* limitless scope to request and to convince. From this it should not be inferred that the politician is a victim of the relationship; he is not obliged to accept *Cosa Nostra*'s votes, but if he does accept them, he cannot be unaware of the requests or of the issues that interest his *partners.* [17]

Referring to Salvo Lima, the Sicilian Euro-MP murdered by *Cosa Nostra* in March 1992, the report noted,

> In the Commission's view, Salvo Lima's connections with the men of *Cosa Nostra* have been ascertained. He was the most senior representative in Sicily of the faction of the Christian Democratic Party led by Giulio Andreotti. As far as Senator Andreotti is concerned, Parliament will have to decide on any political responsibility deriving from his relations with Salvo Lima.[18]

In June 1993 (before parliamentary immunity from investigation had been formally abolished) a parliamentary committee would, at Andreotti's own request, waive his parliamentary privilege and authorize the Palermo prosecution office to proceed with its investigation (see Chapter 7).

In the winter of 1992–93 the Antimafia Commission met in secret locations to put wide-ranging questions to six of the most important state's witnesses. In the public interest the transcripts of the sessions were later released and made a notable contribution to an understanding of the Mafia's activities, structure and objectives. In the course of a ten-hour session, Gaspare Mutolo, a key member of the Palermo clan of Partanna Mondello, explained the context of the 1992 massacres:

> I knew that for any problems requiring a solution in Rome, Lima was the man we turned to [..] Lima was killed because he did not uphold, or couldn't uphold, the commitments he had made in Palermo [..] The verdict of the Supreme Court was a disaster. After the Supreme Court verdict we felt we were lost. That verdict was like a dose of poison for the *mafiosi*, who felt like wounded animals. That's why they carried out the massacres. Something had to happen. I was surprised when people who had eight years of a prison sentence still to serve started giving themselves up. Then they killed Lima and I understood.[19]

The description of *Cosa Nostra*'s anger at being betrayed by erstwhile allies who could no longer guarantee impunity was an indication of how corrupted Italian institutional life had become. Mutolo, who had only begun to talk of Mafia–political links after the arrest of Totò Riina in January 1993, also warned the Antimafia Commission in February of the likelihood that further attacks were being planned on the mainland, as indeed was the case.

Several state's witnesses told the Commission about the function of secret Masonic lodges, the nexus of the relationship between Mafia, the judiciary and the business world. An investigation carried out by the previous Antimafia Commission under Gherardo Chiaromonte had revealed that there was a total of 113 Masonic lodges in Sicily comprising 4600 affiliates. Most of the Mafia members had joined the Masonry between 1976 and 1980 – the period of *Cosa Nostra*'s massive expansion – but there had been two attempts to co-opt the Mafia in right wing *coups d'état* involving Freemasonry in 1970 and 1974. According to the collaborator Leonardo Messina, all the most senior *Cosa Nostra* bosses were affiliated to the Masonry, which represented a 'meeting point for everyone'.[20]

The Mafia–Politics report was approved by an overwhelming majority of the Commission, with only one Radical Party and two MSI commissioners voting against. The contribution of the Commission's deputy chairman, the Christian Democrat Paolo Cabras, was fundamental. With the exception of one DC commissioner who absented herself on the day of the vote with the excuse of an unspecified foreign commitment, all the others voted in favour. Cabras had kept his delegation in line and was proud of the Commission's achievement, stating, ' It is a political act of the greatest importance. The season of culpable distraction and minimization of the Mafia–political link is over. Politics was involved with the Mafia right at the beginning and the delay in realizing this has been one of the factors for the weakness of the State with regard to organized crime.' Asked whether the vote signified a distancing of the DC from Giulio Andreotti, Cabras replied, 'We take a stance against the Mafia, from all that signifies weakness, complicity, contiguity or resignation to the Mafia phenomenon. Establishing criminal responsibilities is a task for the judiciary.'[21]

A conference organized by the Antimafia Commission on the economics of organized crime in May 1993 to commemorate the first anniversary of the Falcone and Borsellino murders was summarized in the report entitled 'Recommendations for a crime-free economy'. It called for greater attention to the privatization process, to the source of funds from which private investment derived, and to the risk of illegal funds being laundered in the legal economy through non-banking financial intermediaries. Among its recommendations were a rationalization and simplification of legislation on taxation, public works, public investments, competition and stock market trading.

The Commission's investigation into Mafia penetration of 'non-traditional' areas of Italy showed not only that organized crime groups were present in the centre-north but that there were 'signs of actual infiltration into the economic structure of the most developed areas'. The report identified 'vast ramifications of various forms of Mafia-type organized crime in practically all the regions of Italy', with 'hardly any of the areas under consideration free from some form of Mafia presence or of infiltration in the economic or business sectors'.[22]

If the Commission's first year of activity was primarily devoted to the *Antimafia dei delitti* – crime and the repression of crime – its second year concentrated on the *Antimafia dei diritti* – the affirmation of citizens' rights and the creation of conditions in which economic enterprise, education and employment could prosper. A working group was set up to safeguard the rights of Mafia victims. The Commission gave priority to initiatives concerning the young, in particular to prevent truancy, improve educational and cultural facilities and to encourage young people to complete their schooling. There was a demonstrable link between the poor state of schools and the areas of greatest Mafia infiltration. Calabria, which had the highest proportion of Mafia members to inhabitants – around two million inhabitants and an estimated 5700 *'Ndrangheta* members, compared to Sicily's five million inhabitants and 5000 *Cosa Nostra* members – also had the lowest educational levels, the poorest sports facilities and was the region least equipped to offer services to the handicapped.[23] Under pressure from the Commission, Parliament approved increased funding for educational materials in the southern regions and in the inner city areas of the north. Twelve new schools were opened in Palermo – the buildings had been ready for use but the essential services had not been connected.[24] A social centre was opened up for young criminals in the Brancaccio district of Palermo, a kind of 'external recreation area' where educational and sporting activities could be carried on in a secure environment. Schools were encouraged to introduce an 'education to antimafia awareness' and in October 1993 this became part of the national school curriculum. An Information Point was opened up in the secretariat of the Commission to provide information for schools, and an 'Antimafia Dossier' was given out to all the regional education authorities – by 12 April 1994, 970 requests for it had been made.[25]

A section of the Final Report dealing with European Community fraud revealed that between 1984 and 1992, Italy had reported the highest number of cases of fraudulently obtained agricultural subsidies. Of the frauds perpetrated in the olive oil and citrus fruit sectors between 1987 and 1992, 83 per cent and 98 per cent respectively had been carried on in the four southern regions, and in them the involvement of organized crime had been ascertained.[26]

The Final Report concluded with an assessment of improvements since the Commission's work had begun. Important legislation had been introduced or modified with regard to money laundering, witness protection and on greater transparency in monitoring the allocation and execution of public works contracts. All of these had brought results. In the judicial field, the Commission had called for an increase in the numbers of magistrates as vacancies were high in the four southern regions, especially in Calabria, where 30 per cent of posts were unfilled. A law passed in 1993 had created 600 new posts, of which 50 per cent were in the south.[27] The Commission had encouraged the growth of anti-racketeering associations, of which there were then a total of 29 – 19 in Sicily, 5 in Apulia, 2 in Calabria and one each in Lombardy, Lazio and Campania. The existence of these associations had strengthened the resistance of those who suffered extortion attempts.

Since the passing of a law in 1991, municipal councils could be dissolved on grounds of Mafia infiltration, after which special commissioners were appointed to run the councils until new elections could be held. But their work had been made extremely difficult by the non-cooperation of local townspeople and bureaucrats and under pressure from the Antimafia Commission, a committee had been set up to support and monitor the work of the special commissioners. At the end of 1993, Campania had the highest number of dissolved councils (32), of public administrators removed for abuse of office (64), of magistrates under investigation (16 out of a national total of 41), and the highest number of parliamentarians under suspicion of collusion with the Mafia (8 out of 16).[28]

The Commission had held meetings with police chiefs from Spain, France and Germany and had developed particularly fruitful contacts with the German Federal Parliament. In June 1993 there had also been a meeting between the Commission and the head of the Russian Parliamentary Antimafia Commission. Discussions with West European colleagues had indicated that Italy's antimafia legislation was more advanced than elsewhere, and that it was judged by her partners to be adequate. There had been general agreement over the desirability of creating a European antimafia judicial 'space' within which criminal investigations could be carried on.[29]

At the end of the parliamentary term in February 1994, the Antimafia Commission proposed that a series of outstanding issues be given urgent attention. The most important were

1. The transfer to court trial of the important criminal investigations of the previous few years; centralization of Mafia trials in designated prosecution offices and more efficient deployment of magistrates within the judicial system.

2. More incisive action against Mafia finances. Whereas Italy was able to deal adequately with the purely criminal–military aspects of the Mafia, measures to tackle organized crime wealth were insufficient. A new conceptual approach was required to deal with the interpenetration between criminality and the legal economy, especially within the credit sector.

3. Improved administrative controls in the public sector. Control of public works contracts embodied the essence of the Mafia – domination of territory through economic control. Public administration, its spending mechanisms and the systematic attention that organized crime paid to these called for specific measures to reduce the risk of criminal penetration in public works contracts. It was necessary to prevent the formation of a new circuit between contracted public works and criminal entrepreneurs through a blend of transparency and efficiency. Despite the volume of legislation passed to deal with public works contracts and subcontracts since the start of the 'Bribesville' investigations, they had dealt almost exclusively with procedures at the post-contract stage, and did not tackle the problem of Mafia pressure at pre-selection stage. Many rules of entry were simply ignored.

The Antimafia Commission had worked prodigiously for the 17 months of the legislative period. Party differences did not sap the determination to make a major contribution to the antimafia struggle at the time when, objectively, the battle to save Italy's democracy from criminal subversion was at a critical stage. Violante's greatest achievement lay in the fact that the most important reports were backed by all the major parties instead, as in the past, of producing majority (government) and minority (opposition) reports on the same theme. Credit for this unity of purpose was also due to the DC deputy chairman Senator Paolo Cabras who, when faced with incontrovertible evidence of political degradation, had won over the support of his party colleagues.

Any attempt to defend the dignity of the political system would in fact have been rendered risible by statistics – in February 1994, two years from the first political corruption arrests, 2993 arrest warrants had been issued; 6059 individuals were under investigation including 873 businessmen, 1978 local administrators and 438 parliamentarians of whom four were former prime ministers.[30] Ten suspects had committed suicide. In the legislative period from 1992 to 1994 alone there had been 851

Italian Governments, 1989–99

Period of office	PM	Interior Min.	Justice Min.	Antimafia Com. Chair.
July 89–Feb 92 (gen. election 5/4/92)	Giulio Andreotti	Vincenzo Scotti	Claudio Martelli	Gherardo Chiaromonte
June 92–April 93	Giuliano Amato	Nicola Mancino	Claudio Martelli/Giovanni Conso	Luciano Violante
April 93–March 94 (gen. election 27/3/94)	Carlo Azeglio Ciampi	Nicola Mancino	Giovanni Conso	Luciano Violante
May–Dec 94	Silvio Berlusconi	Roberto Maroni	Alfredo Biondi	Tiziana Parenti
Jan– Dec 95 (gen. election 21/4/96)	Lamberto Dini	Antonio Brancaccio/ Giovanni Coronas	Filippo Mancuso	Tiziana Parenti
May 96–Oct 98	Romano Prodi	Giorgio Napolitano	Giovanni Maria Flick	Ottaviano Del Turco
Oct 98–	Massimo D'Alema	Rosa Russo Jervolino	Oliviero Diliberto	Ottaviano Del Turco

requests from the judiciary to proceed against sitting members of Parliament plus 11 concerning current or former government ministers. At the expiry of the parliamentary term, 44 sitting MPs could expect immediate arrest if they were not re-elected in the forthcoming general election.[31] Authorization to proceed with the investigation of Giulio Andreotti was given by the Senate on 10 June 1993 and he was formally committed for trial in Palermo on 2 March 1995. On 18 July 1995 former Interior Minister Antonio Gava, frequently referred to by the press as 'Don Antonio' for his godfather-like influence over the Naples area, was committed for trial on charges of Mafia association of a *Camorra* type, together with four other parliamentarians, of whom one was a former under-secretary of state, another a former deputy chairman of the Justice Commission of the Chamber of Deputies. Gava was accused of being 'the highest point of reference' for the powerful Alfieri clan in Campania.

Italy's 'Second Republic'

After the general election of 27 March 1994 political initiatives against the Mafia underwent a transformation. Two years on from the murder of Falcone and Borsellino, it was clear that Italy was ready for a new approach to politics and that it had become weary of the Mafia 'emergency'. Sicily voted overwhelmingly for the new political partnership known as the Freedom Alliance *(Polo delle Libertà)* formed by Silvio Berlusconi's new *Forza Italia* party, Gianfranco Fini's reformed fascists, the National Alliance *(Alleanza Nazionale*, AN) and Umberto Bossi's Northern League *(Lega Nord)*. With 21 per cent of the vote nationally, *Forza Italia* had come from nowhere to become the largest party in Parliament. Even Antonino Caponnetto, the retired judge who had become a symbol of national grief after the Palermo atrocities, failed to win election for Leoluca Orlando's Net party in Sicily.

Before and after the general election, rumours circulated about possible Mafia support for the Freedom Alliance. Two collaborators claimed that Berlusconi's company Fininvest had paid *Cosa Nostra* substantial sums to be able to operate in Sicily.[32] Prominent campaigners for the Freedom Alliance had tried to discredit the contribution of the state's witnesses and proposed radical alterations to the legislation. Before the election, Antimafia Commission chairman Violante pointed out that it was less important whether or not the Mafia voted for *Forza Italia* than that it perceived certain of *Forza Italia's* pronouncements as being indicative of a less determined approach to combat it, and called on Berlusconi to distance himself publicly from the acceptability of Mafia votes. The suggestion was ignored.

There seems little doubt that, whether or not *Forza Italia* candidates sought or knowingly accepted Mafia votes, the Mafia perceived *Forza Italia* as a party which was non-hostile or even sympathetic to certain of the organization's own political objectives. Independent statements from several state's witnesses indicate that *Cosa Nostra* 'orders' were to vote *Forza Italia* in Sicily in the hope that the legislation on state's witnesses and the 41 *bis* regime would be abolished.[33] One of them, Filippo Malvagna, told the court in the Falcone murder trial that *Cosa Nostra* bosses believed *Forza Italia* would be 'the saviour of the *mafiosi*'.[34]

At least one of Salvo Lima's former followers was elected on a *Forza Italia* ticket, and two others were elected by the Democratic Christian Centre (*Centro Cristiano Democratico*,CCD) a splinter party which had emerged from the old DC – dissolved in January 1994 – and allied with the Freedom Alliance.[35] On 13 December 1994 Pino Mandalari, political activist, Mason and financial adviser to Totò Riina, was arrested. Transcripts of intercepted telephone conversations showed unequivocally that in the March 1994 general election, in the European elections and in the local Sicilian elections of 1994, Mandalari and associates had been campaigning on behalf of *Forza Italia* and National Alliance (AN) candidates in Sicily and was in regular contact with them. None seemed to refuse or to have been embarrassed by his offers of help. A frequent link between Mandalari and his contacts was Freemasonry, in which Mandalari apparently held a high position, being respectfully called *maestro* by some of his interlocutors.[36] Immediately after the general election, on 29 March, he was heard to say, 'Wonderful, all the candidates are my friends, all of them got elected!'[37] During a telephone call made to newly elected Senator Filiberto Scalone, Scalone was heard to thank him profusely, using the familiar *tu* form. Subsequently, those for whom Mandalari had campaigned professed ignorance as to his Mafia connections. Yet he had been investigated and arrested in 1983 for Mafia association; between 1984 and 1987 he was subjected to special police surveillance from which his close contacts with the Riina family emerged; and he had been committed for trial and convicted in 1990 for profiting from illegally derived funds. Mandalari was convicted of Mafia association in 1997.

In October 1996 Marcello Dell'Utri, the Sicilian former managing director of Fininvest's advertising company, Publitalia, elected to the Chamber of Deputies in June of that year for *Forza Italia*, was committed for trial for money laundering and for favouring *Cosa Nostra*. The Palermo prosecutors listed 57 separate incidents as indicative of his alleged collusion, including numerous meetings with prominent *Cosa Nostra* bosses.[38] In 1980 Dell'Utri, by his own admission,[39] attended the wedding in London of a presumed international drugs trafficker at which three other prominent *mafiosi* were present, one of whom would later be suspected of the murder of *Banco Ambrosiano* chairman Roberto Calvi, found hanging under Blackfriars Bridge in 1982. It was alleged that through Dell'Utri's Mafia contacts, Silvio Berlusconi's family had been protected from kidnap attempts by Calabrian gangs operating in Milan in the 1970s, and Berlusconi's companies had been able to operate without hindrance in Sicily, at least until 1990. In that year the Fininvest-owned Standa supermarket chain suffered a series of arson attacks in Catania which ceased, according to prosecutors, when favours and sums of money were forthcoming. Dell'Utri's trial opened in Palermo in November 1997. In mid-trial, in February 1999, the Palermo prosecution office requested authorization to arrest him on new charges of slander and attempted extortion, but in April Parliament rejected the request by a margin of 22 votes. In the European elections in June 1999 Marcello Dell'Utri was among the three most voted candidates for *Forza Italia*, which won the largest share of the vote in Sicily and nationally. A candidate in several constituencies, he was expected to take up his seat for North-west Italy rather than for the South and Islands.

With the victory of the Freedom Alliance and the start of Silvio Berlusconi's premiership in May 1994, the fight against criminality continued to make rapid progress in terms of law enforcement but its political impetus slowed down. A week before the general election, Berlusconi had sent a formal complaint to the Milan chief prosecutor about the methods of the city's 'clean hands' anti-corruption judges who, he believed, were deliberately discrediting his political ambitions by ordering repeated raids on the Milan offices of his Fininvest conglomerate. On becoming Prime Minister, he began a personal crusade against what he saw as the excesses of the corruption investigations, and several of his key appointees were a direct reflection of this endeavour. His personal campaign against the judiciary had important repercussions for the antimafia fight. Tiziana Parenti, the new *Forza Italia* chairwoman of the Antimafia Commission, had no Mafia experience but had been a member of the 'clean hands' team in Milan which she had abandoned after disagreements with her colleagues. Having protested vehemently about allegations of Mafia infiltration of *Forza Italia* in Sicily prior to the election, Parenti later admitted the possibility and many *Forza Italia* offices or 'clubs' set up in Sicily were subsequently closed down.

Berlusconi had tried to co-opt another prominent 'clean hands' judge, Antonio Di Pietro, into his cabinet as Interior Minister but the offer was refused. His appointee as chairman of the Cultural Affairs Commission of the Chamber, Vittorio Sgarbi, used a nightly programme on a Berlusconi-owned television channel to criticize the 'clean hands' judges, calling them 'assassins' after the suicides in prison of several prominent businessmen held in pre-trial custody. The new *Forza Italia* chairwoman of the Justice Commission of the Chamber of Deputies, Tiziana Maiolo, was a strong critic of the antimafia laws passed in the previous two years and, on taking office, began to speak out publicly against the legislation on state's witnesses and the 41 *bis* prison regime; she also proposed that the crime of Mafia association be abolished from the criminal code. Her proposals were resisted by Berlusconi's Interior Minister, Roberto Maroni of the Northern League, whose commitment to the antimafia fight was unequivocal.

In October, Berlusconi assured the Antimafia Commission that he had no intention of rethinking or going back on previous legislation, that the 41 *bis* would only be revoked when the threat was significantly reduced and that he believed the laws on collaboration to be necessary. In a foretaste of the Italian Government's statement to the World Ministerial Conference against Organized Transnational Crime to be hosted in Naples the following month, he promised a 'globally coordinated strategy' against the Mafia, 'which does not merely consist of strengthening the investigative structures or supporting judicial investigations. The Government's commitment must be developed prior to and independently of the repression of crime.'[40] The main pillars of his government's strategy were:

- strengthening of crime prevention and investigative structures;
- 'grass roots' prevention measures in the form of social support mechanisms;
- improvement of judicial and trial procedures;
- attack on illicit profits;
- development of international cooperation.

In the course of 1994 a number of factors increased the vulnerability of those most committed to the antimafia fight. In May, two weeks after Berlusconi's government had taken office, *Cosa Nostra*'s *capo dei capi* Totò Riina used his appearance in a Reggio Calabria courtroom to issue a direct threat to his institutional enemies. Referring to the Deputy Speaker of the Chamber, Luciano Violante, to Palermo chief prosecutor Gian Carlo

Caselli and to Mafia expert Pino Arlacchi, recently elected to Parliament for the PDS, he announced,

> All governments are the same. But the new government should beware of the Communists. There's *Signor* Violante, *Signor* Caselli in Palermo, *Signor* Arlacchi. *Signor* Arlacchi writes, but what does he write? Communist things. I'm sorry if there are some Communists among you. But the government should be careful of all that revolves around Communists.

In the mouth of the Mafia boss, these apparently innocuous remarks were laden with meaning. Firstly, they pretended a bond of complicity between *Cosa Nostra* and the new government through a mutual enemy: in the run-up to the election Berlusconi had repeatedly warned of the 'Communist' threat from the Left, even though the old *Partito Comunista Italiano* had become the Democratic Left Party in 1991. Secondly, it was a clear invitation to *Cosa Nostra* to assassinate the individuals concerned. On this occasion Berlusconi and his government colleagues reacted with immediate condemnation.

In July 1994 one of the first judicial indicators from the new government came in the form of a law decree drawn up by Justice Minster Alfredo Biondi which abolished pre-trial imprisonment for specific categories of crime, including those relating to active and passive corruption, and reduced the maximum time period within which pre-liminary criminal investigations could be carried out to three months, instead of the two years granted (for Mafia investigations only) by Law Decree 306 of June 1992. The decree provoked a chorus of opposition from judges around the country and the request for transfers to other offices by the members of the Milan anti-corruption team, while thousands of Milanese staged a solidarity sit-in outside the Milan lawcourts. After a heated debate in Parliament the decree was found not to have the necessary criteria of urgency and it was dropped.

In October 1994 Silvio Berlusconi made a second formal denunciation of the methods employed by the Milan prosecution office to President Oscar Luigi Scalfaro, this time in his capacity as Prime Minister, in which he alleged an 'attack on the functioning of the constitutional organs of the State'. Shortly afterwards Berlusconi's successor as chairman of the Fininvest Group (a title Berlusconi relinquished when he entered Parliament) claimed the company was being persecuted; on 18 October Justice Minister Biondi ordered a ministerial inspection of the work of the Milan prosecution office. A Commission set up inside the CSM to assess the correctness of the inspection later reported that the minister-ial team had carried out 'numerous and serious violations of the limits beyond which the Ministry cannot go without interfering with the inde-pendence of the judiciary'.

Berlusconi received notification that he was under investigation for fiscal fraud on 22 November 1994, while he was presiding over the World Ministerial Conference against Organized Transnational Crime in Naples. His resignation as Prime Minister in December, caused primarily by the withdrawal from his coalition of the Northern League, was hastened by continuing allegations of impropriety.

After leaving office, Berlusconi's conviction that he had been a victim of a deliberate campaign to unseat him continued: in May 1998 he made a third formal denunciation of the anti-corruption judges in Milan, claiming that the charges against him and the Fininvest Group had been deliberately aimed at causing his government to fall, and that the techniques used had included 'political intimidation, persecution, and judicial determination' to bring down himself and his company.[41] Judges in Brescia were investigating the substance of the allegations.

The alternating, contradictory messages emanating from the Berlusconi administration undoubtedly slowed the political momentum of the antimafia movement. The drop in attention was felt elsewhere: between May and September 1994 the number of prisoners detained under article 41 *bis* dropped from 733 to 445.[42] The Antimafia Commission was paralysed by internal conflict and ineffective leadership and no reports were approved during Berlusconi's tenure of office. In February 1995 the centre-left members of the Commission presented a motion of no confidence in the presidency which was passed a month later but Tiziana Parenti refused to resign since, according to the terms of her appointment, the motion of no confidence was inadmissible.

Berlusconi's successor, his Foreign Minister Lamberto Dini, was sworn in as Prime Minister in January 1995. In his inaugural address to Parliament Dini promised to continue the antimafia fight with deter-mination, but in practice political antimafia efforts were dominated by the increasingly acerbic conflict between judiciary and Parliament. In just nine months of holding office, Dini's Justice Minister Filippo Mancuso called for a total of 217 inspections of the working methods of the judiciary, with Milan as his main target.[43] Palermo also came under scrutiny.

Lamberto Dini was careful not to take Mancuso's side against mounting criticism from the PDS, which had voted his government into power, but Mancuso hung on until October 1995 when a parliamentary vote of no confidence drove him out of office. Dini himself took over the Justice Ministry until he offered his own resignation at the end of the year.

Mafia issues did not play a significant part in the run-up to the 1996 general election and there were few party polemics on the subject. In advance of any electioneering, Gianfranco Fini, President of the right-wing National Alliance (AN) distanced himself from his Freedom Alliance partner Silvio Berlusconi. In December 1995 Fini pledged his party's support for the work of the Palermo prosecution office during a conference on the Mafia organized by AN and attended by Palermo chief prosecutor Gian Carlo Caselli. Unlike *Forza Italia*, whose members had criticized Caselli for being a 'red' judge and suggested he was planning to place Berlusconi under investigation just as the electoral campaign got under way, Fini said of him, 'Without Caselli the antimafia fight would be going less well or else would not be going at all [...] Gian Carlo Caselli is a true professional and an extremely dedicated man, very well aware of the great responsibilities he bears on his shoulders.' In contrast to Berlusconi, Fini made a public rejection of Mafia votes on behalf of his own party: 'On one point Caselli and I agree totally – the clans are looking for new points of reference. And they certainly won't be looking for them among the opposition. Therefore we all have a responsibility to block any infiltration. Better to lose the election in some seats rather than offer new opportunities to the Mafia bosses.'[44] *Forza Italia* remained the strongest party in Sicily after the election but there were no indications that *Cosa Nostra* had campaigned on its behalf.

The Net

The one political party directly founded on an antimafia commitment, the Net, has experienced mixed fortunes since its creation in March 1991. Leoluca Orlando entered politics as DC city councillor shortly after the assassination of Piersanti Mattarella in 1980, determined to pursue Mattarella's objectives of breaking the bonds of complicity between the DC and the Mafia. In July 1985 he became mayor of Palermo. The four and a half years of his unorthodox administration – comprising Christian Democrats, Communists, Greens and a Jesuit-inspired movement called *Città per l'Uomo* (City for Mankind) – known as the 'Palermo Spring', was marked by a new sense of citizen participation, greater transparency in local government, and by an antimafia commitment symbolized by Orlando's unprecedented step of entering Palermo City Council as civil plaintiff in the Mafia maxi-trial. The DC party hierarchy in Rome disapproved of Orlando's hybrid city government and was embarrassed by his repeated denunciations of the party's infiltration by the Mafia. Orlando refused to stand as DC candidate for the 1989 European elections together with Salvo Lima but in the local elections of 1990 he headed the DC list with a candidate from the Lima faction as number two. Despite his personal triumph and his oft-repeated wish 'to change the party, not to change parties', he was unable to remould it as he wished and in mid-1990 he turned his back on the DC.

The Net drew its initial inspiration from individuals with first-hand experience of Mafia violence – three of the party's co-founders with Orlando had had their fathers murdered by *Cosa Nostra*; a fourth, a former judge, had been the target of a Mafia car bomb in 1985 which in missing him had killed a mother and her twin sons. The Net's first election campaign in 1992 called for an overhaul of the electoral system, the accountability of public figures, including the abolition of parliamentary immunity, stronger defence of the weaker social classes and the independence of the judiciary and of the media from political interference. The party won a total of 12 seats in Parliament, with Orlando the third most voted politician in the country. But the successful debut was not sustained, partly because of a clash of personalities among its original founders, and because its original goals of ethical reform and political accountability were not sufficient to attract a loyal voter constituency at national level in the absence of an identifiable independent economic and political programme.

In the 1996 general election Italy's gradual transformation from political fragmentation towards two political poles of centre-left and centre-right obliged the Net to come under the umbrella of the centre-left 'Olive Tree' coalition and deprived it of an independent voice in the Rome Parliament. The Net remains a protest party but its original *raison d'être* as scourge of corruption and political misdeeds has gradually been sidelined by the work of the judiciary.

Orlando's political career advanced independently of the Net thanks to the single most important political innovation since 1993 – the introduction of a new voting system for local elections which allows inhabitants of the larger cities to elect their mayors directly. The closer link between elector and elected brought effective accountability and responsibility to local government for the first time, and in the south, reduced the risk of Mafia influence over the vote. Leoluca Orlando was returned as mayor of Palermo in 1993 and again in 1997, on both occasions taking more than 70 per cent of the vote. To date, he has emerged unscathed from judicial investigations into the awarding of sub-contracts for the reconstruction of Palermo's *Teatro Massimo*, from revelations of illicit activities by former members of his City Council and from statements by collaborators that in the 1980s he had contacts with *Cosa Nostra*. With no regrets about the decline of the Net,[45] Orlando's political aspirations were focused on furthering international antimafia cooperation in the EU through his membership of the European Parliament and on the creation of a single, centre-left party on the model of the 'Olive Tree' coalition, comprising amongst others former PM Romano Prodi, the former judge, now Senator, Antonio Di Pietro and several city mayors of the centre-left including Orlando himself and those of Catania, Venice and Rome, all of whom will be barred from re-election to mayoral office in 2001. Orlando stood as a candidate with Prodi's new party, the Democrats, in the June 1999 European elections, but was not re-elected to Strasbourg.

Contrary to general expectations, the centre-left coalition led by Romano Prodi from 1996 to 1998 did not advance the antimafia fight politically. Virtually all the initiatives undertaken by PDS Interior Minister Giorgio Napolitano were *ad hoc* responses to specific crises as they arose – such as a surge of *Camorra* violence in Naples and a spate of kidnappings in northern Italy – while the government was frequently sidetracked by the new and apparently unstoppable problem of illegal immigration. Prodi's government did not fulfil its promises on stimulating employment or on the provision of economic incentives in southern Italy, nor did he ever visit Palermo in his two-and-a-half-year premiership. Election results in Sicily in May 1998 reflected voter disillusionment with a government perceived as being obsessed with meeting the economic requirements for European monetary union at the expense of social infrastructures and economic investment. Many voters felt that far from having improved, the economic situation in Sicily had declined drastically, while the offer of packets of pasta as an inducement to vote made its reappearance in Palermo for the first time in 30 years.

The Antimafia Commission of the current Parliament began its activities on 4 December 1996 with the best-qualified candidate for chairman being discarded in favour of a compromise nomination with no first-hand experience of Mafia matters. For months the Commission appeared rudderless and largely ineffective, and its chairman's utterances either banal or misinformed. After nearly three years of operation its competence has slowly improved and some valuable documentation and analyses have been generated, divided more or less evenly between prevention and repression. As a former trade-union leader, chairman Ottaviano Del Turco has concentrated on low-profile but particularly destructive forms of Mafia activity such as racketeering, extortion and usury, and the Commission operates a telephone line which can be used for reporting such attempts. The commitment to assist youth and school communities has been maintained through an information desk which answers requests and provides educational material. The Commission has also been monitoring the workings of the asset seizure and confiscation legislation, from which recommendations will be made as to how the legislation can be improved.[46] Laudable as these initiatives may be the Commission, like the Prodi Government, has been reactive rather than proactive and has done little to elaborate a long-term antimafia strategy which can deal with the internationalization and technological sophistication of contemporary criminality and meet the challenges of the coming decade.

Prodi's Justice Minister Giovanni Maria Flick, an astute and politically non-aligned lawyer who represented several families of Mafia victims during the Palermo maxi-trial, found his efforts to drive through legislation continually frustrated. He was handicapped partly by political inexperience, but most of all because his supposed advantage of political independence turned out to have the disadvantage of depriving him of the continuous support of any of the government parties. The PDS in particular, the largest party in government, frequently voiced views which either contradicted or were critical of Flick's position. It was also his misfortune to have to try to arbitrate in the ongoing conflict between judicial and executive power that had deepened with the Bribesville scandals. Judges who risked their lives every day came under frequent attack from political quarters, in particular from *Forza Italia*. Throughout 1997 Palermo chief prosecutor Gian Carlo Caselli talked of 'repeated, continuous aggression towards the Palermo prosecution office' and a 'systematic falsification of reality' which he compared to the marginalization of Falcone some ten years earlier.[47]

The conflict between judicial and executive power in Italy goes back many years. In the 1970s and 1980s Parliament effectively delegated the front-line management of the two most important challenges to postwar democracy – terrorism and the Mafia – to the magistrates, many of whom were murdered for their tenacity. Parliament encouraged the judiciary and provided legislative support because the threat was external to the institutions and its own members seen as targets or victims rather than accomplices. But corruption – the third important challenge – changed the balance of power and in doing so exacerbated Italy's institutional crisis. The corruption investigations put politicians in the position of being simultaneously subordinate to the judiciary as objects of investigation and, as the legislative arm of the state, threatened by a constitutional power with which they stood on equal footing. As a result the criminal justice system in Italy has been transformed into an institutional battlefield for unresolved contradictions in areas not of its competence. The judiciary has been obliged to respond to the criminalization and degradation of politics but is powerless to reform the system which gave rise to the crimes. Until these contradictions are resolved by Parliament and until constitutional and electoral reform make strong, full-term government a possibility, it is likely that antimafia policies in Italy will continue to be driven by stop-gap political measures provoked by emergency situations – policies which merely react to, rather than pre-empt, the organized crime threat.

Annex

Since the first emergency package of legislation passed in the summer of 1992, the principal antimafia legislation has been as follows:

Law 119 of 29 March 1993, to permit a change of identity for collaborators and their families.

Law 256 of 24 July 1993, to modify the law on compulsory domicile for those convicted or suspected of belonging to a Mafia association, such that they are no longer required to reside in a place other than their usual place of abode. This was modified because Mafia suspects 'exiled' from the southern regions to other parts of Italy frequently transferred their criminal activities to the new area.

Law 328 of 9 August 1993, to permit ratification of the Council of Europe Convention on the Laundering, Search, Seizure and Confiscation of the Proceeds from Crime. It extended the range of predicate crimes for money laundering from four – aggravated robbery, aggravated extortion, kidnap for ransom and drug trafficking – to all forms of crime. Ratification opened up the possibility of international collaboration in money-laundering investigations despite differences in judicial systems.

Law 310 of 12 August 1993, concerning the transfer of ownership of shares in companies and of commercial business and property. Transfer of interest in companies of limited liability must be documented within 30 days in a register of businesses. Notification of directors, administrators and of anyone with a financial interest in the business is also necessary.

Law 382 of 27 September 1993, concerning the creation of a support fund for victims of extortion.

Law 109 of 19 February 1994, regulating the procedures for public works contracts. The law sets standards for efficiency, transparency and for the freedom of competition; it establishes conditions and limits on private bidding and on the permissible variations to an original contract. It insists on respect for time clauses, minimum attributes for companies competing for public works contracts, clear-cut contractual responsibilities for participants. An independent commission was established to oversee the correct application of the new norms. A 12-month period was given for companies to adhere to the new standards, after which the law entered into force. An amendment to prevent companies under criminal investigation from participating in public tenders was rejected.[48]

Law 501 of 8 August 1994, concerning asset confiscation. Confiscation of assets became obligatory if the person convicted of serious crimes could not justify their source and if that person had in his possession or at his disposal assets which were out of proportion to his income.

Law 36 of 15 February 1995, to extend the duration of article 41 *bis* of law 354 1975 until 31 December 1999.

Law 216 of 2 June 1995, concerning public works contracts. In particular, if a competitor in a public tender makes an offer which is discounted by more than 20 per cent of the average of all the other discounts, the sum of the guarantees requested of all the participants in the tender is raised by 50 per cent.

Law 332 of 8 August 1995, to reduce the maximum length of pre-trial detention. By this law the maximum period was reduced from 20 years to 9, with an upper limit of 3 years for each grade of justice (Court of Assizes, Court of Appeal, Supreme Court). It also made provision for the interrogation of imprisoned persons to be recorded or video-recorded.

Law 107 of March 1996, to set up a fund of solidarity for victims of usury; to assist in relations between banks and clients who are victims of usury; with regard to confiscated assets, to protect lawful activities and workers who might suffer from the cessation of activities and to arrange for the administration of frozen or confiscated assets by competent authorities; to assign assets confiscated from Mafia convicts to socially useful projects.

Law 97 of 10 April 1997, constituting a parliamentary commission of enquiry into the waste disposal industry and into the extent of criminal and organized crime infiltration into it.

Law 267 of 7 August 1997, reforming article 513 of the code of criminal procedure. Henceforth statements made by state's witnesses in preliminary hearings or during preliminary investigations could no longer be used as evidence in trials for related crimes if the collaborators did not repeat their statements in open court (see Chapter 4 for discussion and further modification of this law).

Law 282 of 28 August 1997, permitting the temporary use of the armed forces in support of civil police in the Naples area.

Law 11 of 7 January 1998, to permit use of video testimony in court trials in the case of extremely complex proceedings or when there are particular concerns for public safety. Video testimony can be ordered for those detained under article 41 *bis* and for state's witnesses.

Plate 1   Judge Giovanni Falcone.

Plate 2   The conference on 12 May 1992 in Rome at which Giovanni Falcone spoke in public for the last time. On the podium, left to right, are Giovanni Falcone, Daniele Ripeto (chair, adnkronos), Professor Francesco Bruno (criminologist), the author, Henry Marsden (Director, Office of Research, Office of National Drug Control Policy, Executive Office of the President, The White House).

Plate 3   Giovanni Falcone, immediately after receiving an anonymous letter at the conference in Rome on 12 May 1992.

Plate 4   The motorway at Capaci, with the bulletproof Fiat Croma in which Giovanni Falcone, his wife Francesca and bodyguard Giuseppe Costanzo were travelling when the bomb exploded.

Plate 5   Via D'Amelio, Palermo, scene of the car bomb which killed Paolo Borsellino and bodyguards Agostino Catalano, Walter Cusina, Vincenzo Li Muli, Claudio Traina and Emanuela Loi.

Plate 6   Judge Paolo Borsellino.

Plate 7 Mafia boss Salvatore (Totò) Riina photographed just after his arrest in Palermo on the morning of 15 January 1993.

Plate 8 Father Luigi Ciotti with friends at a ceremony to commemorate victims of the Mafia.

AMERICAN CONSULATE GENERAL

Palermo, Italy - November 21, 1944.

SUBJECT: Meeting of Maffia Leaders with General Giuseppe
Castellano and formation of group favoring
autonomy.

SECRET

THE HONORABLE

THE SECRETARY OF STATE,

WASHINGTON.

SIR:

I have the honor to report that on November 18,
1944 General Giuseppe Castellano, together with Maffia
leaders including Calogero Vizzini conferred with
Virgilio Nasi, head of the well-known Nasi family in
Trapani and asked him to take over the leadership of a
Maffia-backed movement for Sicilian autonomy which will
have the cooperation of the FDOS and the Legge Agricul-
tura.

This movement has not yet matured to the point
where a full report can be made and the following information is based on such data as have come to hand,
but it is reliable.

General Castellano, who is a Sicilian, took command of the re-activated Aosta Division in the beginning of October and since that time has been very active
in studying the Sicilian problem and looking for a
solution. He has developed close contacts with the
Maffia leaders and has met them on frequent occasions.

As reported in my despatch No. 375 dated November
18, 1944, prominent members of the Maffia met in Palermo
and one of the results of this conference was the decision to ask Virgilio Nasi of Trapani to head up this
movement with the ultimate intention of his becoming
High Commissioner. The Nasi family have been well
known in the Province of Trapani for at least two generations and are highly respected by all classes. It
is understood that Nasi is a Labor Democrat but he has
played little part in the political upheavals on the
island throughout the past year.

During the next few weeks an active campaign will
get underway to gain more adherents to the movement.
The FDOS, which as already reported is very strong, will,
of course, cooperate and I believe it quite likely that
many of the followers of Finocchiaro-Aprile, who is
losing popularity and the confidence of the people, will
join with the Nasi followers. Their platform has not
yet

Plate 9   Document from American Consulate General (see page 15).

4
The Law-enforcement Response

The most important law-enforcement initiatives introduced after the Palermo atrocities concern the implementation of the new or modified legislation adopted by Parliament; the full activation of the national antimafia police force, the *Direzione Investigativa Antimafia*, (DIA) and of the national antimafia prosecution service, the *Direzione Nazionale Antimafia*, (DNA); and the sending of military detachments to Sicily in support of the civil authorities. This chapter aims to analyse the effectiveness of the measures which were adopted and to examine the contribution to the antimafia fight of each of the institutions having direct law-enforcement responsibilities.

The army

The decision taken by Giuliano Amato's government in July 1992 to send 7000 army troops to Sicily for public order duties had numerous precedents in the history of the Italian Republic: troops had been used in the 1960s in the north-eastern region of Alto Adige where irredentist groups were active; during civil unrest in Calabria in 1970; to set up roadblocks during the kidnap of Christian Democrat Party Chairman Aldo Moro in 1978; in surveillance of the Rome–Florence railway line after a terrorist bomb had exploded in Bologna station in 1980; in 1988 in the Calabrian Aspromonte mountains where kidnap victims were believed to be held hostage; in the surveillance of key buildings for the duration of the Gulf War in 1991 and in August of that year to assist coastguard patrols in the Adriatic during an influx of Albanian refugees.

The aim of 'Operation Sicilian Vespers' was to deploy soldiers in surveillance and general public order functions, thereby freeing the regular police and *carabinieri* units for investigative duties. Under the terms of Law Decree 349 of 25 July, converted into Law 386 on 23 September, military personnel were granted temporary police status and had the power to identify and search vehicles and individuals *in situ* when circumstances were of an exceptional and urgent nature and related to the specific likelihood of possession of arms, explosives or a risk to life and safety, and when prior authorization from a public prosecutor was impossible. Military officers could make arrests and accompany persons who had been searched to the nearest police station or *carabinieri* barracks to permit completion of identity procedures, after which they were required to inform the judicial authorities immediately. Other tasks were of a more static nature, such as surveillance of sensitive buildings – courthouses, prisons, the houses of judges and politicians – and of the principal roads linking Palermo to the airport and to the other main Sicilian towns. Some 158 sites were denoted as 'sensitive locations'. By the end of July 1992, the addition of the military units brought the total number of personnel with public order functions in Sicily to 27 000,[1] approximately one for every 185 inhabitants. The command headquarters for the 'Sicilian Vespers' mission was established in Palermo's twelfth-century Norman palace, seat of the Sicilian regional government. Goffredo Canino, Chief of the Armed Forces, described the army's task as a 'Colombian-type operation' aimed at isolating *Cosa Nostra* in its own territory by making it dangerous for people to connive with and protect it: 'Mao used to say that to poison the enemy you need to pollute the water in which he swims. That is what we intend to do. Perhaps we will have our own dead but we must accept the rules of battle. Today more than ever we need to say that the most important thing is not to win a battle, but to win the war.'[2]

Despite the reservations of many Sicilians that the troops would 'militarize' the island, the integration with civil society was handled with care and a conspicuous drop in general crime levels occurred. In the first month of the army's presence 1272 crimes were reported, 60 per cent fewer than in the same period of 1991. Thefts dropped during the month from 2553 in the same period of 1991 to 999 in 1992; car thefts from 411 to 109; property thefts from 144 to 80, and robberies by 50 per cent. The incidence of petty crimes such as bag snatching and pocket picking dropped from 144 to 45 and from 227 to 99 respectively.[3]

In the 12-month period from June 1992 to June 1993, thefts in Sicily fell by 12 per cent and serious robberies by 18 per cent.[4] By September

1995, the army had been responsible for checking the identity of 622 350 individuals and for making 1060 arrests.[5] The provisions of the law were extended until 30 June 1998, after which the army troops were replaced by regular police units. The soldiers' departure was regretted by many private citizens as well as by the public authorities. In general, Sicilian judges saw the army presence as a symbol of the State's reacquisition of the monopoly of force and of the repossession of Mafia-controlled territory, and feared the departure would send a 'message' to *Cosa Nostra* that the period of special vigilance was over.[6] The mayor of Palermo, Leoluca Orlando, requested in vain that a 'rapid reaction force' of some 500 men be retained for emergencies.[7]

Police operations

The murder of eight police bodyguards in the Falcone and Borsellino attacks provoked furious reactions within the ranks of their colleagues. After the Borsellino attack, 108 of the 400 Sicilian bodyguards requested a transfer to other locations, refusing to remain as 'cannon fodder' for the Mafia.[8] Some called for the total suspension of the service on the grounds that bullet-proof vests and machine guns were useless against Mafia bombs. Emotions were particularly aroused by the first murder in the course of duty of a female bodyguard, 25-year-old Sardinian Emanuela Loi, who had been transferred to the Borsellino team only a few days beforehand. Many colleagues refused to go into church during the state funeral of the five Borsellino bodyguards and stood outside jeering as the institutional representatives filed in. When Italy's police chief Vincenzo Parisi left the church together with President Oscar Luigi Scalfaro, he nearly fell to the ground from the blows rained on his back and shoulders. On 24 July the largest police union, SIULP, called for the introduction of the death penalty and the military occupation of Sicily. Its Sicilian branch passed a motion asking that Parisi's position be reconsidered, given that 'in recent years the antimafia fight has yielded results of minimal importance' . Parisi's offer to resign was refused, but both the Questor (police chief) and the Prefect of Palermo were transferred at the end of July.

The major innovation in the summer of 1992 was the full activation of the *Direzione Investigativa Antimafia*. The DIA had been constituted by Law 410 on 30 December 1991 after the Scopelliti and Grassi murders (see Chapter 2) as an 'urgent response' to the need for improved coordination and greater professionalism in antimafia investigations, but in June 1992 it was struggling with a total staff of 186 to cover its Rome headquarters and six regional offices.[9] By September 1992 it was functioning with some 450 personnel, and in January 1993 the numbers had risen to 1000; the full complement of 1500 personnel was only reached in 1994. In addition to its Rome HQ, the DIA now has 12 operational centres located in Turin, Genoa, Milan, Padua, Florence, Rome, Naples, Bari, Reggio Calabria, Catania, Palermo and Caltanissetta and 5 separate sections located in Agrigento, Trapani, Catanzaro, Lecce and Salerno.

Conceived as the principal repository of expertise in the area of organized crime, the DIA is formally part of the Public Security Department of the Interior Ministry, although it is an interagency body composed of *Carabinieri* (*Arma dei Carabinieri*), State Police (*Polizia di Stato*) and Finance Police (*Guardia di Finanza*). It is responsible for investigating the structural characteristics and subdivisions of criminal organizations, their objectives and operational methods, their domestic and international contacts and any other form of criminal activity connected to them including extortion. The DIA also conducts investigations in its role as judicial police, that is, it acts under instructions from the prosecution service after a crime has been committed. Its operations are divided into three sections: preventive investigations, judicial investigations – those carried out under the instructions of the judiciary – and international relations.

From the end of December 1992, when the office of High Commissioner for the Mafia Fight was abolished, the DIA took over responsibility for preventing infiltration into public institutions, for carrying out asset-tracing investigations and for any operations that might arise from these. Specialized training in dealing with financial crime was provided by the *Libera Università Internazionale degli Studi Sociali* (LUISS) business school in Rome.The director of the DIA receives reports from the intelligence services and expert forensic or ballistic reports and is responsible for the coordination of all preventive investigations by all the police forces in the area of organized crime. For the first time, all sectors of public security were ordered to collaborate with a single agency, whose sole mandate was the area of organized crime.

Another new structure was created at the same time as the DIA, the *Consiglio Generale per la Lotta alla Criminalità Organizzata*, the General Council for the Fight against Organized Crime, headed by the Interior Minister, whose members include the heads of the *Carabinieri*, State Police and Finance Police and the directors of the domestic and military intelligence services, SISDE and SISMI. The Director of the DIA is a designated participant. This became and remains the body responsible for (a) setting the broad strategies for the fight against organized crime, (b) setting the objectives to be reached for each force, (c) the rationalization of the resources and instruments available and (d) the evaluation of results, with proposals for improvements.

Prior to the creation of the DIA, all three police forces already had specialized units to deal with typical Mafia-type crimes, including kidnap for ransom. These were: the *Servizio Centrale Operativo* (SCO), the Central Operational Service of the State Police, the *Raggruppamento Operativo Speciale* (ROS), the Special Operational Group of the *Carabinieri* and the *Gruppi di Investigazione sulla Criminalità Organizzata* (GICO), the Organized Crime Investigation Groups of the Finance Police. In 1993 the Finance Police set up the *Servizio Centrale di Investigazione sulla Criminalità Organizzata* (SCICO), Central Service of Investigation of Organized Crime to which GICO was attached. SCICO's tasks were to undertake work for the National Antimafia Prosecution Service, the DNA, to ensure collaboration with other centralized police forces and interagency groups and to centralize the information and intelligence collected by GICO.

The DIA was created on the assumption that it would centralize all police work on organized crime, yet the law did not require the specialized organized crime units of the individual forces to be dismantled. The commanders of the existing units were reluctant to give up their best officers to the new interagency force and, fearing for their autonomy, reinforced their own capabilities. In January 1993 the structure of the antimafia police forces was as follows:[10]

DIA	CARABINIERI	STATE POLICE	FINANCE POLICE
1000 interagency staff	*Special Operational* Group (ROS) 1000 staff	*Central Operational* *Service* (SCO) 200 staff	*Organized Crime* *Investigation Groups* (GICO) 600 staff

Specifically, officers of the special units and the DIA could:[11]

(a) Infiltrate clandestine networks and participate in undercover operations within them in order to gather proof for drug trafficking, money laundering and arms trafficking investigations. Such operations might include 'buy-bust' operations, simulated money laundering and simulated receipt of arms.

(b) As delegated by the Minister of the Interior, local chiefs of police, the head of the DIA and the heads of the central and interagency police services could request a district antimafia prosecutor (see below) to authorize the interception of telephone conversations or other forms of interception (such as electronic surveillance) when this was considered necessary for preventing and gathering information on Mafia crimes (as per Law Decree 306 of 1992).

(c) Ask the national antimafia prosecutor to order the preventive detention of those believed to be preparing to commit serious Mafia-type crimes (as per Law Decree 306).

(d) Supply the national antimafia prosecutor with any useful piece of information about current Mafia contacts of convicted persons who might be about to gain prison concessions (reduced sentence, parole, day leave and so on).

(e) Conduct 'investigative conversations' with prison inmates in order to obtain confidential information concerning organized crime with regard to crimes committed or about to be committed. The national antimafia prosecutor also has this facility, in which case the purpose is mainly to encourage the prisoner to collaborate.

The first important law-enforcement successes began in the autumn of 1992. In September, the presumed second-in-command of the *Cosa Nostra* Interprovincial Commission, Giuseppe Madonia, was arrested near Vicenza after ten years on the run; in the same month a major international money-laundering network was dismantled, leading to 152 arrests worldwide and the seizure of assets to the value of US$44 million from the Colombian Cali cartel, thanks to cooperation between seven countries in Europe, North and South America. In this joint operation, known as 'Green Ice', DIA officers made 29 arrests and seized $1.3 million. The contribution of the domestic intelligence service SISDE to the operation is discussed below. International cooperation made further advances in September with the arrest in Argentina of *Cosa Nostra* boss Gaetano Fidanzati and the extradition from Venezuela of the Cuntrera brothers Paolo, Gaspare and Pasquale, wanted since 1984 for trafficking massive quantities of heroin between Italy and the Americas. Around 200 new arrest warrants were issued in November thanks to the testimony of a *Cosa Nostra* collaborator, Leonardo Messina. In January 1993, *capo dei capi* Totò Riina was arrested in Palermo, after 23 years on the run.

Table 4.1   Persons reported and arrested for serious crimes (theft, robbery, arson, drug-related crimes, extortion, murder/attempted murder, Mafia association) in Sicily, 1990–95

	1990	1991	1992	1993	1994	1995
Persons reported	34 326	37 729	46 368	49 836	50 216	52 100
Persons arrested	4 850	6 866	9 305	10 534	11 223	11 223

Source: Interior Ministry annual reports on organized crime, 1993–95.

From Table 4.2, which shows the number of persons reported in Sicily for the crime of Mafia association over a longer time period, the watershed of 1992 is even more apparent:

Table 4.2   Persons reported in Sicily for the crime of Mafia association (according to article 416 *bis* of the criminal code), 1983–97

Year	Persons reported in Sicily for Mafia association
1983	573
1984	1 421
1985	724
1986	290
1987	305
1988	455
1989	537
1990	501
1991	818
1992	1 306
1993	1 786
1994	1 645
1995	1 347
1996	1 145
1997	1 189

Source: Parliamentary Antimafia Commission, annual report, July 1998. Interior Minister's Annual Report to Parliament on Police Activities, September 1998.

A total of 54 organized crime fugitives were arrested in the second half of 1992 and 117 in the first six months of 1993. In 1992 and the first half of 1993, a total of 4423 persons were being investigated for Mafia-related crimes and 19 of the 30 most wanted criminals had been arrested, including important members of mainland crime groups.[12]

A clear consequence of the law-enforcement drive was a dramatic reduction in the number of organized crime murders between 1992 and 1993, as Table 4.3 shows: in Sicily in 1993, 85 Mafia-type assassinations were carried out, compared to 200 in 1992, a 57.5 per cent drop, and a 66.4 per cent fall from 1991, the year with the highest ever number of murders – 253. This must be seen in the light of a fall in the national murder rate by 27.1 per cent over 1992 and 44.1 per cent over 1991.[13] The sharp fall in the murder rate in Calabria between 1991 and 1992 can be traced to a truce in a decade-long clan war which was agreed in the month of October.[14] In 1997 a total of 190 organized crime murders were committed in Italy, of which almost all were in the south.[15]

Table 4.3   Murder rates in Italy and in the four southern regions, 1991–97

Murders	1991	1992	1993	1994	1995	1996	1997
Italy, total	1 916	1 461	1 065	952	1 000	943	863
Sicily	481	399	251	249	223	180	131
(of which, Mafia-related)	(253)	(200)	(85)	(90)	(88)	(66)	(34)
Calabria	277	151	127	121	95	103	100
(of which, Mafia-related)	(165)	(46)	(42)	(42)	(24)	(30)	(32)
Campania,	378	290	196	165	228	204	185
(of which, Mafia-related)	(232)	(181)	(86)	(65)	(113)	(94)	(103)
Apulia	188	135	100	72	86	73	82
(of which, Mafia-related)	(29)	(10)	(3)	(5)	(5)	(3)	(18)

Source: Interior Ministry, annual reports on organized crime 1993–97.

In March 1993, 56 arrest warrants were issued for murders in Palermo on the basis of testimonies made by collaborators Gaspare Mutolo and Pino Marchese. Many other arrests followed in the spring of 1993, including that of the head of *Cosa Nostra* in Catania, Nitto Santapaola. DIA investigations resulted in the issue of 1444 arrest warrants in the course of 1993, 554 in the first half and 890 in the second half of the year.[16]

Table 4.4   Persons arrested for the crime of Mafia association (article 416 *bis*), 1988–97

Year	1988	1989	1990	1991	1992	1993	1994	1995	1996	1997
Persons arrested	821	788	585	874	1 217	1 990	2 136	1 412	1 777	1 324

Source: Interior Ministry.

A total of 867 'major' organized criminals were arrested in the period 1994–96, of which 65 per cent by the State Police, 30 per cent by the *Carabinieri*, 2.6 per cent by the DIA and around 1 per cent by the Finance Police.[17] In the course of 1996, a further 292 important organized criminals were arrested, of whom 8 were in the category of 'the 30 most wanted fugitives' and in 1997 the trend continued: 200 important crime bosses were arrested, of whom 8 were on the '30 most wanted' list.[18]

The extended powers given to the police forces under the 1992 legislation to intercept telephone conversations and carry out electronic surveillance were used extensively (See Table 4. 5). To provide some statistical comparison, the 20 539 intrusive operations that the Italian Justice Ministry acknowledged were carried out in 1995 can be seen against only 2 350 operations carried out by UK Police and Customs in the same year.[19] But since, in addition to these official data, one can assume that a significant number of unreported operations were carried out by the intelligence services in both countries, they are unlikely to be directly comparable.

Table 4.5   Operations of electronic surveillance/telephone interception authorized in Italy, 1992–96

Year	Number of operations
1992	15 360
1993	17 133
1994	18 103
1995	20 539
1996	44 176

Source: La Repubblica, 22 October 1997.

The provision to hold 'investigative conversations' with imprisoned Mafia members introduced by Law Decree 306 was envisaged as a means of informally acquiring information for a particular investigation from persons informed about Mafia crimes who had either indicated a willingness to talk or were felt to be approachable in this sense. It was used on 62 occasions from June to December 1992, after which 13 Mafia members decided to collaborate with the authorities.[20] But problems of a procedural nature have frequently arisen for the police forces involved. In order to conduct investigative conversations, authorization is necessary from all the prosecutors of all the proceedings in which the subject is involved, which in practice can mean delaying the appointment by several months and allowing a line of investigation to go cold. Another potential problem occurs when a prisoner refers details of a crime to his police confidant. The conversation is off the record and therefore there is no formal record of it – other than the fact that it took place and had the appropriate authorization – but a police officer is obliged by law to inform a prosecutor if he learns of a crime and the prosecutor in turn is obliged to proceed, which breaks the intended confidentiality of the conversation and places the prisoner at risk from his fellow detainees.[21] For this reason prisoners considered to be potential collaborators are generally approached for investigative conversations in prisons in central or northern Italy where the Mafia 'grapevine' is less effective.[22]

There is no doubt that the Mafia organizations in Italy, in particular *Cosa Nostra*, were severely damaged after 1992 by intelligent and painstaking work by all the police agencies. The DIA has emerged as a professional body of considerable prestige and expertise with the internal obstacles to its interagency structure largely overcome, for which credit is due to the Director of the service during 1993 and 1994, later Deputy Chief of Police, Gianni De Gennaro. The research and analysis section has been expanded and an intelligence database regularly generates up-to-date information on the various Mafia clans, their tactics and their economic interests. This enables the rapid analysis of specific events, such as the spate of bombings carried out on the Italian mainland in 1993 (see Chapter 7), which was attributed to *Cosa Nostra* within the context of the organization's new strategy. The international section has been responsible for setting up a series of important links with investigative agencies abroad, in particular where Italian Mafia groups have settled. These are discussed in Chapter 6.

On the negative side, the DIA's financial autonomy, generous salaries and flexible working schedules and its image as a dynamic, technologically sophisticated agency exacerbated competitiveness between it and the other specialized police agencies. While some competition could be seen as desirable, an excess has occasionally led to the non-sharing of information and a strategic use of informants within the context of interagency rivalry. Ambiguities in the relationship between officers and informants in the *Carabinieri* ROS units have cast a shadow over an otherwise distinguished record of arresting Mafia fugitives.

A legislative decree issued by the Interior Minister in March 1998 reorganized the structure and functions of the specialized agency units. From June onwards, the headquarters of the antimafia units of the three police forces became 'centres of analysis and of logistic–technical support' and lost their national operational capacity. At provincial level, ROS, SCO and GICO were absorbed into the territorial command structures of their local force (*Carabinieri*, State Police or Finance Police as appropriate). By this decree it was hoped, firstly, to end the confusion for the prosecution offices, which had often found themselves having to coordinate units which belonged to the same force but did not communicate,[23] secondly to avoid the wasteful replication or overlap of functions and thirdly to rein-in what was seen as excessive discretionality and autonomy. In addition, a formal recognition of a *de facto* situation was begun whereby the State Police became more concentrated in the cities and the *Carabineri* in the countryside. The functions of the DIA remained unchanged, except in the area of money-laundering controls (see below), although the exact nature of its future role was under discussion. Two possibilities under review were that the DIA might become a specialized antimafia intelligence service, released from the obligations of a judicial police force, or that it might merge with the antimafia units of the other police forces and the interagency Central Antidrugs Directorate to become a single national structure dealing with serious crime along the lines of the FBI or UK National Crime Squad, but neither seemed imminent in 1999.

The almost unbroken record of police successes has inevitably been punctuated by lapses. Organized crime groups constantly seek to neutralize law-enforcement efforts through intimidation and corruption and, not infrequently, they succeed. In 1997 it emerged that anti-*Camorra* efforts in Naples had been severely compromised by several police officers whose 'salaries' from the leading crime families ranged from $1300 to $2800 per month. Nineteen officers were arrested in January. In February the former head of the Naples Flying Squad was arrested, followed by three more officers from the city's drugs squad in May. It was alleged that the men regularly faked investigations into the criminal activities of the *Camorra* factions who were paying them, while arresting members of rival clans. Between 1994 and 1996, 1586 members of the State Police had been subject to criminal investigation, amounting to 1.55 per cent of the total force. Of them 609 had been convicted in the first grade of trial, the Court of Assizes.[24]

The need for a conspicuous police presence to deal with organized crime in the four southern regions is likely to continue, but perhaps even more important for the overall wellbeing of the majority of citizens is a police presence which restores a sense of security to city streets at night-time, to outlying city suburbs, and to the ill-lit quarters of old city centres. With a a national total of 261 000 police officers of the three principal forces, or an average of one to every 212 inhabitants in 1997, Italy had the highest ratio of police per head of population in the European Union. In Sicily the ratio was 1:191; in Calabria 1:172; in Campania 1:237.[25] In 1995 the average level of policing to population in the EU was 1:281, but there were wide margins of difference, with the lowest, Norway and Finland, having 597 and 594 inhabitants per police officer respectively.[26]

The capacity of the police forces to perform a genuine public security service for Italian society seems to be limited firstly by the fact that many of its armed and uniformed personnel have desk functions which in most countries are performed by public administration – keeping registers of non-Italian residents, issuing work and residence permits, driving licences and other types of authorization – and secondly by the extraordinary personnel requirements involved in serious criminal investigations: the 40 000 communication intercepts each year are a striking example. Given the increasing demands on the resources of conventional policing, some cost-benefit evaluation of the role and activities of the police forces might be of considerable value for the future.

The intelligence services

The principal Italian intelligence agencies are SISDE (Service for Intelligence and Democratic Security) and SISMI (Service for Military Intelligence and Security). SISDE is responsible for intelligence and security functions relating to the preservation of democracy and protecting the integrity of Italian institutions, and is formally part of the Ministry of the Interior. SISMI is responsible for all intelligence and security functions relating to national defence, including counter-espionage, and reports to the Ministry of Defence. The two services are coordinated by the Executive Committee for the Intelligence and Security Services (CESIS) which is chaired by the Prime Minister, who decides its composition; the directors of the two services are permanent members. The Army, Navy and Air Force also have their own intelligence-gathering sections.

Italy's intelligence services were last restructured in 1977, and were given no new powers as a specific consequence of the Palermo massacres of 1992. In 1991, under the terms of the law which created the DIA, SISDE and SISMI were given designated responsibility in the area of organized crime, namely, '[...] the task of carrying out intelligence and security activities regarding any danger or form of subversion of organized crime groups which threaten the institutions and the development of civil coexistence'.[27] Prior to this, according to the directors of the two intelligence services who testified before the Parliamentary Antimafia Commission in 1993, SISMI had 'never dealt with organized crime' while SISDE 'was not activated on a permanent basis but only at particular moments'.[28] Given that the Mafia has represented the major threat to Italian democracy at least since the early 1980s if not before, these statements aroused some surprise.

After the passing of Law Decree 306 in June 1992 the intelligence services had their scope for action reduced in relation to that of the specialized police forces, who were given powers to infiltrate, engage in undercover operations and carry out telephone and electronic surveillance. But an important disparity between police forces and intelligence services remains – intelligence agents are not obliged to inform the prosecution service of their actions and take no orders from them, unlike the police forces which, in their capacity as judicial police, follow the instructions of the public prosecution service.

Following the 1991 legislation, an organized crime department was set up within SISMI. It has contributed to organized crime investigations mainly through the exchange of assistance and intelligence with the intelligence services of other countries. In particular, it studies the transnational aspects of organized crime in different political, socio-economic and geographical contexts.

SISDE has a more diversified role. It has provided a backup service to the judicial police in providing technology and technical experts and in facilitating access to places where electronic eavesdropping and other surveillance operations are carried out. It also provides intelligence by using informants – who are often contiguous with organized crime – in non-conventional operations. More recently, given that organized crime produces and manages considerable wealth and infiltrates the legitimate economy, SISDE has begun to cultivate informants among economic and financial operators who have privileged access to or observation of the economic sectors where the legal and illegal worlds intersect. Nowadays economic intelligence is the service's principal contribution to organized crime investigations. In early 1995, a 'Division of Economic and Industrial Countermeasures' was created inside SISDE's Operations Division. It is divided into three sections, one of which is dedicated to following illicit financial flows.

Almost all the organized crime operations in which SISDE has been involved since the summer of 1992 have been conducted jointly with specialized units of the three police forces or with the DIA. Two such operations are described below.

Operation Green Ice[29]

The investigation began in 1991 with the aim of studying the methods by which the Colombian cocaine cartels Pereira and Cali laundered money from drug sales in Europe. It transpired that the traffickers were having difficulty in transferring the large quantities of cash to Colombia.

The US Drug Enforcement Administration, Italy's Central Operational Service (SCO) and the Central Antidrugs Directorate asked SISDE to create a number of financial brokerage companies and import–export companies as fronts to launder funds. Once these were established, DEA undercover agents promoted them in Colombia and arranged for contact to be made. A company was set up in Rome comprising two DEA agents and one SISDE agent. As Italian law forbids intelligence agents to use false documents, the SISDE agent had to use his own, and set himself up as company manager with an apartment, a bank account and a car leased to the new firm. He took space in a suite of offices with a centralized secretariat and fitted it out with telephone and electronic eavesdropping devices. He took out subscriptions to appropriate trade journals and opened a bank account to be used for laundering. The company, which had begun to operate in March 1992, received the first requests from Colombia in June via contacts in Italian organized crime groups. At this point Italian prosecutors were informed and three controlled deliveries of money took place. The company took 8 per cent of money laundered as commission. As these funds could not be utilized under Italian law (being the proceeds of a crime) the commission was transferred to a DEA account. A Dutch courier made regular visits to the office with bags of cash. Eventually relations with her became so harmonious that she was given a mobile phone and an apartment, which, being bugged, provided the certainty of her contacts with *Cosa Nostra* in Palermo and with the top echelons of the Cali and Pereira cartels. Two top money-laundering operatives in the cartels were persuaded to come over to Europe, Orlando Ospina Cediel Vargas and Pedro Felipe Villaquiran. The former went to the Rome office and proposed to intensify business contacts by offering deliveries of cocaine, and was about to send 300 kilogrammes of cocaine to Italy on the day before his arrest. The drug was seized in Cartagena, Colombia. In Italy 48 arrest warrants were issued (4 of which were carried out abroad) and a major money-laundering network was broken up. The Dutch money courier Bettein Martens turned state's witness and assisted in the identification of 136 drug traffickers and described the structure of the Colombian drug cartels. The operation, which concluded at the end of September 1992, had led to the seizure of more than US$44 million worth of money and assets and 152 arrests in different parts of the world.

Operation Strongbox[30]

The particular focus of study was an examination of transactions involving off-shore havens which had aroused suspicion either because they had no obvious cause or they used shell corporations. The name of

Giovanni Cannizzo came to attention in early 1993. Cannizzo had no schooling beyond primary education, was officially unemployed and had not declared an income for tax purposes for some ten years. Before that he had been registered as a mechanic and as a travelling salesman in clothing. Between April and May 1993, close surveillance of his movements indicated that he was a member of the powerful Santapaola clan in Catania. He was moving large sums of capital – around a billion dollars, estimated to be the volume of business done by the Santapaola clan – around financial markets in Switzerland, Austria, Luxembourg, Monaco and San Marino and travelled frequently to continental European destinations. SISDE set up a working group together with the Bank of Italy to study his laundering methods.

Cannizzo set up a company to front his operations, then made an agreement, first with an international financial intermediation agency and then with an individual broker, to set up a joint venture. Its purpose was to find a finance house which would be prepared, on payment of a commission, to act as a front for fictitious financial transactions. The intermediation agency then began to acquire prime bank guarantees (PBGs), credit certificates with which a bank guarantees an obligation. The shell corporation asked the joint venture to acquire the PBGs at a percentage of the face value, and the cash to be laundered was moved to the account of the shell corporation, which acquired the PBGs with a fictitious contract. This served only to justify the movement of the cash because in reality the PBGs remained in the possession of the joint venture. Money was paid out by the shell corporation from a Swiss safe deposit box to mediators and companies of the joint venture owned by Cannizzo. The intention was to use part of the laundered money for investments in real estate, tourism facilities and casinos abroad. The remainder was to be returned to Italy to finance criminal activities: an account had been opened in the name of a Catania housewife with the local branch of a large northern bank to which $24 million was to be sent. The financial experts in SISDE worked together for months with the Bank of Italy and with the Finance Police unit SCICO. Cannizzo's fax and telephone lines were intercepted. It transpired that he was running two distinct operations involving banks and companies in Germany, the USA, Canada and Britain with sums of over a million dollars. In the first, Cannizzo transferred sums of 10 million dollars daily to the *Credito Svizzero* in Zurich from a company in Milan. The second involved the same Milan company together with others in Panama and in Zug, in Switzerland, in the purchase of five PBGs issued by the Rochester, New York State branch of the Russian-owned Commercial Stockholding Bank-Himbank. The final destination of the money was Brazil. Later Cannizzo was also offered PBGs from the Royal Bank of Canada and Hambros Bank in Germany. The company he was using to purchase them was registered in Liberia with an office in the UK. This last operation was in fact blocked by the *Union des Banques Suisses* (UBS) which had been monitoring the entire process. According to SISDE, Cannizzo was in contact with the Philippines and with 'the highest institutional sectors in Chile'. As the Bank of Italy would report, he enjoyed 'an extraordinary freedom of movement in buying up companies, signing contracts and opening bank accounts in his name at all stages of these financial operations'.[31]

A final impetus to the investigation, which removed any doubt about Cannizzo's awareness of the source of the profits he was laundering, came from a number of *Cosa Nostra* collaborators who confirmed that he was a member of the Santapaola clan. He was arrested in February 1995.

Although the overall contribution of the security services to organized crime investigations since 1992 should be evaluated positively, like the police they have not been immune from the Mafia's corruptive influence. The former deputy head of SISDE in Sicily, Bruno Contrada, was arrested on Christmas Eve in 1992, charged with collusion with *Cosa Nostra*. After being detained pending trial in a military prison for 31 months and then granted house arrest on health grounds, he was found guilty and sentenced by the Palermo Court of Assizes to ten years' imprisonment. According to the testimonies of four state's witnesses, corroborated independently, Contrada had been 'totally at the disposal of *Cosa Nostra*' from 1979 until his arrest. His assistance apparently consisted of giving early warning of investigations, arrest warrants and police raids. The Appeal trial had not concluded at the time of writing. The head of SISDE for the Genoa area, Augusto Citanna, was arrested in October 1993 on charges of subversion: he had allegedly arranged with members of the *Camorra* for a bomb to be placed on the Palermo–Turin night train a month previously. The bomb was 'discovered' during a halt in Rome after Citanna's office in Genoa picked up a 'rumour' that a bomb had been planted on the train.

In July 1999 the D'Alema government introduced a draft law on the reform of the intelligence services by which two new 'agencies' (no longer 'services'), corresponding to the existing domestic/foreign distinction, would be created under the direct responsibility of the prime minister's office. A parliamentary watchdog committee would have greater powers than at present to scrutinize expenditure, but detailed discussion of political responsibility, accountability and of how the new control mechanisms would operate was postponed for parliamentary debate.

The judicial response

The Sicilian magistrates, in particular those of the younger generation who had worked with Giovanni Falcone and Paolo Borsellino, were devastated by the personal and professional loss of their colleagues. In a joint letter of resignation written to Palermo chief prosecutor Pietro Giammanco and delivered to his home on 23 July, eight members of the Palermo district antimafia prosecution office requested a transfer to other offices. The letter was a passionate *j'accuse* of anger and despair and gave a negative response to an appeal, made to the Sicilian judges two days previously by President Scalfaro, to stand firm at their posts. The letter's principal targets were the inadequacies of the state security apparatus and the insuperable conflicts that had arisen with chief prosecutor Pietro Giammanco. It criticized the Interior Ministry and the security forces which had been 'unable to provide an efficient defence against Mafia terrorism such as to protect the most exposed targets and prevent foreseeable massacres'. The Sicilian judges were 'abandoned to their fate of death [..] on a tragic waiting list which is destined to lengthen indefinitely', while political–institutional sectors were 'always ready to cover up responsibilities and inefficiencies, to mislead public opinion with law-manifestos and solemn statements of intent which are regularly forgotten'. The apparent ease with which the attacks had been perpetrated was 'an incentive to *Cosa Nostra*'s strategy of systematically eliminating all those who will not yield to Mafia intimidation'. The demand for a new chief prosecutor was explicit: the letter talked of 'differences and rifts which only an authoritative and uncontroversial leadership could overcome and repair'. The letter concluded,

> It is unacceptable that those responsible for all that has happened remain in their jobs, and that such glaring omissions and inadequacies do not lead to resignations and dismissals at all levels. The State has betrayed Paolo Borsellino. It has betrayed him by the negligence and the moral indifference with which it failed to prevent *Cosa Nostra* from carrying out a death sentence which was totally predictable. This is why we resign from the district antimafia directorate. In Palermo and in Sicily the minimum conditions for the exercise of criminal justice are not being met.[32]

After publication of the letter in the press the Superior Judicial Council (CSM) summoned all 34 members of the Palermo prosecution office to Rome over a three-day period to provide a complete overview of the situation. Pietro Giammanco's position as chief prosecutor, which had become difficult after Falcone's death, became untenable. The conflictual relationship between Falcone and his superior had been demonstrated by the publication on 24 June of extracts from Falcone's diary which he had given to a trusted journalist a year before his death, with such an eventuality in mind. The diary entries showed Falcone's bitterness at the working methods of his superior, who had deliberately obstructed his investigations by failing to inform him of developments in specific cases, by transferring cases to colleagues without consulting him and, according to the diary, bowing to political pressure by ensuring that a case would effectively be buried.[33] On 28 July Giammanco requested a transfer to the Supreme Court; the resignations of the eight judges were subsequently withdrawn.

The autumn brought progress in the form of several crucial appointments. The vacant post of national antimafia prosecutor – which had been blocked for months by the divergent views of the CSM and the Justice Minister on the choice of appointee – was readvertised and candidates with the appropriate experience and seniority invited to apply. As an interim measure, the CSM invited Supreme Court judge and former Executive Director of the United Nations International Drug Control Programme Giuseppe Di Gennaro to become acting national prosecutor. Di Gennaro, an ambitious, outspoken judge with extensive international experience and one of four who was eventually short-listed for the job of 'super prosecutor', immediately proclaimed a set of objectives which would in his words have the Mafia 'with its back to the wall' inside two years. He saw the task as being to provide a 'systematic and unitary perception of the Mafia phenomenon and of its sister organizations, and a plan for a national and international strategy'.[34] On 30 October 1992, 11 months after the DNA had been created by law, the appointment was announced. It went neither to Di Gennaro nor to the candidate whom the majority of the CSM had preferred to Falcone, chief prosecutor of Palmi (Calabria) Agostino Cordova, but to Bruno Siclari, 67-year-old Prosecutor General of the Palermo Court of Appeal.

At the end of August 1992, Giovanni Falcone's deputy at the Ministry of Justice, judge Liliana Ferraro, was appointed as his successor as Director of Criminal Affairs. Among her achievements during 22 years in the Ministry was the supervision of the construction and security of the courtroom-prison built for the Palermo maxi-trial in 1986. Ferraro promised that she would pursue Falcone's own objectives, in particular (a) to propose improvements to the code of criminal procedure introduced in 1989; (b) to improve the judicial apparatus for dealing with organized crime; and (c) to introduce a methodology that would permit constant monitoring of the new techniques introduced in the prosecution offices.[35]

The third key appointment of 1992 was that in December of Turin judge Gian Carlo Caselli as chief prosecutor of Palermo. Caselli, who offered his services in recognition of a debt owed to his murdered colleagues, had little or no direct experience of Mafia investigations, but his dedication and his abilities in the investigation of terrorism in Turin during the 1970s had earned him widespread admiration, while his tenure of office in the CSM between 1986 and 1990 had brought him first-hand experience of the tensions within the Sicilian judiciary. His appointment was approved unanimously and the Palermo prosecution office gave him an unqualified welcome. It was no coincidence that *Cosa Nostra's capo dei capi* Totò Riina was arrested on Caselli's first day at work in Palermo on 15 January 1993.

An important indicator of change in September 1992 was the CSM's decision to open an investigation into the work of Corrado Carnevale, who had presided over the First Section of the Supreme Court since 1986. The First Section, which habitually dealt with cases of organized criminality, had overturned numerous guilty verdicts of the Courts of Assizes or Appeal, frequently on the slenderest of technicalities. A few weeks before the CSM decided to act, the First Section had overruled two convictions concerning a renowned drug trafficker and had ordered the trials to be rerun from the beginning on the grounds that one of the defendant's two lawyers had not been informed about a particular interrogation and thus had not been present, even though the lawyer in question had not raised any objection.

Three strands of investigation were opened into Carnevale's work: one was based on a study carried out by the Communist Party (PCI) delegation of the Antimafia Commission in 1990 into five trials and ten verdicts relating to the Mafia in which examples of procedural errors had been alleged, these being the only area in which the Supreme Court can intervene. The second related to alleged improprieties in Carnevale's involvement with the bankruptcy proceedings of the Lauro shipping fleet in Naples. The third strand dealt with a possible abuse of authority in a conflict between Carnevale and a Naples prosecutor, Paolo Mancuso. The first two led to criminal investigations. In April 1993 Carnevale was suspended without salary from the judiciary for his involvement in the Lauro affair; in 1996 he was sent for trial and convicted on the charge of having favoured two businessmen in the acquisition of the Lauro fleet while he was chairman of the watchdog committee set up to oversee correct observance of the bankruptcy procedures. An investigation carried out by the Palermo prosecution office concluded that his decisions in Mafia cases had been corruptly influenced by *Cosa Nostra* and he was committed for trial in Palermo on 6 April 1998 on the charge of favouring the Mafia. Altogether 15 state's witnesses provided incriminating evidence against him. (At the time of writing the trial had not concluded.)

The National Antimafia Directorate

With the appointment of Bruno Siclari, the DNA (*Direzione Nazionale Antimafia*) or National Antimafia Directorate finally began to function. Under the terms of Law Decree 367 of 20 November 1991 (converted into Law 8 of 20 January 1992), the DNA exists inside the office of the Prosecutor General within the Supreme Court and is located in Rome. Its primary tasks are to provide *coordination* and *impetus* for Mafia investigations nationally and internationally in order to avoid the dissipation of knowledge and experience that can occur when investigations are carried out in different prosecution offices. Twenty judges are assigned to the DNA for a minimum of two years, selected on the basis of proven teamwork and experience of Mafia investigations. Their appointment must meet with the approval of the national prosecutor. The national antimafia prosecutor is appointed for a term of four years, renewable once.

The DNA is responsible for coordinating the work of the district antimafia directorates, *(direzione distrettuale antimafia,* DDA*)* or prosecution offices, which, under the same law of 1992, had been created to deal with specific Mafia-type crimes, including kidnap for ransom, in each of the 26 cities in which there was a Court of Appeal. Thus the DDA in Palermo is competent for all Mafia-related crimes committed in the provinces of Palermo, Termini Imerese, Sciacca, Trapani, Marsala and Agrigento; the Rome DDA for all Mafia crimes committed in the Lazio region, where there is only one Court of Appeal. The judges within each DDA are seconded to it for a period of two years, with the possibility of renewal.

Among the requirements of the law was that a computerized database be set up for storing and analysing intelligence and information on organized crime, to be made available to the DDAs as appropriate. The database was to be built up from court documents, arrest warrants, statements from state's witnesses and other official sources. Each DDA was to set up a database using similar methodology which would be linked to the DNA's central computer in Rome.

The 'impetus' functions of the national antimafia prosecutor are extremely wide-ranging: he or she can issue instructions to the DDAs on a variety of matters, including the most efficient use of the judicial police in the prevention and repression of organized crime; call meetings of DDA prosecutors to discuss problems; assign magistrates from the central DNA office to the DDAs for a specific investigation; even take personal charge of an investigation from a DDA if it reaches an *impasse* or if the instructions issued are not being followed, although this is considered an extreme remedy and to date has not occurred. The overall function of the office is to ensure efficiency, continuity and timeliness in judicial action against the Mafia.

Less than a year after its inauguration, the DNA was in difficulties. In early October 1993, 18 of the 20 magistrates assigned to it wrote a letter to the CSM, copied to Siclari, in which they complained about the lack of direction and the inefficiencies of the DNA, and cast doubt on whether in its current form it could ever be made to function. It was a common view in judicial circles at that time, shared by the 18 signatories of the letter, that the DNA had been Giovanni Falcone's brainchild and that he had been the only one capable of leading it. The letter described Siclari as 'correct' and 'not linked to any particular political power structure', but he was described as 'absolutely inadequate' to his task. According to the signatories, the DNA had an inherently ambiguous legislative structure without clear guidelines on procedures. There was no sense of the DNA's overall function, which up to that time had been based on individual initiatives; in the absence of a common goal, day-to-day exigencies and the desire to obtain instant results had prevailed over the work of analysis and methodological development. Of the 20 magistrates 11 had been temporarily assigned to DDAs around the country and only 7 were working on a full-time basis in Rome. The resources to set up a sound database had not been forthcoming.[36]

Some of the criticisms were justified, particularly those concerning the ambiguity of roles of the DNA and of the national antimafia prosecutor. Falcone's original vision of the DNA had been as a management structure for Mafia prosecutions in which the national prosecutor was responsible for directing and prioritizing investigations, but in the passage of the law through Parliament, opposition from the judiciary that the DNA might become politicized under the influence of the Justice Ministry had caused its powers to be considerably diluted.

The DNA's responsibilities for setting up a database had been loosely defined, and merely called for 'the acquisition and elaboration of facts, information and data relative to organized crime'. To serve a useful purpose such information needed to be carefully applied to specific tasks, enabling the DNA to become a repository of expertise on which investigators could draw to facilitate an understanding of the Mafia, its command and support structures, financial outlets, its contacts with the economy, finance, public administration and politics.

After a difficult running-in period the DNA gradually improved its capabilities. Doubts remained about its intrinsic value as an institution, but expertise was being developed in the analysis of economic crime and money laundering and of specific sectors, including organized criminal involvement in non-traditional activities such as industrial waste disposal – the so-called 'eco-Mafia'. The appointment of Pier Luigi Vigna, formerly chief prosecutor of Florence and head of the Florence DDA as national antimafia prosecutor at the end of 1996, brought a new dynamism to the office: studies have been undertaken of the use by organized crime of new technologies and, conversely, of how investigating authorities can utilize these as investigative tools; special emphasis has been devoted to inter-national collaboration and to the threat from foreign Mafia groups, in particular Chinese, Russian, Colombian and Albanian organizations. Vigna is convinced that Mafia groups around the world now collaborate on the basis of 'strategic agreements' according to which certain activities are subdivided by sector or geographical area, and others such as money laundering are centralized. A process of specialization and division of tasks has taken place in Italy and one can presume as a 'logical conse-quence ' that a similar transformation has occurred at international level, hence the need for a coordinated international response.[37] The DNA has a department devoted to relations with overseas counterparts and receives them regularly in Rome. The long-term aim is the establishment of an EU-wide network of judicial investigators who deal with organized crime, with a focal point in each country.[38]

Although Vigna's more interventionist style has brought the DNA greater visibility in the antimafia fight, it has also highlighted a source of possible tension – that the decision of the national antimafia prosecutor to give a particular impetus to an investigation may be taken by the DDA concerned to be undue criticism of or interference in its work. The risk was evident in early 1998 during two prolonged kidnaps, one in Sardinia and the other on the mainland, when Vigna offered to assign prosecu-tors from the DNA to assist the DDAs in Cagliari and Brescia respectively. In both cases the DDAs declined the offer on the grounds that they were competent to handle the investigations.

The ambiguity of the DNA's position in straddling both criminal justice policy management and the impartial application of the law remains the most delicate aspect of its functions, given the fine balance between the Italian obligation to proceed against every notified crime and the inde-pendence of the judiciary from political direction. This was highlighted in early 1998 by proposals contained in a draft law which would allow the national antimafia prosecutor to order asset-tracing, freezing and confiscation measures for suspected Mafia members, a power hitherto confined to the prosecution office and the police chief in the town of residence of the suspect. Vigna argues that the extension of his powers is a natural one, given that he already receives information concerning suspicious transactions relating to money laundering. As the ordinary DDAs and the officials currently responsible for these measures are over-burdened and unable to carry out all the necessary checks, he proposes that these should be ordered and carried out by the DNA and the DDA responsible for the area.[39]

Judicial investigations

After the Capaci and via D'Amelio attacks in which judges from Palermo had been murdered, the DDA in Caltanissetta, as the adjacent prosecu-tion office to Palermo, took charge of both investigations. In May 1992 the Caltanissetta prosecution office comprised only three deputies, one of whom was about to depart for maternity leave, and it was awaiting the nomination of a new chief. Judge Giovanni Tinebra was appointed chief prosecutor immediately after the Falcone murder and arrived in Caltanissetta on 15 July 1992, four days before the Borsellino attack. He quickly acquired four extra prosecutors, transferred from Messina and Catania, and in November he was joined by judges Ilda Boccassini from Milan and Fausto Cardella from Perugia, at their express wish. Ilda Boccassini had prosecuted *Cosa Nostra*'s activities in Milan and had had a long professional friendship with Falcone. She described the need to separate the emotionally lacerating aspects of investigating a friend's murder from the dispassionate approach required to carry it out as 'dev-astating and traumatic' but ultimately 'exhilarating' when the investigation concluded with indictments for those responsible.[40]

Tinebra set up a core group of DIA agents within his office to coordinate all the documentation and the telephone intercepts. Then he proceeded to computerize every item of the investigative work according to a model which would later be adopted by all the DDAs around the country.[41] Reconstructing the progress of the Falcone enquiry, judge Boccassini described how it had begun like any other murder case, by careful exam-ination of the scene of the crime and by trying to understand the dynamics of the attack, the logistical bases, the location of the remote control detonator and the method of activation. The work was divided up between the DIA, the organized crime group of the *Carabinieri* – ROS – and a specialized police unit known as the Falcone–Borsellino group which had been set up by the new Questor of Palermo, Arnaldo La Barbera. Each group was given precise tasks. On the working supposition that it was a *Cosa Nostra* attack, enquiries were oriented towards the clans whose leaders were still at liberty and who could be presumed to have taken part in the deliberations, the preparatory phase and the execution of the attack. This led to the placing of a series of telephonic and electronic eavesdropping devices and to the observation of specific targets. ROS surveillance operatives took some 3600 hours of film. A bug placed by the DIA in the house of *mafioso* Gioacchino La Barbera permitted the interception in March 1993 of a conversation, one sentence of which led to the identification of the executive command. It would later transpire that La Barbera had made and received many telephone calls on 23 May from prominent *Cosa Nostra* members in Rome and in Sicily. It became clear that Falcone's movements had been carefully monitored throughout the day of his murder.

Every item of potential evidence was studied, including a series of anonymous letters which had been circulated after the bombing. All the material found around the site of the attack and in the course of house raids was examined. Use was made of technically sophisticated techniques and expert analysis such as the DNA examination of 53 cigarette butts found on the hillside overlooking the motorway near Capaci, carried out by a team sent over from the USA by the Federal Bureau of Investigation. A torch, a pair of rubber gloves, a tube of strong glue and a paper bag advertising a pharmaceutical product were found near the culvert where the bomb explosive had been hidden. The bag was traced back to the advertiser, from there to medical connections in Sicily and then to doctors considered close to *Cosa Nostra*. Following Falcone's own working methods, a broad approach to the crime was taken which looked not just for the material authors of the crime but for their sympathizers, their financiers, and their points of reference in- and outside the criminal underworld. The team did not exclude the possible involvement of institutional contacts or of instigators to the crime who belonged to criminal groups with business and financial interests.[42] As Falcone had always insisted,

> Only the professional rigour of magistrates and investigators will give the Mafia the sense that Sicily is no longer its own backyard, and consequently will serve to deprive the Mafia of its aura of impunity and invincibility [and to] dismantle the insolence and arrogance of the *mafioso* who will not bow to the State's authority.[43]

The first state's witness to contribute to the Falcone enquiry was Santo Di Matteo, a close associate of Totò Riina and used by him as a killer, who had participated in the early preparations for the Falcone attack. His collaboration was followed by that of Gioacchino La Barbera, arrested in March 1993, whose contribution was unique in that he had participated at every stage. The collaborators' testimonies helped to reconstruct the details of the attack in terms that only an insider could know, for example in explaining that two skateboards had been used at Capaci, one to lie on and the other to slide the drums of explosive into the culvert. They also gave details of the surveillance operation of Falcone's departure from Rome and his arrival in Sicily, and revealed that the butcher's shop belonging to the Ganci Mafia family, with a clear view of Falcone's apartment in via Notarbartolo, had been used to observe the departure of his armoured convoy for Palermo airport.

Scientific and technical analyses provided independent corroboration. In September 1992, before any state's witnesses had begun to talk, explosives experts from the Scientific Police built a replica of the motorway section at Capaci, complete with culvert, on a stretch of wasteland near Livorno, and performed a controlled explosion to assess the quantity and type of explosive used.[44] Collaborators later confirmed that approximately 500 kilogrammes of explosive, comprising TNT, Semtex – a combination of T4 and pentaerythritol tetranitrate (PETN) – and blasting gelatine of the type used in quarries, had been packed into 13 plastic drums, sealed with adhesive and pushed into the culvert under the 11-metre-wide carriageway. An old mattress had been thrown over the entrance. The work had been done by night at the end of April over a period of several hours, hence the torch. During the operation a two-man *carabiniere* patrol had stopped 100 metres away on a call of nature, but had noticed nothing. Trials to gauge the speed of the Falcone convoy for timing, distance and detonation purposes had been carried out, and tests of explosives buried underground were made on property belonging to Santo Di Matteo at Altofonte, near Palermo, where the noise was drowned by blasting from a nearby quarry. A fridge dumped in the field beside the motorway was removed to a spot some 25 metres forward from the culvert, in view of the three-man team on the hillside, as a marker for the point at which to detonate the bomb. This was done by a radio-controlled device of the type used to guide model aircraft. The team had waited for their target for three weekends in a row, and nearly missed it on 23 May when the convoy slowed down suddenly from 140 to 90 kilometres – due, as they learned later, to Falcone's removal of the car keys from the ignition. After every previous wait on the hillside, all cigarette ends had been carefully collected, but in the tension of the moment the precaution was forgotten, leaving a vital clue for investigators.[45]

Only one direct participant in the Borsellino murder turned state's witness, and his testimony, later retracted, was of doubtful validity. Nonetheless investigators succeeded in establishing the essential details of the bomb attack, in which 90 kilogrammes of Semtex were used, detonated by a sophisticated electronic timing device from behind a wall some 30–40 metres away. Almost every window in via D'Amelio was broken by the explosion, two dozen vehicles were badly damaged and a further 12 vehicles were totally destroyed, their parts scattered over a wide radius, causing problems for the identification of the car in which the bomb had been placed. But the area was sealed off within a short time and the street combed for fragments of evidence, from which an inventory of cars present in the street was compiled. The discovery of a cylinder block without an apparent 'parent' vehicle led to the identification of a Fiat 126 which had been stolen two weeks before. Its number plate had been stolen from a different car on the night before the attack.

Tinebra's team in Caltanissetta achieved remarkable results within a timespan that was unprecedented for organized crime investigations in Sicily, notwithstanding the delay caused by a ruling of the Constitutional Court on incompatibility of judicial functions (see below). The trial for the Falcone attack opened in Caltanissetta in September 1994 and concluded on 26 September 1997 with 24 sentences of life imprisonment for the 37 defendants. In October 1994, 20 individuals were charged with the murders of Paolo Borsellino and his five bodyguards; the first grade trial concluded on 27 January 1996 with life imprisonment for the principal defendants; the Appeal trial concluded in January 1999.

Elsewhere in Italy those with material responsibility for the major organized crime attacks of the 1990s were identified, arrested and committed for trial, and many of the trials of the 1980s came to a definitive conclusion in the Supreme Court. On 21 October 1992, 24 arrest warrants were issued for the murder of Salvo Lima. For the first time in a murder indictment, a clear link was made between a Mafia victim and his political–Mafia links. Although Lima was not considered a *Cosa Nostra* affiliate he had been valuable to the organization as a link between the organization and Giulio Andreotti. The Palermo Court of Assizes reached a verdict in the first grade trial for the murder of Ignazio Salvo on 11 January 1996, also with life sentences for the principal defendants. On 11 May 1996 the trial for the murder of judge Antonino Scopelliti – due to represent the prosecution's case in the Supreme Court hearing for the maxi-trial in January 1992 – concluded with life sentences for Totò Riina and nine others. (The verdict was overturned on Appeal as the evidence was not considered conclusive.) On 10 June 1996 the Supreme

Court confirmed life sentences for Riina and nine other members of the Commission for the murders perpetrated in the 1980s of Flying Squad chief Boris Giuliano, of General Carlo Alberto Dalla Chiesa and of other institutional figures.

In January 1996 the first arrest warrants were issued for the 1993 bombs in Rome, Florence and Milan (see Chapter 7) and in April and June, 35 individuals, including the principal *Cosa Nostra* bosses Riina, Provenzano, Brusca, Bagarella and the Graviano brothers, were committed for trial in the Florence Court of Assizes. The trial ran from November 1996 until June 1998 and resulted in 14 sentences of life imprisonment. Table 4.6 shows the numbers of prisoners who were awaiting trial or convicted for Mafia crimes between 1992 and 1996.

Table 4.6   Survey of prisoners (awaiting trial or definitively convicted) under article 416 *bis* (Mafia-type association) and article 74 of Law 309/90 (criminal association with the aim of drug trafficking), 1992–96

Date	Mafia association	Drug trafficking
31.07.1992	2 060	2 172
05.10.1992	2 130	2 252
13.03.1993	2 173	2 330
21.12.1993	3 340	2 925
17.01.1994	3 416	2 886
30.06.1994	4 115	3 222
31.01.1995	3 935	2 987
30.06.1995	4 085	2 855
31.12.1995	3 809	2 476
31.12.1996	3 877	2 497

Source: Ministero di Grazia e Giustizia, Dipartimento dell'amministrazione penitenziaria.

Table 4.7   Criminal proceedings relating to Mafia-type crimes, 1994–97 (P = Pending, D = Definitive)

	1994		1995		1996		1997*	
	P	D	P	D	P	D	P	D
North	193	73	613	158	569	276	580	138
Centre	32	12	503	82	403	189	405	74
South	381	143	1 301	371	1 471	658	1 541	388
Islands	651	101	1 061	126	1 356	1 127	1 372	590
Italy (total)	*1 257*	*329*	*3 478*	*737*	*3 799*	*2 250*	*3 898*	*1 190*

Source: Ministero di Grazia e Giustizia – Direzione Generale degli Affari Penali.
* first six months only.

In December 1997 the Palermo DDA presented a list of its activities since Gian Carlo Caselli's appointment as chief prosecutor from January 1993 to November 1997:

Table 4.8   Investigative activities of the Palermo DDA (District Prosecution Office), 1993–97

Number of investigations opened	611
Persons Investigated	5 062
Arrest warrants requested	1 255
Arrest warrants issued	999
Number of persons arrested	762
Number of persons sent for trial	1 255

Source: Tribunale di Palermo, 1997.

Implementation of legislation

The successes achieved by the judiciary were facilitated by modifications to existing legislation which had been introduced in the aftermath of the Palermo massacres and by the application of new legislation.

State's witnesses

Judges Falcone and Borsellino had insisted since the mid-1980s on the need for legislation to regularize the position of Mafia collaborators within the Italian judicial system. Falcone's experience of working with US counterparts, and the contribution made by collaborating Italian and US *mafiosi* to the 'Pizza Connection' trial in New York in 1985 and later to the first maxi-trial in Palermo, had convinced him that well-defined measures with clear-cut responsibilities on both sides were an indispensable tool in organized crime investigations. In 1989 he told the author,

> On the one hand we need clarity in the areas of judicial treatment and of sentencing, and on the other we need to be able to guarantee minimum conditions of personal security for collaborators and their families. Above all we must continue to be able to use what I consider to be an irreplaceable investigative tool, because only the voices from inside can help us to understand properly what is happening. To do all this we need absolute clarity and most of all we must avoid any possibility of occult manoeuvres or obscure deals between the State and certain people. Everything must be done in the light of day, everything must be clear and everything must be codified. The law must establish

clearly what can and what cannot be done, and as soon as possible. Our system permits a whole series of sentence reductions quite separately from collaboration so that sometimes the absurd thing happens that those who collaborate often receive worse treatment than those who do not. This simply must stop otherwise we won't have any more collaborators. The most important thing is to remove all powers of discretion from those who must decide whether and how much to reduce prison sentences or the time that must actually be spent in prison. I am in no doubt whatsoever about the need for a new form of judicial procedure which is in keeping with today's new conditions, because there is simply no time to lose.[46]

Legislation on state's witnesses was only passed in 1991, and for two years afterwards was technically unworkable because corresponding modifications to the criminal code had not been made. Moreover certain eventualities, such as the possibility that a *mafioso* could begin to collaborate after his conviction and sentencing had been definitively established by the Supreme Court, had not been foreseen by the law's drafters.[47] Only in 1993 did it become legally possible for a collaborator to change his name and use false identity documents.

A criminal's decision to collaborate with the authorities arises from a series of factors which depend upon how the potential collaborator views both the State and the organization of affiliation. The decision usually coincides with a personal crisis in which the values and identity of the individual come to be viewed, perhaps for the first time, as separate from and directly conflicting with those of the group. Other important factors include:[48]

- the wish for revenge;
- a loss of consensus: the rejection of the criminal organization by a significant sector of society which had once explicitly or implicitly tolerated or supported its activities;
- internal conflict, such that the group identity and solidarity are weakened;
- a perceived breaking of the rules or betrayal of the values for which an individual joined the group;
- altered perceptions of victory and defeat such that the organization loses credibility and/or legitimacy in the eyes of its own members at the same time as the authority of the State is growing (the act of collaboration being an implicit recognition of the State's superiority);

- the fear of a long prison sentence;
- the individual's fear for the physical safety, inside or outside prison, of himself and/or his family.

Table 4.9   Numbers of state's witnesses in Italy, 1992–97

November 1992	40
December 1992	58
January 1993	250
February 1993	270
March 1993	286
April 1993	320
May 1993	388
June 1993	420
mid-August 1993	500
31 December 1993	602
31 December 1994	774
31 December 1995	1 052
31 December 1996	1 231
31 December 1997	1 028

Sources: Il Mondo 10/17 May 1993; *La Repubblica*, 30 May 1993, *L'Espresso* 30 May 1993; *Ministero dell'Interno* various; *Servizio Centrale di Protezione* in *Panorama* 16 January 1997; *Direzione Investigativa Antimafia.*

As Table 4.9 shows, the number of collaborators grew exponentially throughout 1993 and continued to rise for the following two years. In addition to the generic influences described above, the trend is attributable to three specific factors: the Supreme Court verdict of January 1992 which conferred juridical validity on the testimonies of the state's witnesses in the maxi-trial, the incentive to collaborate provided by new legislation and the harsh prison regime which the 41 *bis* regulations imposed. There was a general perception that Italy's commitment to the antimafia fight was genuine, and that the State might win. From July 1992 until 30 June 1996 over 5 per cent of all 41 *bis* prisoners had decided to collaborate.[49]

The numbers of collaborators of different affiliations can be studied in relation to the overall size of the organization concerned.

If the estimates of organizational size in Table 4.10 are accurate, and are compared with the total number of collaborators in the four groups in Table 4.11 below, in 1997 *Cosa Nostra* collaborators represented 6.6 per cent of the total membership of the organization, those of the United Holy Crown 4.76 per cent, of the *'Ndrangheta* 2.73 per cent and of the

Camorra 2.67 per cent, figures which belie the popular view of *Cosa Nostra* as the most impermeable and disciplined of the four crime groups.

Table 4.10   Numbers of presumed members of Italian Mafia-type organizations, 1995–97

Mafia Organizations	on 31.12.95	on 31.12.96	on 31.12.97
Sicily	5 400	5 700	5 500
Campania	7 200	7 541	6 700
Calabria	5 600	5 616	6 000
Apulia	2 000	2 000	1 951

Source: Direzione Investigativa Antimafia.

Table 4.11   Numbers of state's witnesses and their affiliation, 1995–97

Year/Organization	1995	1996	1997
Cosa Nostra	381	424	363
Camorra	192	224	179
'Ndrangheta	133	159	164
United Holy Crown	85	100	93
Others[a]	261	324	229
Total	1 052	1 231	1 028[b]

Source: Direzione Investigativa Antimafia, 1998.
[a]   State's witnesses not belonging to organized crime groups.
[b]   On 31 December 1997, of the total of 1028 collaborators, 195 were held in prison, 618 were at liberty, 2 were under arrest but not in prison, and 4 were at liberty abroad.

Only a more precise analysis would provide a satisfactory explanation for these data, but they suggest that proportionally, *Cosa Nostra* has been more damaged by the efforts of law enforcement and by internal conflict, or by a confluence of the factors described above, than the other organizations. The strategy of divide and rule practised successfully by Totò Riina to win supremacy for the *Corleonesi* after the second Mafia war and the strategy of massacres undertaken in his name in 1992–93 may contain the seeds of *Cosa Nostra*'s temporary or even definitive fragmentation. The higher percentage of UHC collaborators may be related to the fact that it is relatively new within the organized crime spectrum – having been founded only in 1980 – and therefore has less tradition to defend. The low percentages of the *Camorra* and *'Ndrangheta* may be due to the extreme fragmentation of the former, such that would-be collaborators are less able to provide a relevant contribution to investigations; in the case of the latter, the fact that biological families form the core of the

'*Ndrangheta* has created a greater impermeability and reluctance to collaborate. For this and other reasons the '*Ndrangheta* is likely to be the most dangerous Italian crime group in the years to come.

The problems of evaluating the contribution of state's witnesses and the credibility of the testimonies of lifelong criminals whose decision to collaborate may be dominated by the desire for revenge are evident. There is a constant risk that collaborators harmonize their testimonies or manipulate their evidence in such a way as to deceive a court. Article 192 of the Italian code of criminal procedure requires Italian courts to seek independent corroboration of accomplice evidence (*chiamata di correo*), but the testimonies of two collaborators can constitute proof if the testimonies are precise, concrete, if they coincide factually and if it can be shown that they could not have been coordinated. The presiding judge is permitted to exercise the principle of *libero convincimento* or 'freely reached conviction'. This constitutes a synthesis of the evidence in the specific case with the 'maximum of judicial experience' (roughly corresponding to precedent in common law). Written motivation is obligatory within a given period after a court verdict and this is scrutinized by the Supreme Court for procedural inaccuracies.

The Falcone murder investigation was a textbook case of the professional use of collaborators, in that their statements reinforced evidence which had been collected independently. A synthesis of the contributions made by the most important state's witnesses is given below.

The value of the state's witnesses to Italy's antimafia investigations since 1992 has been offset by a series of complex judicial, economic and social problems which have placed the entire system under considerable strain. In contrast to the United States, where protected witnesses can be relocated and absorbed in a new community without attracting undue attention, Italy is geographically too small to cope with over one thousand

Principal Collaborators since 1992[50]		
Collaborator and Mafia 'family'	Start of collaboration	Nature of contribution
Leonardo Messina San Cataldo (Caltanissetta)	June 1992	Important essentially for *Cosa Nostra*–political links and context of 1992 murders, in particular points to a Lima–Andreotti–Carnevale connection.

Giuseppe Marchese Corso dei Mille (Palermo)	September 1992	Until August 1992 one of Riina's most trusted associates despite being in prison virtually without a break for ten years. His contribution concerned (a) the attempts by Riina to influence the maxi-trial; (b) the role of Lima as intermediary; (c) the significance of Lima's murder.
Gaspare Mutolo Partanna Mondello (Palermo)	July 1992	Important for CN–institutional links. His testimony led to the arrest of SISDE deputy director, Bruno Contrada, to the indictment of Giulio Andreotti and to an understanding of the context in which the 1992 murders occurred.
Baldassare Di Maggio San Giuseppe Jato	January 1993	His information led directly to the arrest of Riina, and contributed to the incrimination of Giulio Andreotti. Also recounted CN–political links through Salvo cousins.
Salvatore Cancemi Porta Nuova (Palermo)	July 1993	He gave himself up spontaneously. Took part in the Falcone attack. His statements led to the incrimination of Marcello Dell'Utri.
Santo Di Matteo Altofonte	October 1993	A killer for Riina. Provided details of Falcone murder preparations.
Gioacchino La Barbera Altofonte	November 1993	Admitted to killing of Salvo Lima. Gave full details of all stages of Falcone attack.
Maurizio Avola Santapaola (Catania)	1994	Information leading to arrests of Catania Santapaola clan. Gave details of planning of 1993 bombing campaign.
Filippo Malvagna Pulvirenti (Catania)	1994	Gave information on Mafia–political links; on 1993 bombing campaign.

collaborators, each with an average of four family members: in addition to the 1028 collaborators from Mafia groups at the end of 1997, 4181 family members including 2025 minors were also receiving protection. Entire families are uprooted, sometimes at no notice, and are removed to other areas of Italy where numerous problems of housing, health care, schooling and employment must be resolved. The sudden arrival of a family from southern Italy without work, family ties in the area or any other apparent reason for settling arouses suspicions which are aggravated if compulsory secretiveness is perceived as unfriendliness. Small communities have protested when news of a collaborator's relocation has leaked out. The greatest problems concern children: almost 40 per cent of the family members of collaborators are under the age of 18. A wife may refuse to relocate with her collaborator husband, and this can lead to the breakup of families. The current Questor of Palermo, formerly director of Italy's protection programme, describes the situation in terms of the many southern families who emigrated to northern Italy during the 1950s and 1960s, but admits the problems are greater because of the need for total anonymity and because all ties with the south must be completely severed.[51] In February 1996 a new structure was set up which, among its other tasks, became responsible for the social and psychological aspects of family relocation and change of identity.

A different category of problem has been created by the existence of approximately 60 non-criminal witnesses of criminal events, obliged by their own courage in testifying in court against murderers and extortionists to give up their work and homes. This category of witness has been neglected and inadequately appreciated, such that many have either retracted their testimonies or have regretted making the sacrifice.

The cost to the public purse of the witness protection programme up to 1997 was officially estimated at around 110 billion lire, or $66 million, although Achille Serra, Prefect of Palermo from 1995 to 1996, speculated that the true cost might run into several hundred or even thousands of billions of lire.[52] The official breakdown of costs is given in Table 4.12.

Table 4.12   Breakdown of costs for Italian Witness Protection Programme

legal costs	12.6%
monthly payments	35.4%
medical costs	1.3%
hotels	6.1%
rental of apartments	31.6%
other	13.0%

Source: Servizio Centrale di Protezione in *Panorama* 16 January 1997.

Another problem that has caused widespread public concern concerns the arrangements for the economic maintenance of state's witnesses and the alleged link between financial support and the willingness to give testimony. Salvatore Cancemi admitted during questioning in court that his monthly salary, which had been $300 at the start of his collaboration, had been increased to $1680, excluding the costs for his accommodation, taxes, his children's schooling and transport. It was claimed, and not denied, that Francesco Marino Mannoia, an important *Cosa Nostra* collaborator since 1989, received $600 000 when he gave evidence against Giulio Andreotti in the spring of 1993. Marino Mannoia was living at liberty in the USA on $3000 per month plus his father's pension, all paid from Italy.[53] Felice Maniero, a collaborator from the so-called 'Brenta Mafia' operating in north-east Italy, whose statements put his entire organization in prison, had his prison sentence cut from 33 to 11 years and had his villa and his yacht returned to him.[54] Maniero was expelled from the witness protection programme in August 1996 after giving a series of interviews, but was readmitted a month later when it emerged that an attack on his life was being planned. He was rearrested for subsequent crimes in April 1998.

Two *Camorra* collaborators, Carmine Alfieri and Pasquale Galasso, also had their frozen assets returned to them – in the case of Galasso, who was released from prison in May 1993, the value of the assets restored to him was estimated at $25.2 million. The reversal of asset restraint orders was technically justified on the grounds that they had been imposed as a preventive measure as a consequence of the danger he was presumed to represent to society – a clause which can hardly be invoked when an individual lives under state protection. Preventive freezing is quite separate from measures of freezing and confiscation applied after a defendant is convicted in court.

In December 1996 the collaborator Baldassare Di Maggio, whose contribution had led to the arrest of Totò Riina, admitted in court that he had received a lump sum of $300 000 from the State. It had been given him with the idea that he would start a business and thereafter be economically independent. During the Falcone murder trial in Caltanissetta, Di Maggio declined to answer questions put to him – some said the silence was linked to a demand for more money, others that it was due to pressure exerted on him or to other inducements not to confirm his testimony in the trial of former Prime Minister Giulio Andreotti (see Chapter 7).

The general impression of insufficient supervision over state's witnesses was reinforced during 1997 when several collaborators – including Baldassare Di Maggio, Gioacchino La Barbera and Santo Di Matteo, all key witnesses in important trials then under way and living freely outside prison – were rearrested. They had returned to their home bases to recommence criminal activities, to make money and to avenge atrocities carried out on family members or close associates. Altogether 144 protection programmes were revoked in 1997 when collaborators broke the terms of their agreement.

A few days after his rearrest Baldassare Di Maggio told Palermo prosecutors that he had been under pressure to retract his testimony concerning a kiss of greeting which had allegedly taken place between Andreotti and Riina in 1987, and that he had been introduced by a Palermo lawyer to two men who offered him $3.6 million. Palermo assistant chief prosecutor Guido Lo Forte commented, 'Very refined minds have studied an extremely sophisticated plan. On the one hand they have used Baldassare Di Maggio manipulatively to get rid of some dead wood in the organization. On the other they have destabilized the system by delegitimizing the collaborators.'[55] However Di Maggio repeated his evidence against Andreotti in court in Palermo on 27 January 1998.

In August 1997 Parliament revised article 513 of the code of criminal procedure so that accomplice evidence, given either in a previous trial or before a prosecutor prior to a public court hearing, ceased to be usable as evidence if the defendant making the accusation chose either to deny or not to repeat it. This constituted a reversal of the provision made by Law Decree 306 in 1992. In February 1998 the Supreme Court ruled that the modification to article 513 could be applied retrospectively, after two individuals who had been convicted in the Court of Appeal on the evidence of criminal associates who had testified in the Court of Assizes but had refused to repeat their statements in court, appealed against their conviction. The Supreme Court ruled in their favour. This meant that any trial verdicts up to the level of Court of Appeal could be annulled if they had been based on accomplice evidence which was not repeated in open court. While in theory this should have been a guarantee for the defence, in practice it allowed state's witnesses to determine the outcome of trial proceedings either by repeating allegations or by remaining silent. The judges most affected – the antimafia judges in Sicily and those dealing with corruption cases in Milan where many investigations involved accomplice evidence – strongly opposed the ruling.

The ultimate arbiter of Italy's laws, the Constitutional Court, pronounced on the validity of article 513 in November 1998. It ruled that article 513 as revised in 1997 was not constitutionally valid because it caused the outcome of a trial to be dependent upon the whim of a defendant to remain silent, which in turn prevented evidence being challenged in court – the essential function of the trial and the principal means of arriving at the truth. The new ruling stated that accomplice evidence given either in previous trials or during pre-court testimony before a prosecutor could be presented as evidence; the defendant making the accusations was not obliged to repeat the evidence in court but the statements could be read out and contested in open court by the defence lawyers of the person accused. Whereas from 1997 the statements made earlier and not repeated had ceased to have any value for the trial under way, henceforth the transcribed statements, whether repeated or not, would remain with the court documents and could be examined by judges and jury. In so doing the Court preserved the right of the accomplice to remain silent, and therefore preserved his status of defendant, but allowed the defence to challenge the evidence presented. In this sense the Constitutional Court took a middle way between protecting the oral component of the accusatorial system and reverting to the pre-trial written basis of the inquisitorial system. General dissatisfaction with the compromise position, and a feeling that the Constitutional Court had rewritten the law rather than interpret it, caused Parliament to propose further modifications to the code of criminal procedure which were being debated in 1999. Article 192 has remained a source of controversy and has been particularly opposed by defence lawyers in Mafia trials.

Since 1997 a draft law containing substantial changes in the collaboration legislation has been under discussion in Parliament. With possible minor amendments, the future law will be as follows:

- A clear distinction will be made between (a) the benefits that can accrue to the collaborator – to be assessed by the prosecutor in terms of the value of the contribution – and (b) the degree of economic and physical protection that can be provided, to be decided by a separate protection programme management committee. Even a small infringement will signify breaking the terms of the programme and expulsion from it.
- Public prosecutors will propose potential entrants to a protection programme. If there are conflicting opinions within two DDAs the national antimafia prosecutor will make the final decision. The power to make provisional acceptance, currently decided by the Chief of Police, will pass to a committee within the Interior Ministry which will also assess the value of assets held by the collaborator.
- A collaborator will be required to declare at the outset of the collaboration all the assets at his disposal without waiting for a freezing

or confiscation order. A proportion may be allocated to witness protection while another share may go to a fund for the victims of Mafia aggression. The State will decide what proportion of assets may remain for the collaborator's own use.

- More collaborators will be kept in specially designated prisons, and therefore fewer will live at liberty.
- A differentiation will be made between prisoners who confess and those who come forward spontaneously.
- A time limit will be established, of between six months and one year, within which collaborators must tell what they know or else justify the delay. (This is a controversial issue and one contested on the grounds that it takes time for the collaborative process to mature.)
- A collaborator will only qualify for a protection programme if new facts are provided.
- For the first six months collaborators will be detained in a 'soft' prison.
- Increased measures will be taken to avoid the possibility of collaborators coordinating their accounts.

Asset-tracing and money-laundering legislation

The identification, seizure and confiscation of criminal assets is held to be one of the most incisive means of fighting organized crime, although one of the most difficult to apply. Wealth accumulation, together with the exercise of power, are organized crime's primary objectives, and in the decades since the drug-trafficking boom of the late 1970s criminals have devoted major efforts to the concealment and management of illicit capital. Estimates of criminal income in Italy vary widely, and, given all the variables of an underground economy, should be regarded with scepticism. A middle-range guess for the annual turnover of Italian organized crime in 1996 was 109 trillion lire, or US$65.4 billion. Of this, illicit drugs sales were estimated at $30 billion, the revenue from extortion and usury at $6.9 billion and from illicit arms sales $2.4 billion.[56] But even using a low estimate of the average income of Italian organized crime from 1983 to 1997 of $30 billion per annum, the share of criminal wealth seized by the authorities is minimal: as a ratio of estimated turnover, assets seized over the period represent only 0.8 per cent, confiscations 0.2 per cent and definitive confiscations 0.06 per cent.[57]

Asset-tracing, freezing and confiscation measures for individuals considered socially dangerous were in place in Italy as early as 1965; they were applied effectively from 1982 with regard to Mafia suspects and from 1990 for those suspected of other profit-generating activities (see Chapter 2). Article 12 *quinquies* of Law 356 in August 1992 (converted from Law Decree 306 of 8 June) established that for those accused of specific Mafia-related crimes and who had assets out of proportion to their declared income or to their stated economic activities of which they were unable to justify the legitimate source, confiscation of the share of assets representing the unjustified source of income was *obligatory*. Because the confiscation was applied to persons *accused* rather than *convicted*, this article of the law was judged to be invalid by the Italian Constitutional Court in February 1994, and it was modified by Law Decree 246 in April of that year. The new article 12 *sexies* of Law 356 imposes the obligation to confiscate assets, money or other utilities when a person is convicted or receives a sentence by plea-bargaining for specific Mafia-related crimes when there is a discrepancy between the assets at an individual's disposal and his declared income, and when the individual cannot justify the source of assets of which he is title holder or which are at his disposal, either directly or through a physical or juridical person. As can be seen from Table 4.13, the value of seized assets rose considerably during the years 1992–94, although the confiscation totals are difficult to interpret, given the average period of four years that passes between seizure and confiscation, and of ten years from seizure before the assets pass definitively into state possession.

Table 4.13   Assets seized and confiscated in Italy, 1990–97

Year	Value of assets seized (in US$)	Value of assets confiscated (in US$)
1990	39 946 200	5 252 400
1991	168 103 200	3 370 200
1992	652 279 800	7 841 400
1993	789 243 000	37 584 000
1994	837 548 400	45 007 200
1995	527 774 400	53 549 400
1996	269 658 600	58 233 600
1997	107 988 600	29 662 200
Total	3 392 542 200	240 500 400

Source: Italian Interior Ministry 1998 figures; own dollar calculations based on exchange rate of 1700 LIT = 1 US$.

As Table 4.13 shows, the total value of assets seized at the end of 1997 was around $3.4 billion compared to $240 million confiscated, giving a ratio of confiscated to seized assets of around 7 per cent. If one looks at asset seizures, confiscations subject to legal recourse and definitive confiscations from Mafia suspects during the entire period from 1983 to 1997 (Table 4.14), a similar pattern emerges. Assets confiscated subject to legal recourse are 26.1 per cent of those seized, assets definitively confiscated are 7.5 per cent of those seized.

Table 4.14   Indirect estimates of criminal assets seized, confiscated and confiscated definitively[c] in Italy, 1983–97, in US$m.

Seizures (A)	10 790 868
Confiscations (B) (subject to legal recourse)	2 820 920
B/A	26.1%
Definitive confiscations (D)	817 123
D/B	28.9%
D/A	7.5%

[c]   The values are considered estimates and may be subject to revision.

Source: M. Centorrino in Violante (ed.) 1998.

Conversion into US$ by the author, using an exchange rate of 1700 LIT = 1 US$.

Part of the discrepancy between assets seized and confiscated is inevitable. Firstly, because assets may be frozen preventively and thus the measure is applied before a defence against it can be put up. Secondly, the value of an asset on seizure may not correspond to its actual value when finally realized. Thirdly, an individual may succeed in proving the legitimate source of a significant proportion of the assets seized, either that they are his by right or that they belong to a third party. Third-party interests are one of the most delicate areas of asset-tracing investigations. For many years Italian law was considered defective with regard to safeguarding the interests and employment of third parties, as for example the *bona fide* workforce of a company taken into commissaryship as a result of asset freezing or confiscation,[58] but a law of 1996 attempted to remedy the situation (see Annex to Chapter 3). A loophole that has not been closed leaves the authorities powerless to pursue the assets of a criminal who dies before a confiscation order is made.

Money-laundering legislation was introduced in Italy in 1990, with the obligation to report suspicious transactions created in 1991. Initially the crime of money laundering could only be linked to four predicate crimes: aggravated robbery, aggravated extortion, kidnapping for ransom or crimes concerning the production or trafficking of drugs; but was extended to cover all crimes on Italy's ratification of the Council of Europe Convention on the Laundering, Search, Seizure and Confiscation of the Proceeds from Crime in August 1993. Until 1996, Italian procedures for reporting suspicious transactions were cumbersome: a bank employee or other financial intermediary who believed a client's transaction might be linked to money laundering sent a suspicious transaction disclosure to the bank's legal representative who decided whether or not to pass it on to the local police chief, who would in turn transmit the report to the appropriate sector of the Finance Police or financial sector of the State Police. Anonymity was not guaranteed and there was no central repository of suspicious disclosures. A record of all large cash transactions was kept by the Italian Exchange Office (*Ufficio Italiano dei Cambi*, UIC) which was entitled to perform arbitrary checks on the proper functioning of the system and to carry out statistical analyses – of the aggregate data only – provided by each intermediary in order to identify possible anomalies in a given geographical region. If anomalies emerged, the UIC informed the Treasury Ministry which in turn informed the competent investigative authorities. According to the Financial Action Task Force (FATF), set up in 1989 by the G7 group to monitor international money-laundering trends and advise countries accordingly, in 1993 Italy's system represented a 'preliminary stage, rather than the completion, of a system with a crucial central agency with responsibilities of intelligence and coordination of anti-money-laundering activities.'[59]

There was little enthusiasm for the money-laundering legislation on the part of the banking sector on account of the labour and administrative costs involved, and cooperation was poor in the early years, as a study by the economists Centorrino and Giorgianni shows:[60] from February 1991 until 31 December 1996 there had been a total of only 7134 suspicious disclosures, of which almost 80 per cent were made in the years 1995 and 1996. But almost all – 94 per cent – came from the banking sector (see Table 4.15).

Table 4.15   Suspicious disclosures in Italy to 31 December 1996

Year	Reports
1991	29
1992	131
1993	334
1994	1 029
1995	2 891
1996	2 720
Total	7 134

Source: Centorrino and Giorgianni.

The South and Islands had supplied only 19 per cent of the total, despite higher levels of criminality, probably due to fear of reprisals against bank staff in these areas. In proportion to its population Tuscany was the most diligent region in that it accounted for 36 per cent of disclosures, of which a large proportion was from the Arezzo area. The statistics had been distorted by the repercussions of a much publicized money-laundering operation in Arezzo in January 1994 which had raised levels of awareness of the phenomenon. Campania accounted for only 8 per cent of reports, Calabria for 3.6 per cent and Sicily for 3.1 per cent. The region that had supplied the highest number of reports overall was Lombardy, with 41 per cent.

The number of suspicious disclosures in Italy was compared unfavourably with the approximately 16 000 reports made in the UK in 1994; but only about 10 per cent of the UK reports had been considered worthy of follow-up, and rarely referred to large sums. In Italy, only 39 disclosures had not been followed up and 447 criminal investigations had been initiated. The Finance Police had reported at the end of July 1996 that 78 per cent of all cases followed up were undergoing closer investigation, which suggested that in most cases the suspicions of laundering activity were well-founded.[61] A total of 611 individuals were reported in Italy for money-laundering offences in 1996, compared to 797 in 1995 and 648 in 1994. The highest number of suspects came from Calabria, followed by Tuscany.[62]

Centorrino and Giorgianni's study concluded that there was a need to make reporting criteria more objective and to encourage staff to cooperate. Italian banking personnel were reluctant to report out of a lack of corporate loyalty, for fear of losing the client or of the client knowing about the disclosure. Intimidation of clients by threatening to disclose irregular transactions was also a potential weapon in the hands of an unscrupulous bank worker. But even an honest bank-teller was an inappropriate detective to deal with the complexity of money-laundering operations in a country with some 50 million current and savings accounts and at least 10 million deposit share accounts.[63]

According to a survey of 300 bank managers throughout Italy carried out by the Rome-based research institute Eurispes, 78 per cent of respondents had been 'aware of' operations which had aroused suspicions of illegal activity. The affirmative answers were spread uniformly throughout different types of bank around the country, although the majority (81 per cent) of suspicions were aroused in towns of 100–250 000 inhabitants. The percentage of those who 'frequently' found themselves in these situations ranged from 11 per cent in the north-east to 3 per cent in the north-west, 8 per cent in central Italy and 7 per cent in the south. Eurispes researchers warned that generalizations should not be made from such a limited sample.[64]

There are objective difficulties in prosecuting the crime of money laundering which relate to the professionalization and internationalization which have characterized the activity in recent years. Italy's legislation, like that of most other countries, requires evidence of several elements in order to bring a successful money-laundering prosecution – the predicate crime, the launderer's awareness of the illegal source of the proceeds, the action of removing, disguising or concealing funds, and their reinvestment.

Although the Italian money-laundering legislation has had positive effects in that the cost of money laundering has risen from 5 to 15 per cent,[65] it is a multifaceted activity and one which is in constant flux. The tripartite model which separates the process of money laundering into *placement* (cash deposits, usually of small sums), *layering,* (disguising the criminal source of the money by passing it through a series of filters) and *integration* (reinsertion into the legal economy) may no longer be relevant. Criminal organizations now prefer to outsource their financial management to full-time professional money launderers without criminal records who transfer sums of money and other financial instruments around the world in complex, multiple and often undetectable operations. Italian criminals use apparently respectable accountants, lawyers or professional businessmen as receivers and reinvestment agents, and these individuals provide all the necessary cover and guarantees within the legal financial and commercial sectors. Criminals are increasingly distancing their criminally derived assets from criminal acts and from themselves, and rarely make use of assets of which they cannot show a legitimate provenance. A study of the assets seized and confiscated in Italy shows a consistent pattern – property is by far the most common asset seized, followed by mobile assets (cars, yachts and so on), financial assets and commercial activities. But a study carried out by the Italian Finance Police in a specific area of Sicily in 1993 showed that 60 per cent of investments were in financial markets and only 17 per cent in property. Whereas property is a highly visible asset, financial assets are harder to detect.

Italy's ratification of the Council of Europe Convention on the Laundering, Search, Seizure and Confiscation of the Proceeds from Crime was intended to facilitate money-laundering investigations where money or the criminal, or both, had crossed borders. In practice, international judicial cooperation in this field has been sluggish and in Italy the Convention has been of little direct use in prosecutions.[66] One problem is that the crime of Mafia association as defined under Italian law is not covered in most legislative systems. Consequently an Italian request for assets to be frozen based on article 416 *bis* of the criminal code may not be valid grounds for the requested state to comply unless it is proven that a specific crime deriving from the association has been committed there.[67] This emphasizes the difference between the crime of Mafia association and the Anglo-Saxon concept of conspiracy, where it is assumed that at least one of the participants in a conspiracy has committed an overt act in relation to the crime which it is intended to commit.

The legislative gap might be overcome in the future by ratification of a new European Convention on Extradition drawn up in Brussels in September 1996. The Convention states that extradition for an offence which is classified by the requesting State as an association or conspiracy to commit offences of an organized crime nature shall not be refused on the grounds that the law of the requested party does not provide for the same facts to be an offence, provided that the offence is punishable in the requesting country by a maximum term of deprivation of liberty of at least 12 months.[68] The Joint Action adopted by the Council of the European Union in March 1998 on making it an offence to participate in a criminal organization may be another means for overcoming the problem. International cooperation in this area is discussed in Chapter 6.

With Legislative Decree 125 of 25 May 1997, Italy further integrated its money-laundering reporting procedures with the requirements of the EU Directive on money laundering (91/308/CEE). The Italian Exchange Office (UIC) was designated as the recipient office for all suspect financial operations; incentives to report suspicious transactions were provided by guarantees of anonymity for those disclosing, and a constant monitoring facility for confiscated and frozen assets was established within the Justice Ministry. From June 1999 all types of financial inter-mediaries, credit recovery agents, estate agents, casinos, jewellers, art galleries, auction houses and antique dealers have been obliged to keep customer records and details of large sums transacted and, with the exception of the last four-mentioned categories, are required to notify any suspicious transactions to the appropriate authorities.

The UIC performs a preliminary analysis of the suspicious disclosures using a system known as 'Dbinspector', which studies liquidity ratios and cash flows through financial institutions. Once the preliminary analyses have been carried out, the UIC filters out the disclosures considered not relevant then forwards the rest to the appropriate inves-tigative agencies. If they concern organized crime the disclosures are sent to the DIA and to the DNA, otherwise they go to the Department of Fiscal Police of the Finance Police. In the course of the first year's work, Dbinspector had detected anomalies indicating money-laundering activity in unusual and unexplained cash flows in southern Italian banks, and in cash flows to Albania and the former Yugoslavia.[69]

Italy's most experienced police investigator into economic crime was doubtful that the new procedures would make a significant difference to money-laundering investigations. In his view Parliament had not 'taken account of new developments in [money-laundering] investigations but has made exclusive reference to an obsolete framework created to deal with typologies which were out of date several years ago'. The legislative changes only focused on money laundering as a cash-based phenomonon, and had ignored factors such as the internationalization of the activity and the heterogeneous figure of the launderer. Money laundering was no longer prevalently conducted within the banking system but within money markets, in financial futures and options and in the commercial sector. The sectors affected by money laundering were not simply credit institutions but those concerning taxation, commerce, financial inter-mediation and civil law. The presence of foreign Mafia groups in Italy had clouded the picture even further. The most significant results in the area of money laundering had come from repression rather than prevention, and in particular from highly professional police operations involving undercover operations and sophisticated surveillance technology. Until prevention could be more effective, he argued, the only way forward was to concentrate on improving investigative techniques.[70]

The crime of usury, or loansharking, which is linked to money laundering, is commonly practised by organized crime. The illegal provision of high-interest loans is a means of simultaneously laundering illicit capital, of making a financial profit and, frequently, of acquiring a commercial interest in a clean business which can be used as a front for illegal activity because its proprietors have been intimidated into not reporting the loans or the illegal operations. A support fund was set up by law for the victims of usury in 1996 after a series of tragic episodes when small traders, unable to tolerate the pressures from their money-lenders, committed suicide. Justice Minister Giovanni Maria Flick also promised that a register of all credit intermediaries would be drawn up. Other evidence suggests that a more thorough overhaul of the credit sector in southern Italy may be required.[71]

While economic recession and credit squeezes are the most common features that cause the recourse to loansharks,[72] within this economic environment, the higher cost of borrowing and the instability of the banking sector in the south are significant. Interest on a loan of up to $60 000 varied in 1996 from the lowest rate of 14.6 per cent in northern Italy to almost 21 per cent in the south-east.[73] The official rate of bad loans in southern Italy is over 20 per cent, but in practice it is nearer 55–60 per cent. Between 1985 and 1994, three-quarters of all banks taken into emergency administration or forced liquidation in Italy were in the south. Analysts concluded that this was due to a combination of a high risk to the lender – due to the expected poor quality of the borrower – and the poor quality of the lender – the inefficiency of the banks.[74] In fact the number of independent banks operating in the south is steadily decreasing, with more and more takeovers from northern institutions. A buoyant, viable banking sector is a yardstick for a healthy economy, and is considered a crucial factor in the liberation of the south from organized crime.[75]

Prison regime/article 41 bis

The introduction of article 41 *bis* for Mafia prisoners considered particularly dangerous was introduced in July 1992 as a means of severing the connections by which organized criminals could coordinate strategies and communicate with each other and the outside world. It was also intended as a strong message to Mafia leaders that their privileges and impunity had come to an end. With the passing of time both the numbers of prisoners subject to the regime (Table 4.16) and the severity of the measure have declined.

Table 4.16   Prisoners subject to special regime with application of article 41 *bis*

Date	No. of prisoners
(As of) July 1992	369
September 1992*	1 102
May 1994	733
September 1994	445
April 1995	471
December 1995	485
December 1996	464
December 1997	435

Source: *Ministero di Grazia e Giustizia, Dipartimento dell'amministrazione penitenziaria*, in Violante, 1998, *op. cit.* * *L'Espresso*, 1 July 1994.

In part the decline has occurred because of more lenient attitudes taken by 'custody judges' (*giudici di sorveglianza*) towards appeals made by defence lawyers against the imposition of 41 *bis* rules. More importantly, the Constitutional Court ruled in November 1996 that the aim of the 41 *bis* regime should be to sever a *mafioso*'s contacts with the external criminal world, not make life intolerable for him. Accordingly, a law of February 1997 introduced three modifications: the monthly family visit could be replaced by a (monitored) telephone call; prisoners could prepare their own meals on gas cookers at lunchtime (a privilege which had only been granted to Totò Riina for fear of his being poisoned) and permission was granted to receive extra food parcels from the family. A year later, a circular from the Prison Administration Department ordered that children under 12 could visit their imprisoned parent without a glass screen between them, although a video camera would film the visit. The fresh air period was increased from two to four hours per day and could include team sport; 41 *bis* prisoners were also granted access to a library for up to two hours per day. The government's reasoning was that the concessions were balanced in security terms by the obligation for all 41 *bis* prisoners to testify in court by video testimony. This would prevent their contact with the outside world and with former associates and avoid the practice of 'courtroom tourism' whereby top security prisoners were moved from prison to prison around the country in order to appear in court.[76] The concessions permitting greater socialization in prison were generally criticized by the antimafia judges and by national antimafia prosecutor Pier Luigi Vigna. Their fears were partially borne out in June 1998 when it was learned that one 41 *bis* prisoner was issuing orders from a mobile phone which had been smuggled into his cell and that another had given murder instructions to his 11-year-old son to be passed on to an outside associate. It is also claimed that the use of video testimony does not necessarily prevent association between prisoners, since *mafiosi* waiting to testify are kept together and communicate by expressions and gestures which cannot be understood by prison warders.[77]

Other decisions of the Constitutional Court have served to attenuate the repressive tendency that criminal justice took in the 1990s and to re-establish greater guarantees for criminal suspects. In April 1996 the Court – composed of 15 members of whom 5 are elected by Parliament, 5 by the Supreme Court and 5 by the Head of State – ruled that a magistrate who had made a judgement about a specific defendant – in an appeal for release from prison, or to have specific restrictive measures lifted – and therefore who had already expressed an opinion about the suspect's presumed social dangerousness, did not possess sufficient impartiality to preside over a court trial in which that individual was on trial. The Court's ruling of incompatibility, while welcomed in principle, caused many trials in progress to be abandoned and reconvened with different judges, creating heavy workloads for the courts concerned. The trial in Caltanissetta for the Falcone murder was halted in June 1996 and had to be reconvened entirely a month later; the trial which had opened in Palermo for the murder of Salvo Lima was also restarted.

In May 1996 the Court ruled that Law 55 of 1990, which prevented an individual who had been committed for trial or had been convicted in the Courts of Assizes or Appeal for Mafia-related crimes from becoming a candidate for public office in administrative elections, was invalid and that the ban could only apply if the individual was definitively convicted, that is, after the sentence of the Supreme Court. Nonetheless, in the event of such a person being elected, the Prefect could suspend the individual concerned without waiting for a definitive conviction. The ruling was criticized by Mafia expert Pino Arlacchi, who pointed out that the same court had approved the 1991 law on the dissolution of Mafia-infiltrated town councils, in which the premise of Mafia-linked public-office holders was implicit, even though not necessarily definitively proven. In Arlacchi's view therefore, lower standards of proof were required by the law that had been approved than by the law that had been judged to be unconstitutional.

The criminal justice system since 1992 – outstanding problems for the antimafia fight

The time that must pass before trials reach their conclusion in Italy – both in the civil and in the criminal courts – remains one of Italy's most intractable problems. The delays in criminal trials are due in part to the three-tier process by which cases go through the Court of Assizes, the Court of Appeal and the Supreme Court and because the Supreme Court, in overturning previous verdicts for procedural reasons, frequently causes the trials of the earlier grades to be rerun. Italy accounts for over 70 per cent of all cases that come before the European Court of Justice for violation of a 'reasonable time' in which trials should take place. Other reasons for the slowness of criminal procedures are to be found in the profusion and complexity of Italy's laws and in the mandatory prosecution principle which requires criminal proceedings to be initiated whenever a crime is reported. Measures were introduced in 1999 to depenalize minor crimes and to permit more single-judge courts, but a long-term solution is unlikely until judicial–political tensions (see Chapter 3) are resolved.

In terms of organized crime trials, the courts in Calabria and Campania have worse problems than those in Sicily. At the Tribunal of Santa Maria Capua Vetere – competent for crimes committed in the Caserta area of Campania and the sixth largest court in Italy – lawyers were on strike for more than 700 days between 1992 and 1997. Although Calabria accounts for only 3.7 per cent of the national population, its share of murders over the 1983–93 period lay between 10.3 and 18.4 per cent of the national total. From the mid-1980s until 1991 *'Ndrangheta* clans carried out around 600 murders in the province of Reggio Calabria alone.[78] As the trials for these murders began to go through the courts in the mid-1990s, the court system came under increasing pressure. At the end of August 1993 the head of the Reggio Calabria DDA, Salvatore Boemi, warned about the desperate problems in Calabria and the paralysis of the judicial process in Reggio, where some 300 defendants were awaiting trial. 'Some bosses', he noted ironically, 'have died in their beds not knowing whether they were Mafia members or not'. His protests continued and in 1998 he announced his resignation as head of the Reggio Calabria DDA – it was eventually withdrawn after receiving assurances of more support from national antimafia prosecutor Vigna.

In summary, the most acute problems for the Italian criminal justice system concern resources and personnel, the administration of the DDAs and the need to modernize and simplify the judicial process.[79] At the end of 1997 a national average of 12.3 per cent of judicial posts were unfilled; in Sicily the proportion was 13.3 per cent, in Calabria 15.2 per cent and in Campania 11.6 per cent. With the exception of young *uditori* or trainee judges who are compelled to go where they are sent or else resign, magistrates cannot be relocated against their will. Two young trainees chose to resign from the judiciary altogether rather than take up the posts offered them in Gela (southern Sicily), and in 1997 there were no applicants at all for two posts for public prosecutors in Reggio Calabria. As a result, criminal cases are not dealt with in time – for example in the Sicilian provinces of Ragusa, Sciacca, Gela, Agrigento and Caltanissetta, 60 per cent of crimes cannot be prosecuted because of the statute of limitations. In Reggio Calabria, the Court of Appeal could count on only 16 judges to handle 83 trials, one of which had 500 defendants. According to Giovanni Maria Flick, Italy's Justice Minister from 1996–98, the number of magistrates in Calabria had been increased by 67 in the period 1993–96 but out of 480 magistrates' posts 102 were still unfilled. Nationally, there was a need for at least 300 and ideally 700 more judges, but unless the Ministry's share of the national budget were increased from around 1.0 per cent there was little chance of this happening. Relocation incentives in the form of paid trips to the city of origin, subsidies for lodgings and extra pay were introduced in April 1998 to encourage northern judges to move south, but the impact has not yet been felt. In Sicily false economies have been made in essential services: there is no money to pay overtime to administrative staff in the prosecution offices or to pay for petrol for the fuel-intensive bulletproof cars used to protect judges at risk of attack.

The Palermo DDA provides prosecutors to Trapani, Termini Imerese, Agrigento, Sciacca and Marsala. This means that every day, between eight and ten judges travel to these places, usually at fixed times of day and for up to 250 kilometres of predictable route. Not all of these magistrates have proper protection.[80] Calls by magistrates to hold the court trials of the investigations handled by the DDAs in a district courtroom under the auspices of the DDA, rather than in the provincial courthouse as is currently the case, have been refused on the grounds that they violate the constitutional principle that a crime must be tried in its 'natural setting', that is, in the nearest criminal court to the scene of the crime.

With regard to organized crime, substantive legislation and the code of criminal procedure are generally felt to be sound, although in the view of one senior Italian official, the mechanisms by which the varying investigating authorities coordinate parallel enquiries are 'hopelessly inadequate'. Other problems concern sentencing policy and practice, and the state of the prisons. Italy's prisons are overpopulated by around one-third, with half of all inmates awaiting trial, and it is often impossible to keep the most dangerous category of prisoners separated from others. Many of the prisons are mediaeval fortresses, and are structurally quite inadequate for their purpose. A tendency has been perceived among prison governors and 'custody judges' to use parole and temporary leave of absence concessions arbitrarily as a means of reducing tension within the prison environment. Sentences served vary considerably for a given offence and do not always correspond to the severity of the crime.[81]

Finally there is a need for a comprehensive review of antimafia legislation and policies in the light of the experiences gained since the *Rognoni–La Torre* law was introduced in 1982. The constant – and continuing – process of modification has created a succession of legislative interventions which partially overlap one another and yet do not meet the new dimensions of organized criminality. For example, prosecutors need a more precise instrument with which to categorize the relationship of collusion with organized crime which goes beyond mere favouring but stops short of actual participation. Currently, the term 'participation from outside' or *concorso esterno*, is used, for which there is no juridical definition.

Under pressure from the judiciary, the first steps have been taken at political level to bring together the entire body of antimafia legislation – including Mafia association, criminal collusion, accomplice testimony, money laundering, and asset tracing, seizure and confiscation – into a single unified text. Although the process may take years it should be encouraged, not only in the national interest but as a working, empirical model for organized crime legislation from which the international community could learn. Most of all it would constitute the demonstration of Italy's political will to consolidate the administration of the antimafia fight outside the straightjacket of national emergency in which it has traditionally operated. As the statistics in this chapter show, Italian organized crime has continued to maintain its manpower and its economic strength despite the admirable efforts made in the last seven years by the judiciary and law-enforcement bodies. The sacrifice of so many loyal servants of the state can only be repaid if those who now represent it continue the fight with determination and constancy.

Annex

The Italian judicial system

The Italian judicial system is based on Roman law and is almost entirely codified. Under the Italian Constitution judges are (a) subject only to the law, (b) independent of every other power of the State and (c) appointed for life unless by order of the Superior Judicial Council. Although they are independent of political power, inspections and disciplinary measures can be instigated by the Justice Minister. This independence is balanced by an obligation to prosecute every crime that is reported. Criminal proceedings are dealt with in the first grade either by the single-judge authority of the *Pretura*, by the three-judge college of the *Tribunale* or by the Court of Assizes, which sits with a jury comprising one professional judge and 12 lay jurors. Proceedings are allocated to one of these three courts according to the offences concerned. Prosecutions are initiated and carried out by the *pubblico ministero* or public prosecutor. The prosecution makes a request for arrest or committal for trial to the *giudice per le indagini preliminari* (GIP), the judge for preliminary investigations, who decides on the evidence presented whether to grant or refuse the request. The second grade of trial is represented by the Court of Appeal and third and final grade by the Supreme Court. A verdict is only definitive after the Supreme Court has ruled on matters of procedural correctness. The Supreme Court can rule a retrial at either of the two lower levels if errors of procedure emerge. A new code of criminal procedure was introduced in 1989 which shifted the balance from an inquisitorial criminal justice system towards an adversarial system, although in practice this process has been incomplete. Italy's judicial system presents a number of unusual features: firstly, there is no career separation between judges who are prosecutors and judges who preside over courts in the Anglo-Saxon sense; secondly, career promotion is virtually automatic and is primarily based on age; thirdly, the existence and powers of the *Consiglio Superiore della Magistratura* (CSM), the Superior Judicial Council. The CSM, presided over by the Head of State, appoints, transfers, disciplines and promotes judges. It is a kind of mini-parliament which reflects the bias of each of its two elements – the bias of Parliament in office at the time of its four-yearly elections (one-third of its members are elected by Parliament) – and the political positions of the judiciary themselves, who vote for two-thirds of its members on the basis of factions. The ultimate arbiter of the actions of the judiciary and of the CSM is the Constitutional Court, whose 15 members are elected one-third by Parliament, one-third by the Head of State and one-third by the Supreme Court. The principal function of the Constitutional Court is to judge the conformity of the laws passed by Parliament with the Constitution.

5
The Grassroots Antimafia

The removal of the causes that constitute the strength of *Cosa Nostra* can only be accomplished by the restoration of faith in public administration. No influx of financial resources, however massive, will produce beneficial effects if the State and the institutions in general are not able and do not appear to be impartial holders and distributors of the trust necessary for the free and orderly progression of civil life. Otherwise the recourse to alternative organizations that ensure materialistic advantages will continue and the consensus around them, whether expressed or passive, will continue.

Paolo Borsellino, January 1989[1]

Chapter 4 focused on the '*Antimafia dei delitti*', literally the 'Antimafia of crimes', or the means by which the tools of investigation and prosecution of organized crime were strengthened after the Palermo murders of 1992. We now turn to the 'grassroots' Antimafia or *Antimafia dei diritti* – literally 'of rights' – to examine how different sectors of Italian society reacted to the atrocities and whether grassroots activism, by refusing cohabitation with criminality and reclaiming rights that had been surrendered to the Mafia, has set in motion an irreversible cultural transformation.

The work of judges Borsellino and Falcone was not confined to the courthouses and to the interrogation rooms of Italy's prisons. Both men regularly added to their heavy work schedules by writing and lecturing and by going into schools to talk about the Mafia and the means to combat it, an activity that gave Borsellino in particular great satisfaction. He talked to schoolchildren without legal pomposity but with a simplicity and spontaneity that held their attention. In the weeks before he was killed Falcone was advising the makers of a television series about the Mafia for which he would have provided commentary on camera to a studio presenter. (The programmes were later broadcast with an empty chair beside that of the presenter.) Borsellino and Falcone were public figures who saw themselves as having public duties, convinced that without the awareness and support of society there could be no antimafia fight.

The murders of the two judges were experienced by thousands of Italians with a sense of deep personal loss, as if friends had been killed. The murder of Borsellino immediately after that of Falcone produced a collective shame for a country which was so wretchedly unable – or unwilling – to protect its finest representatives. Giovanni and Francesca Falcone and their three bodyguards were given a state funeral as were the five bodyguards murdered with Borsellino, whose family opted for a private ceremony. The two state funerals were large-scale public events, followed on television by several million viewers. On the morning of the Falcone funeral on 25 May thousands of Sicilians lined the route of the cortège from the courthouse to the thirteenth-century Basilica of San Domenico and remained outside in torrential rain throughout the funeral service. At the conclusion of the ceremony, as the institutional dignitaries began to leave, cries of 'Assassins!' and 'Justice!' roared by the crowd outside in the square were taken up by the weeping congregation in the Basilica. The five coffins were applauded loudly as they were brought out through the doors.

On 27 June more than 100 000 demonstrators comprising trade union delegations, political parties, youth, cultural and community associations as well as many thousands of ordinary citizens converged on Palermo from all over the country in specially chartered trains, buses and planes. The magnolia tree outside Falcone's apartment in via Notarbartolo became a focal point and shrine for visitors, many of them children, who wished to leave a message of solidarity or protest. A photograph of the two judges with their heads close together, smiling at a shared confidence, appeared on posters all over the city accompanied by slogans of affection or of defiance: 'You haven't killed them. Their ideas will continue to walk on our legs.'

Within a matter of days after Falcone's murder a petition launched by the youth branch of the Democratic Left (PDS) asking that assets confiscated from the Mafia be put to socially useful purposes had collected

20 000 signatures. On the evening of the Borsellino attack spontaneous demonstrations were held in the Sicilian towns of Trapani and Catania as well as in many mainland cities. For several Sundays in succession, bunches of flowers were laid in via D'Amelio on the site where the car bomb had exploded, and a small shrine was created, adorned with votive candles and photographs of the victims. Candlelight processions, rallies, concerts and conferences have continued to be held on the anniversaries of 23 May and 19 July in Sicily and elsewhere in Italy. On 23 May 1993, more than 15 000 people formed a human chain that stretched from the Palermo courthouse to via Notarbartolo.

On 8 September 1992 a concert was given in Palermo's football stadium by five Sicilian bands who provided their services free – all the takings went towards the building of a school to be named after the two judges. Concert fees from the Bellini music festival held in the composer's home town of Catania were given to the three fatherless children of Borsellino's bodyguard squad. The business community also responded: on 24 July Fiat extended an offer of employment in its Sicilian plant to the widows and offspring of the murdered bodyguards. On 1 August the young industrialists' sector of the employers' association, *Confindustria*, paid for the publication in all the main daily newspapers of an open letter to President Scalfaro and Prime Minister Giuliano Amato. It called for assurances that criminal justice would be done; that the instruments of repression would be strengthened; that institutional reforms would be implemented and that 'signals to the country' would be given. This last was a demand for concrete signs of a serious determination to fight the Mafia, in particular that the work of the First Section of the Supreme Court be investigated and that its president, Corrado Carnevale, be assigned to civil justice duties; that an ongoing strike by criminal lawyers be brought to an end and that the right to strike when clients were in prison be suspended; that every support be given to the army mission in Sicily, with the request that conscripts be sent regularly to the southern regions for training, thereby maintaining a conspicuous state 'presence'; and that all antimafia legislation in Parliament be subject to open, not secret voting.

A joint document on the Mafia problem was presented to the government by the three trade union confederations CGIL, CISL and UIL, together with the police union SIULP and the magistrates' 'trade union', the National Magistrates Association, on 29 September. The document outlined a series of concrete proposals linked to the spheres of economic reform, judicial measures and police activity.

Women's groups

Among the many associations active in the antimafia fight a prominent role has been taken by women's groups, some of which pre-date the 1992 massacres. In 1982 Giovanna Terranova, widow of judge Cesare Terranova, founded the first permanent antimafia association in Italy, the Association of Sicilian Women against the Mafia. It was established as an all-female committee to lobby for the approval of the *Rognoni–La Torre* law, at the time awaiting ratification by Parliament. It evolved into a women's support group when Signora Terranova and a number of other widows of Mafia victims opened a subscription to help pay for the legal costs of women seeking civil remedy in court cases involving the Mafia. Providing moral support has frequently been as important as financial assistance. Michela Buscemi's brother Salvatore was murdered in 1976 in what she believed was a dispute over his share in profits from cigarette smuggling. When another brother, Rodolfo, discovered the truth about Salvatore's murder he was tortured, strangled and thrown into the sea with lead weights on his legs. Michela ignored the advice of friends and family and, with the Association's support, decided to become civil plaintiff in the trial for Rodolfo's murder. She continued to press her case despite being shunned by her friends and relatives, including her mother, until the death threats against her children finally persuaded her to give up the court case, although not her involvement in the Association.

Pietra Lo Verso and her husband Cosimo ran a modestly successful butcher's shop near Palermo until one night in October 1984, when he was murdered with seven others in a cattle barn. His widow could not benefit from regional funds made available for the families of Mafia victims because Lo Verso had had a minor criminal conviction many years before. With the help of the Association she found a lawyer, went to court and publicly named the man she believed was responsible. He was acquitted on grounds of insufficient evidence, the butcher's shop took no custom and went bankrupt and Pietra Lo Verso was obliged to sweep the floor of a Palermo theatre to maintain her family.[2]

Despite these and other setbacks Giovanna Terranova's determination has never wavered. Born the daughter of a baron into a family with extensive landowning interests throughout Sicily, her decision to involve herself in antimafia work was greeted with disbelief, horror and then with outright hostility from many of her contemporaries in genteel Palermo society, which generally feigns complete ignorance of the Mafia and is more interested in games of whist in the comfort of elite clubs and elegant *palazzi* than in the more unsavoury aspects of Sicilian life.

On 22 July 1992, the day after the funeral of the Borsellino bodyguards, the Association of Sicilian Women against the Mafia organized a three-day vigil and hunger strike in Palermo's largest city square, Piazza Politeama. Under the slogan 'We are fasting because we are hungry for justice', a table was set up with a petition calling for the resignations of the public figures considered responsible for not preventing the atrocities – chief prosecutor Pietro Giammanco, Interior Minister Nicola Mancino, Police Chief Vincenzo Parisi and Prefect Mario Jovine. Signatories were invited to add their addresses and telephone numbers and, remarkably for Palermo, most did. The hunger strike began with 11 women but the numbers grew and the vigil continued, drawing comparisons with the women's protest in the *Plaza de Mayo* in Buenos Aires. For a year after the attacks the vigil and hunger strike were renewed from the 19th to the 23rd of each month.

On the same nights that Falcone and Borsellino were killed, three sisters and their daughters hung sheets painted with antimafia slogans from their balconies in Palermo. The gesture of feminist revolt (in contrast to the traditional practice of hanging bloodstained sheets outside a bride's house after her wedding night) developed into 'The Sheets Committee'. Later enlarged to include around 20 women and 6 men, the Committee launched a series of initiatives aimed at exposing corruption and bureaucratic malpractice and at raising awareness of the need for legality in everyday life. It produced T-shirts and television advertisements, organized publicity stunts around its themes and published a pamphlet recommending a code of behaviour for opposing criminality in daily life. It was entitled 'Nine uncomfortable guidelines for the citizen who wants to fight the Mafia'. They were rules which demanded no superhuman heroics but, in Sicily, some tenacity:

1. Learn to do your duty, respect your environment and preserve it from vandalism and destruction.
2. Educate your children to legality, solidarity and tolerance.
3. At work: if you suspect bribery or corruption don't hesitate to take action, go to a judge if necessary. If you are a teacher take every chance to talk about the Mafia and the harm it does. If you are a student, insist on punctuality from your lecturers, report them if they are absent and protest about favouritism.

   If you are in business, and you receive strange offers of protection or requests, turn to one of the anti-racketeering associations. If you're already paying, go to these associations as well.

4. When dealing with public administration, insist on transparency. Don't ask for favours but for your rights.
5. Always ask for a receipt from your doctor, mechanic or in a restaurant.
6. If you witness an attack, help the authorities with their enquiries.
7. Boycott Mafia business – explain to drug-takers that their behaviour is only doing the Mafia a favour; don't buy contraband cigarettes.
8. Refuse to exchange votes for any type of favour.
9. Intervene to prevent young people from acquiring a Mafia mentality; discover solidarity.[3]

These values were promoted in the civic arena by women mayors in several southern Italian towns which have traditional Mafia roots. Mayor Maria Maniscalco of San Giuseppe Jato in Sicily and Mayor Doris Lo Moro of Lamezia Terme in Calabria were elected on a platform of more transparent local government free of criminal influence, and like many colleagues engaged in similar reforms all over the *mezzogiorno,* suffered threats, firebomb attacks and intimidatory letters warning them to desist. But the citizens of San Giuseppe Jato began to perceive the benefits of administrative integrity in improved schools, roads and social services, and when Maria Maniscalco's car was firebombed they taxed themselves and bought her a new one.

Two young women incarnated a new spirit of female revolt against the Mafia: Rosaria Schifani, 22-year-old widow of Vito Schifani, one of Falcone's bodyguards, made an impassioned plea during the funeral service for the victims of Capaci. Having fainted away three times over her husband's coffin, she came forward to the microphone supported on the arm of a priest.

> In the name of all those who have given their lives for the State, first of all I ask that justice be done. Then I turn to the men of the Mafia, because they're here, yes here, inside this church! You should know that even for you there is the possibility of forgiveness. I will forgive you, but you must go down on your knees if you have the courage to change!

The sight of the grief-stricken young widow and the emotional rawness of her appeal amidst the solemn formalities of the state funeral were powerful. A *Cosa Nostra* collaborator was later to admit that his decision to become state's witness had begun at this time.

Rita Atria, a 17-year-old from Partanna in the province of Trapani, had grown up in a Mafia family and had witnessed the murder of her father in 1985. In 1991 her brother Nicola was also murdered. Nicola's wife Piera Aiello – extraneous to *Cosa Nostra* activities – began to collaborate after her husband's death, as did his murderer's mistress, Rosalba Triolo. Rita had decided to follow her sister-in-law's example and was giving evidence to judge Borsellino at the time of his murder. Disowned by her mother and isolated in a safe house near Rome, she flung herself from her third-floor balcony exactly one week after Borsellino, her only friend and protector, had been murdered. Her suicide note stated, 'I am so over-whelmed by the death of Paolo Borsellino. Now there's no one left to protect me, I'm desperate and I can't go on.' At the funeral 12 women carried her coffin but her mother, unrepentant, later desecrated her grave.

At official level, very little help has been offered to women trying to break free from the grip of the Mafia. Unless women can show that their men died in the service of the State there is no official provision for assistance. Felicia Impastato's son Giuseppe was murdered by the Mafia when, in defiance of his *mafioso* father, he continued to denounce Mafia activities in the area of Cinisi, near Palermo, on a local radio station. Although Giuseppe's father threw him out of the house his father's status gave him some protection. But in May 1978, a few months after his father had been knocked over and killed by a car, Giuseppe's mangled body was found on the lines of the Palermo–Trapani railway line; his killers had made it seem as if he had blown himself up while planting a terrorist bomb on the tracks. His mother received a contribution from the Sicilian Region but nothing from the State. Her request in 1992 for compensation was rejected four years later by the Interior Ministry, while her legal representation in the attempt to have her son's murderers brought to justice was dependent on Giovanna Terranova's Association and on the Sicilian study centre which took her son's name (see below). In December 1998, 20 years after the event, the first trial against the Cinisi Mafia clans for Giuseppe Impastato's murder opened in Palermo.

In addition to providing moral and financial support to help break down the wall of silence or *omertà* surrounding Mafia crimes, the women's antimafia associations operate as a constant pressure group for political and legislative changes. They are also active in the field of education, and tour the country giving lectures and participating in conferences and debates. The testimonies of a number of antimafia women were collected in a book entitled '*Nonostante Donna*' (Despite Being Women) published in 1996.[4] The book contains moving accounts of ordinary women – wives, mothers and sisters – driven to action by grief. Several of the contributors were present at a conference to launch the book at the Turin book fair in May 1996, and described how their struggle had developed.[5]

Saveria Antiochia, white-haired elderly mother of police bodyguard Roberto, killed in 1985 with his chief, deputy head of the Palermo Flying Squad Ninni Cassarà, explained,

> There are no words. Words are too small. Most of the time you can't even weep. What has happened is so enormous that the tears won't come. But you find the strength to fight so that this doesn't happen to others, so that our country no longer has this terrible stain on it, the stain of all the blood that has been shed. Here I am, I've survived in order to fight for a better tomorrow; I took courage, I found strength in fighting together with others so that what happened to my son won't happen again. And I believe very humbly that my struggle can give other women courage and then we women will become more numerous. [...] It's as if all the blood that has been shed has made us into a family. I feel we are all part of a family, unfortunately rather a large one, but this also gives us the courage, despite being women, to speak out.

Paolo Borsellino's sister Rita, another contributor, was also present. In the book, she describes her role as Paolo's sister

> [...] not as an indication of status but as the imposition of a duty.[...] By starting to tour round Italy and to talk in public, to reply to people and look them all in the eye, I wanted first of all to show that the assassins have not succeeded in doing what they wanted, in really killing Paolo. From everything I see around me, in what I do, from what I hear and from what I am asked to do, I have this sensation which is a crucial factor and not just for my own life, that my brother Paolo is alive because we all make him live with our commitment, with our intransigence and with our awareness. He will continue to live as long as we keep alive the values that all of us care about and for which he was killed.[6]

> After Paolo's death I met one of the mothers of the *Plaza de Mayo* and she said something that remains engraved in my memory: 'Each one of us knows deep down that we will never see our son again. And yet we continue to struggle because everyone's son, the son of each one of us, has become a son to all of us.' [...] You simply cannot resign yourself, you mustn't be resigned. Resignation is the tomb of everything. Perhaps people expect a woman to withdraw into her grief, to shut herself inside a 'dignified silence' – that much-abused phrase – but it comes in so handy because it's much more convenient when

people don't speak; it's more convenient to say 'poor thing' to a mother who is weeping, to a wife who shuts herself away, to a daughter in despair. It's easier to commiserate with her and feel compassion. It's more difficult to accept it when she speaks out, when she criticizes and continues somehow to do what the relative who was torn from her was trying to do – in her own way of course. [...] I had always followed what my brother did, his work, his activities, I admired him tremendously and loved him dearly. But I had never done anything, anything at all, I had lived my life shut inside my own certainties, incapable of communicating with others. Perhaps I didn't need to, perhaps it was a form of self defence. Maybe it took his death, that atrocious form of his death to open my eyes, to wrench them open. A gash of light that for a moment made me see further, made me see what there was beyond, to the place that Paolo was trying to reach. And I believe that once you have that goal then you don't stop, despite the difficulties, the dangers, the weariness and the criticisms; you don't stop because you can't, because really that is what your life has become. I honestly believe I discovered the meaning of life after Paolo's death. Suddenly, after Paolo's death, I felt the overwhelming need to communicate with others, to communicate what I had inside me, to try to take what other people had to give me, to try to go on together towards that destination that I had glimpsed – and I use a strange expression – thanks to – that explosion, thanks to that death.[7]

The Church

The relationship between Church and Mafia in Italy over the years has been described as lying along a sliding scale from cohabitation through compromise to rejection.[8] There have also been occasions of direct involvement: four Franciscan priests from Mazzarino near Agrigento were sent for trial in 1962 for criminal conspiracy, extortion and murder. Acquitted at their first trial, they were subsequently found guilty and sentenced to 13 years' imprisonment.[9] Another priest, Father Agostino Coppola, was a close associate and cash handler for Corleone boss Luciano Leggio; he performed the marriage ceremony for Totò Riina and was allegedly introduced in *Cosa Nostra* circles as an affiliated man of honour.[10] On his conviction for involvement in several kidnaps he was expelled from the priesthood. More recently Salvatore Cassisa, Bishop of Monreale, was committed for trial in 1994 on charges of fraud and of having accepted bribes from a series of companies in connection with restoration work to the cathedral, and in 1996 for corruption of others.

His private secretary was accused of having favoured the fugitive status of Corleone boss Leoluca Bagarella. A Palermo parish priest, Father Mario Frittitta, was arrested in 1997 on a similar charge with regard to the wanted *mafioso* Pietro Aglieri. It was thought that the Aglieri family had been disturbed by a religious crisis which their relative was experiencing and feared he would give himself up to the authorities, implicating himself and his associates. Intercepted telephone calls indicated the priest's involvement in protecting Aglieri; he was sent for trial and found guilty in October 1998.

In contrast, sectors of the Church and individual priests have taken an influential and courageous stand against the Mafia. Papal interventions in the early 1980s and again after 1992, together with the community-based commitments of many priests in Sicily and on the mainland, have served to put the Church in the forefront of the antimafia fight and consequently to expose it to retaliation.

The Church stands in a crucial position *vis à vis* the Mafia in as much as it represents a large area of intersection between the Mafia as a criminal organization and the society in which it is rooted. A profession of faith in the values of honour, chastity, sacrifice, obedience, respect for the roles of wife and mother and for family unity are common to both, while the rites of baptism, communion, marriage and funeral are rigorously followed in Mafia families, even when participants in these ceremonies are fugitives from justice.

In the postwar period the Catholic Church closely allied itself with the Christian Democratic Party in its opposition to the spread of communism in Italy, and this placed it in an ambiguous role with regard to the Mafia, whose instinctive allegiance also lay with the DC, the largest and most influential political force in Sicily. Nonetheless the clientilistic patterns of power which had grown up around the DC and the degeneration of morality as a result of Mafia activities became a matter of concern within the Sicilian Church. Beginning around 1965 under the influence of the Second Vatican Council, and reinforced from 1973 when Archbishop (later Cardinal) Salvatore Pappalardo became chairman of the Sicilian Council of Bishops, the Church in Sicily preached less about the evils of communism and more about corruption and political malpractice. At the inauguration of the Sicilian Region's legislative assembly on 8 July 1976 Pappalardo warned,

Let no one be deceived. It is impossible to continue with the old clientilistic power games as if nothing had happened. The DC must not be reduced to a federation of factions in continual struggle, each trying to grab its own slice of power. Scandals and misdeeds cannot and must not be covered up and the Party itself should denounce and expel those who are tainted with such actions.[11]

In the early 1980s a sector of the Church in Sicily moved away from traditional DC support in favour of a more pastoral, apolitical and socially-based commitment which transcended the immediate doctrines of the Church. Known as *Città per l'Uomo* (City for Mankind) it took an unequivocal stand against political corruption, administrative malpractice and the Mafia. It also took a strongly pacifist line in its opposition to the installation of Cruise missiles at the NATO base of Comiso, a position in which it was allied with the Communist Party, whose regional secretary, Pio La Torre, led the campaign against the installation of the missiles. In November 1981 Cardinal Pappalardo held a mass for all victims of the Mafia which was intended as an invitation to the city of Palermo to reject the Mafia in favour of pacification and non-violence. In the course of his sermon he described the Mafia as 'a complex and almost inextricable combination of common delinquency which operates in the open and occult manipulators of sordid affairs who act under careful cover and protection'.[12]

In December of that year Pope John Paul II became the first pope publicly to pronounce the word Mafia when he urged bishops to become involved in the struggle to overcome Sicily's problems, and in particular in the antimafia struggle. The following year in September, during the funeral oration for General Carlo Alberto Dalla Chiesa and his wife, amidst whistles and insults directed at the institutional figures present, Cardinal Pappalardo again condemned the Mafia but reserved his harshest criticism for the authorities in Rome. 'A well-known phrase is appropriate here, it comes from Sallustio, I believe: *"Dum Romae consulitur ... Saguntum espugnatur"* – while Rome decides on a course of action, Sagunto is conquered. And this time it is not Sagunto but Palermo! This poor Palermo of ours.'[13] In April 1983 Cardinal Pappalardo went to Palermo's Ucciardone prison to say Easter mass for the prisoners, but *Cosa Nostra* ensured that of more than 800 inmates, not a single one attended.

From this time onwards and for several years, the Church hierarchy refrained from exhortations on Mafia themes. This may have been due to fear in the climate of extreme tension prior to and during the maxitrial; it was also said that Cardinal Pappalardo was afraid of being 'manipulated' and that pressure had been brought to bear on him by individuals in the Vatican who feared that to oppose the Mafia publicly was equivalent to upsetting a certain equilibrium of power in Sicily.[14]

The Pope went to Sicily in November 1982 for the first time but did not pronounce the words against the Mafia which appeared in the text distributed to journalists. When *City for Mankind* took part in administrative elections for the first time in 1984 on an anti-Mafia platform the Church retreated further. The official silence was broken by sporadic denunciations such as those made in 1989 by the Bishop of Agrigento when he described the Mafia as a 'symbol of Satan's power' and by a declaration of excommunication for *mafiosi* made by the Bishop of Catania in 1990.

During a visit to Sicily in November 1991, Pope John Paul II relegitimized the topic: he repeated his invitation to the Sicilian Church to put the Mafia at the centre of attention and stated that organized crime of a Mafia kind was 'a social plague' which constituted 'a serious threat not only to civil society but also to the Church's mission'. In response the Diocese of Agrigento published a text entitled 'The Mafia Emergency: A Pastoral Problem', published in April 1992. The text insisted on the community aspect of the Church's role and urged that it abandon its current practice of generic condemnation – all too often this masked a passivity with regard to the Mafia. Improper forms of behaviour and contiguousness with political power had contributed to

> the murkiness of a social and political system which has constituted the humus of the subculture and the practice of the Mafia. [...] Even today we are suffering from a long silence on the part of the Church which has put the accent on individual salvation and has not used all the means at its disposal to oppose the consolidation of the Mafia phenomenon either at a cultural level (by not favouring the social development of faith) or at a political level (by not always discerning who was in collusion with the Mafia) or at the pastoral level (by too often showing resignation).[15]

In 1992 Cardinal Pappalardo presided over the state funerals of Giovanni and Francesca Falcone and their three bodyguards, and of Borsellino's five bodyguards. On both occasions he made a plea for national unity and for collaboration with the investigations, and called on the institutional authorities to assume the full weight of their responsibilities, but the tone of the funeral orations was more of resignation and trust in God than of belief in earthly remedies.

A powerful denunciation of political corruption appeared in a magazine article of September 1992 written by the Jesuit priest Father Ennio Pintacuda, founder of the Pedro Arrupe Research Istitute in Palermo and spiritual adviser to Leoluca Orlando. In Father Pintacuda's view it was too late to talk of 'reforming' politics:

> We must realize that we are in a pre-revolutionary stage in which reformism has no place [...] we are now beyond the crisis of the representative system, beyond the crisis of partitocracy [...] We have now become a regime. By this term I mean an aggregation of political–economic interests which is suffocating traditional political representation, has crushed the political parties and is destroying the basis of democratic society, aiming at the consolidation of an authoritarian power. Nowadays illegal behaviour prevails among the dominant forces of the regime. [...] It is necessary to break up the front of Masonic–Mafia interests, the new 'historic block' which is oppressing Italy. Not only is there tacit consensus between institutional powers and criminal interests but a veritable pact which aims to establish an authoritarian project and is nourished by a corruption which cannot be reduced to a mere moral problem because it is strangling democracy, reducing it to pure form. To 'reform' is to put the degraded system in an emergency resuscitation unit: this is the characteristic of the Amato government – the government of the emergency resuscitation unit.[16]

Publication of the article caused the expulsion of Father Pintacuda from the Pedro Arrupe Institute on the grounds of its excessive politicization and its evident identification with the proclamations of Leoluca Orlando's Net.

The first official doctrinal statement to come from the Church after the Palermo atrocities was a 21-point document entitled 'Mafia and Evangelization' written by the deputy chairman of the Italian Episcopal Conference and Archbishop of Crotone (Calabria) Monsignor Giuseppe Agostino, which appeared in early October 1992. 'It is true that the *mafiosi* in our territory need to be educated and evangelized, but they must also be shaken up. [...] It is not a question of excommunicating them as some ask, but of finding them and bringing them to the truth.' Henceforth notorious or convicted *mafiosi* were not to be admitted to the sacraments of the Eucharist or of marriage if they had not repented within themselves and had proved their sincerity by putting it to the test; they were not permitted to become godparents or to take an active part in the life of the Church. The funerals of those who died in armed conflict and who were known to be *mafiosi*, or of convicted *mafiosi* who died without showing any sign of real repentance, were to be held without communion.[17]

The final communiqué issued by the Sicilian Episcopal Conference which met in Palermo in early October of the same year stated that among the causes of the crisis of Sicilian society were 'a mafiosity of thought, of behaviour and of structures; a spider's web of personal vested interests; a lack of formative and resolute interventions by state organs; a situation of cultural and economic underdevelopment; a casual approach to public resource management'. The Church should not be resigned but should act 'to purge all such forms of false and compromising behaviour'.[18]

Pope John Paul II visited Sicily in 1993, 1994 and 1995. During his speech in the Valley of the Temples at Agrigento in May 1993, he spoke out strongly against Mafia violence and likened *Cosa Nostra* to the devil. 'God said, "thou shalt not kill". No man, no group or Mafia can change and defy this most saintly God. This people, the Sicilian people – cannot always live under the pressure of a counter-culture, a culture of death. I say to those responsible, "Convert! One day the justice of God will come!"'

After receiving the parents of the young judge Rosario Livatino, murdered in 1990, he announced that lay persons assassinated by the Mafia could also be considered martyrs – 'martyrs of justice and, indirectly, of the faith'. The gesture showed the ecumenical face of the Church and was a statement of belief in the universality of justice. The concept of the Mafia as a perversion of the soul was replaced by a recognition that it was a human phenomenon with social roots. The political context was brought out in another speech made during the same trip, when the Pope invited businessmen and politicians to 'promote the culture of enterprise and solidarity, persevere in the commitment to renew politics, directing it ever more decisively to the objective of the common good and purging it of those obscure clientilistic practices which pollute the experience of democracy'. He urged his audience to fight 'against the Mafia mentality and organization which, although of a dishonourable minority, puts this land to shame and damages its potential'.[19]

In the 1980s and 1990s many priests became involved in community-based antimafia initiatives by addressing the causes that favoured the recruitment of young people into crime such as homelessness, drug addiction, unemployment and the condition of being an immigrant without work or papers. Father Giuseppe Puglisi ran a variety of cultural, social, recreational and sporting activities for young people from the 'Our Father' community centre, next to his church of San Gaetano in the Palermo district of Brancaccio. He tried to discourage children from dropping out of school and from starting to deal in drugs, thieve or sell contraband cigarettes. He ignored a series of 'warnings' to cease his commitment to social resistance and continued with actions considered a provocation to *Cosa Nostra*. He declined to use the firm of builders 'indicated' to him for the restoration of the church and chose another firm – one of its lorries was firebombed and the door of the church was set on fire. He held a commemoration mass on the anniversary of Paolo Borsellino's murder; he was on a committee which had invited a delegation of the Antimafia Commission to a local school debate and he had forbidden a number of local public figures who were under Mafia investigation to write for the parish magazine. In September 1993 *Cosa Nostra* shot him dead at point blank range as he left his house next door to San Gaetano. After Father Puglisi's murder several priests engaged in similar activities were assigned bodyguard protection.

On his next visit to Sicily in November 1994, Pope John Paul praised Father Puglisi as a 'courageous exponent of the Gospel' and urged Sicilians not to allow his death to have been in vain. He warned that silence and passivity in the face of Mafia crimes was tantamount to complicity. Again the Pope made a direct appeal to the Mafia: 'I willingly take this opportunity to address myself once more to the men of the Mafia to say this to them: In the name of God, put an end to violence, put an end to injustice! It is time to open your hearts to that God who is both just and merciful, and who asks of you a sincere change of heart!'

Father Paolo Turturro, whose parish is located in a densely Mafia-populated sector of Palermo beside Ucciardone prison, founded an organization called 'Paint Peace' which as well as professing pacifism, assists down-and-outs, drug addicts, the old and the sick. Every year on 2 November, the day on which the dead are commemorated, Father Turturro organizes a bonfire of toy weapons to educate children against violence. In September 1997 he found two bullets left in the confessional of his church. Father Antonio Garrau works in the Zisa district of Palermo where he tries to keep young people off the streets by engaging them in creative activities, and also organizes summer holidays for children outside Palermo. On All Saints' Day, 1 November 1994, another priest in the Zisa district, Father Mario Scifo, covered all the statues of saints in his church with sheets to symbolize the Church's disapproval of those who feigned devotion to Christianity in church while engaging in criminal activities outside it. He criticized the practice of usury, and urged his congregation to contribute to a fund against it. As he spoke the church emptied; he later received telephone calls warning that a bomb would be planted in the church, and was obliged to leave Palermo a few months later.

The chaplain to the prison of Termini Imerese, Father Gino Sacchetti, encourages *mafiosi* in prison to confess their crimes to the authorities and also runs a drug rehabilitation centre. He has frequently been threatened and had his car firebombed. To coincide with the Pope's arrival in Sicily in November 1994, a lamb with its throat slit was impaled outside his house. A note left beside it said the priest would shortly meet the same fate.

Father Cosimo Scordato runs the San Saverio Community Centre from the baroque church of San Francesco Saverio, in the old Palermo quarter of Albergheria. On Sundays the Centre functions as a church; during the rest of the week it is a meeting hall for trade unionists, pensioners or citizens' groups, an art gallery or concert hall. The Centre has set up a bar and *trattoria* in the square outside the church, cooperatives that provide cleaning services and assistance to the old and a travel agency offering multilingual tours of the city. Father Scordato, who also teaches theology at Palermo University, insists that the Church should not act like a 'parallel state', that it must communicate solidarity and tenderness through humility, not with arrogance, must teach struggle, not hatred. He has enlisted architects and economists on a voluntary basis in his struggle to wrest funds for restoring local housing and to create stable employment in Albergheria, a battle which clearly takes priority over spiritual salvation.[20]

Churchmen in other southern regions have demonstrated courage in opposing the Mafia: Father Edoardo Scordio set up nursery and primary school facilities, centres for the handicapped and pensioners and an ambulance service for his parishioners in the Calabrian town of Capo Isola Rizzuto; he has also used his sermons to accuse '*Ndrangheta* members of violence and hypocrisy and has invited them to surrender their weapons.[21]

After Father Puglisi, a second priest fell victim to organized crime in March 1994 in Casal di Principe, near Caserta. Father Giuseppe Diana had angered local *Camorra* members by his refusal to celebrate the funeral of a crime boss, and was believed to be helping magistrates with their enquiries into local criminality.

The significance of the murders of Father Puglisi and Father Diana should not be underestimated. The Mafia does not murder outside its ranks with indifference, but as a last resort when the individuals concerned represent an insurmountable obstacle to its projects. In the case of the attacks against the Church, to which it has traditionally shown respect and sympathy, the significance is even greater. The murders are a sign of the considerable discomfort that the Church's strong social commitment has produced, and of the threat posed to the Mafia by the potential rejection of upcoming generations. Retaliation against the

Church's defiance of the Mafia may also have been an element in the choice of two churches in Rome as targets for car bomb attacks in 1993 (see Chapter 7).

The churchman who has made the most consistent contribution to the antimafia fight is Father Luigi Ciotti, founder in 1966 of the *Gruppo Abele* in Turin. The *Gruppo Abele* was set up to help minority and marginalized groups in society, particularly the young, to cope with their difficulties. With its defining message of *accoglienza* – hospitality, or welcome – it runs ten communities for individuals with drug- and HIV- or AIDS-related problems, including a centre for HIV-infected babies abandoned by their mothers. It is involved both actively and via a series of publications in a broad range of social concerns such as Mafia-related issues, the rights of immigrants, prisoners and drug-dependent individuals. Despite having a priest at its head, the *Gruppo Abele* does not set itself a proselytizing mission. Asked once whether he tried to encourage youngsters with drug problems towards the Church, Father Ciotti replied that having weaned his charges of one form of dependency he would certainly not push them towards another, but admitted that if some sought this path of their own volition he would willingly assist.[22]

In February 1993 Father Ciotti launched the publication *Narcomafie* in association with the Sicilian Documentation Centre in Palermo and two other associations, the Observatory on the *Camorra* in Naples and the *Observatoire Géopolitique des Drogues* in Paris. *Narcomafie* became a mouthpiece for national opposition to the violence and political corruption symbolized by the Palermo atrocities and the Bribesville scandals; it focuses on drugs and drug-trafficking issues, the problems of the inner cities, on economic and social disparities, on ethnic minorities and on sub-state conflicts around the world; on the phenomenon of 'the Mafias' in Italy and elsewhere and on how organized crime stifles the political, economic and social life of a community. In particular it highlights efforts by private individuals or associations, or by individuals in public life such as priests, teachers or judges to raise public awareness of the harm done by organized crime and who, in their own field, have committed themselves to fighting it. The aim of the publication, according to Father Ciotti, was to attack the 'psychology of dependence' that the Mafia creates: aspects of life that should be taken for granted as rights such as health care, fairness in job recruitment practices and in the allocation of housing, the freedom to set up a business, are seen as favours to be obtained through other people in Mafia-controlled areas. This dependence becomes a filter between needs and resources and erodes cultural consensus from legitimate powers. It was necessary to 'socialize the territory', to empower citizens to repossess their own living and working areas and to control the environmental and social developments within them. *Narcomafie* was to be a facilitator in the exchange of experiences and projects. In 1999, with a print run of 11 000 and 3000 subscribers, the circulation of *Narcomafie* was still growing.

Civic and Community Associations

The contribution to the antimafia effort made by the Italian Church and its representatives inevitably spills over into the category of civic and community efforts. Under the auspices of the *Gruppo Abele*, an association called '*Libera*: Associations, names and numbers against the Mafias' was set up in 1995 to coordinate the 600 antimafia associations that had grown up around the country and to organize initiatives at national level. The president of *Libera* is Father Luigi Ciotti, its vice president is Rita Borsellino. The guidelines of the network of associations were formalized at *Libera*'s constituent assembly in March 1995. A non-profit making, apolitical, lay association, it took as a common denominator the recognition that, quite independently of any specific area of intervention, the defeat of organized crime represented an essential condition for a country's cultural and social development. To defeat the Mafia, repression was necessary but without prevention it would not be enough. *Libera* sets education and legality as principal themes and is committed to action in urban districts, schools and churches and to solidarity with the victims of Mafia violence and intimidation. It runs courses for teachers and has created a computerized information centre which stores all the educational projects carried out in the sector, plus a questionnaire for students which tests the awareness of young people of issues of legality and the Mafia. One of *Libera*'s first actions was to take over coordination of the campaign for a law to allocate assets confiscated from organized criminals towards socially useful projects. Father Ciotti persuaded 23 daily newspapers to publish an editorial appeal written by him asking for signatures, and the goal of one million signatures was reached. The law (109/96) came into force in March 1996; less than two years later, 62 properties had been assigned to local communities for a total value of US$16 277 280, allocated as follows: 31 welfare/solidarity or educational centres, 19 parks or recreational centres, 6 office buildings and 6 other structures.[23]

Libera was also responsible for the establishment of a national day of remembrance for all Mafia victims on 21 March – the first day of spring. On the first remembrance day in 1996, celebrated in Rome's *Piazza del*

Campidoglio, the names of nearly 300 innocent victims of the Mafia were read out. The second was held in Niscemi (Sicily) where two children died in Mafia crossfire in 1987, the third in Reggio Calabria, and the fourth in Corleone.

The slogan 'socialize the territory' was adopted by the *Movimento di Volontariato Italiano* (MoVI), which with 800 groups operating in 37 different areas is the largest voluntary association in Italy. MoVI has taken an active role in the antimafia movement through a campaign to promote civil resistance – as a complement to repression – to the 'integrated layers of the Mafia'. Pointing out in its list of objectives that there was on average one member of the police for every 180–200 inhabitants in the south, but only one social worker for every 40 000 inhabitants, MoVI's aims were: (a) to open up workshops, cultural and recreational areas in the most deprived areas of cities, to be staffed by conscientious objectors [who can opt for voluntary work as an alternative to military service]; (b) to provide advice and assistance to families on educational and employment opportunities, and (c) to encourage the setting up of businesses by young people.[24]

MoVI prepared a document for submission to the Parliamentary Antimafia Commission in April 1993. It called for resources to improve the social and urban structure of cities by the provision of two core services in all the districts of every southern city – a citizens' advice centre and a family health centre. It called for resources for education to prevent children from dropping out of school and to introduce 'education to legality' to the school curriculum. It called on the government to stimulate work opportunities by the provision of professional training and business start-up incentives in preference to welfare subsidies.

The longest-established Italian research centre into the Mafia, the Sicilian Documentation Centre Giuseppe Impastato (CSD) was founded by sociologist Umberto Santino in 1977. It engages in several levels of activity including political lobbying, research on the economic and financial aspects of organized crime and active social involvement. In 1980 it took the name of Giuseppe Impastato in honour of the young activist killed for his denunciation of Mafia activities in Cinisi, near Palermo, on whose behalf it has campaigned in collaboration with the Association of Sicilian Women against the Mafia. In addition to sponsoring support for women harmed by the Mafia who do not receive state compensation, it has promoted specific projects such as a successful application for EU funding to provide a course in screen printing for 20 unemployed women in Palermo. It also collaborates closely with the San Saverio Centre in Albergheria. The CSD has compiled a reading list and volumes of research on drugs and organized crime, and a set of educational materials on the Mafia for universities and schools with audio-visual accompaniment. Despite publishing some of the finest research in the Italian language on Mafia violence, on the economics of organized crime and on Mafia trials,[25] the CSD is more renowned outside Italy than at home, where it has remained on the margins of the mainstream antimafia movement.

In 1984 CSD's Director Umberto Santino prepared a dossier for presentation to the European Parliament entitled 'A Friend at Strasbourg[a]', which described the contacts between Euro-MP Salvo Lima and Mafia members or persons close to it, as detailed in the 1976 Report of the Parliamentary Antimafia Commission (see Chapter 2). A vote on whether to discuss the political implications of the dossier fell through, largely due to the opposition of the Italian Communist Party delegation in Strasbourg, and this soured Santino's relationship with the PCI, later PDS, from then on. In 1988, during the period of Leoluca Orlando's mayorship – which the Centre had welcomed for the declared determination to clean up Palermo politics – a Citizens' Committee of Information and Participation (COCIPA) was formed, open to individuals or groups, with the intention of transcending party political divisions. It met weekly in an office provided by Palermo City Council to discuss problems of traffic, public works contracts, the revitalization of the old city centre and other civic issues. However COCIPA would not give Orlando's administration the uncritical support it demanded and collaboration between the two collapsed. After the split COCIPA devoted itself to analysing the City Council's annual budget; Orlando was found wanting, and COCIPA's meetings were no longer held in the City Hall but in the San Saverio Centre. The PCI's refusal to vote for discussion of the Lima dossier in the European Parliament has remained a running sore in the Centre's relations with the Left, while criticisms of Leoluca Orlando's city administrations and an unwillingness to make political compromises with fellow travellers in the antimafia movement have left it isolated and inadequately funded.

If the CSD has in a sense become a prisoner of its 20 years of political struggle, Palermo citizens seeking a politically non-aligned but socially-rooted antimafia commitment found it after 1992 in the antimafia 'cartel' known as *Palermo Anno Uno* (Palermo Year One). The name originated from a series of initiatives organized to commemorate the first anniver-

---

[a]   Members of the Christian Democratic Party called themselves 'friends' in contrast to the Communist Party 'comrades'.

sary of the atrocities in May 1993 under the slogan 'Palermo Year One – from Anger to Action': church bells and factory sirens were sounded in unison; ships moored in Palermo harbour sounded their sirens and a relay of runners, representing 'the peace Olympics' carried a torch from the southern town of Gela through 16 other Mafia 'strongholds' to the magnolia tree outside the Falcone apartment in via Notarbartolo. Building on this, a network of Palermo-based associations was formed comprising local antimafia groups, pacifist and church-based groups, each with its own priorities but willing to pool resources to achieve common goals. Amongst the first priorities of Palermo Year One were: a campaign to fill all the judicial vacancies in the Palermo courthouse, the revitalization of the Palermo city centre and the creation of new green spaces for recreational purposes; identification of all the unused property owned by the City Council with the objective of creating social and health centres; improvements to the school environment, in particular the inauguration of a new school in the Zen district – the symbol of urban decay in Palermo; the creation of an office of social services and the recruitment of the full quota of social workers – in 1994 there were 10 out of a requirement of 140.[26] By concentrating on actions with a strong symbolic message combined with high-profile 'events', Palermo Year One succeeded in creating a genuinely transversal association which embodies a holistic approach to the antimafia fight, typical of the period since 1992. In recognition of its achievements, Palermo Year One received an award in November 1996 from the Norwegian Thorolf Rafto Foundation, named after an eminent economist committed to the cause of human rights. (Previous recipients had been Aung San Suu Kyi and José Ramos-Horta.)

Palermo Year One currently consists of 40 associations and holds public meetings every two weeks in different locations around the city. Strongly backed by Mayor Leoluca Orlando (although it guards its independence by refusing City Council funding), among its more recent achievements is the repossession of Villa Trabia, a little-used aristocratic residence, which in 1994 became a public library with video and audio library, Internet room and a room for listening to music. In 1995 particular attention was paid to the City of Palermo's statute of planning regulations, unmodified since 1962 when the *mafioso* Vito Ciancimino was City Assessor for Public Works. A new statute had been prepared in the 1980s but the parties could not agree on the format; from 1992 to 1995 it continued to be debated without ever being approved, meanwhile building continued on the areas designated for schools or other social structures. Between February and April 1995 Palermo Year One maintained a constant presence outside the City Hall and built a wall of bricks, each one representing a meeting of the City Council at which the statute had not been approved. It was finally approved in April, but three years later the necessary regulations for implementing it had still not been passed, even though the designated areas could no longer be used for other purposes. Projects for which PYO was lobbying in 1998 included the adoption of a statute of citizens' rights, the provision of a civil ombudsman to represent citizens in disputes with the Council and the creation of a 'Museum of Memory' dedicated to Mafia victims.

Schools/young people

The primary objective of nearly all the Italian antimafia associations is to educate children to know and respect the law and to prevent them from acquiring a 'Mafia mentality' of distrust and antagonism towards public institutions which may lead to a life of crime. Law enforcement has the responsibility for combating the Mafia, but only society can uproot the culture of 'mafiosity' which tolerates and connives with criminality. For this reason particular attention is given to schooling in good citizenship and to the role of educators.

The link between low levels of education, poor quality of school facilities and crime was illustrated by the Parliamentary Antimafia Commission in 1994 (see Chapter 3). Misallocation and misspending of educational resources were also found to be more widespread in the south of Italy, where the cost per school pupil was $3000 per annum compared to $1380 in the north. Calabria had 1500 full-time teachers of further education who provided only a quarter of the number of courses offered by the region of Emilia Romagna with fewer staff.

The number of young people in southern Italy who do not complete the eight years of compulsory schooling from 6–14 years is almost double the number in the north. The highest share – 30 per cent – is Sicilian, 23 per cent are from Campania, 18 per cent from Apulia and 8 per cent from Calabria.[27] A bare 10 per cent of children in the slums of Palermo stay on at school beyond the compulsory minimum.[28] Research also shows that 76 per cent of minors who commit crimes in Italy are either formally illiterate or have at the most an elementary school diploma.

Sicily has one-quarter of Italy's institutionalized minors, Campania 14 per cent. In Naples 1355 adolescents were imprisoned in 1992; of them, 81.6 per cent had not completed obligatory schooling and 5 per cent were illiterate; 54 per cent had been imprisoned for theft and/or robbery, 20 per cent for drug law violations and 12 per cent for possession of firearms.[29]

Antimafia awareness programmes have nominally been provided in Sicilian schools since 1980 but until 1992 were not widely implemented. Under pressure from the Antimafia Commission, 'education to good citizenship' and antimafia programmes formally entered the national school curriculum in October 1993, and were expanded from 1995 with the involvement of *Libera*. By 1998, 620 schools had undertaken this type of programme and 1000 projects were under way, involving 8000 teachers and 800 000 students.[30] Examples abound: a link was set up between a classics high school in Milan and its counterpart in Corleone to exchange 'letters' by video cassette. More than two hundred pupils in a secondary school in Turin participated in after-hours sessions twice a week to study the history and geography of the Mafia, its economic activities and criminal profile. An association called 'I Care' was formed in Castellamare di Stabia near Naples which arranges for older children to help younger ones with learning difficulties. In Secondigliano, a run-down suburb of Naples, an association of former pupils, all of whom had stimulating jobs, began regular visits to the school to talk about their work and to reassure pupils that coming from a working-class city suburb was not a bar to finding a good job. A group calling itself GIOVARE (Young Volunteers to Assist in Educational Rehabilitation) – literally, 'to be useful' – was formed at the end of 1994 by former pupils to help 11–12-year-olds with learning difficulties for one or two afternoons per week. The Centre for Study and Research into Southern Issues in Potenza (in the region of Basilicata) put together an educational leaflet on justice and legality which was distributed in local schools.

Most of the school-based programmes were devised on the principle that the main function of a school is to foster the ability to think and to make independent judgements rather than simply to learn. A 'self-governing cooperative' was set up by a school in Palermo to supply particular goods and services, including the sale of snacks and drinks for lesson breaks, the provision of stationery, the running of a games club and a disco on alternating afternoons in the school hall.[31] Each cooperative had a committee whose members had specific responsibilities for management of the activities, accounting and publicity.

The Giancarlo Siani school in Gragnano, Naples, was named after a young journalist murdered by the *Camorra* in 1985. The school, which is located in a depressed quarter of the city, introduced a project entitled 'Educate to legality' in the 1994–95 curriculum.[32] The project focused on the theme of justice, and included visits to the Naples courthouse and studies of the criminal law. A simulated trial was staged around the theft of a moped to help pupils understand the law and the functions within the legal process of the defence lawyer, the police, the civil plaintiff, the prosecutor and the president of the court. As part of the preparation, a prosecutor from the criminal court was invited to give lessons on trial procedures. Pupils were split into groups to research the different phases of the court proceedings and were allocated roles; a courtroom was set up and the trial enacted.

A local antimafia association, also named after Siani, offers prizes for degree theses and for educational projects on the theme of criminality and violence. It organizes mobilization days in schools (particularly on the anniversary of Siani's murder), debates on specific subjects and meetings between students and judges, police officers and journalists.[33]

The courtroom scenario has been a popular classroom model: a school in Modena inserted the history and economics of the Mafia into its civic education project and studied the use of investigation techniques through a mock-up of the Andreotti trial (see Chapter 7), with some students taking the defence, others the prosecution.[34]

At a more abstract level, a school in Florence encouraged pupils to identify the rights and duties that they considered most important for society, and a comparison was made with the rights and duties associated with school life and with those enshrined in the Italian constitution. Using improvisation and story-telling, a scenario was developed describing how a group of young people broke the law and how the problems were resolved.[35] Even very young children can participate in 'education to good citizenship' projects: in Catania a little elephant called *Gino l'Educhino* was adopted as a classroom mascot to support a programme of lessons on civic education.

One of the more imaginative school projects was launched in Naples in December 1992 under the auspices of a European Community project entitled 'Schools adopt a monument'. It developed into a national network in 1994 involving 65 city councils, 100 schools and almost 600 000 students.[36] The project invites schools to take over the physical care and maintenance of a monument such as a villa, church, gateway, garden, fountain or other historical site. Students research the monument's historical and cultural significance and act as guides to visitors from other schools and from the adult world. The research leads to play and essay writing, art exhibitions and the production of postcards, T-shirts and guidebooks, and brings the pupils into contact with the local area and its administrators, taking them physically and spiritually outside the school and projecting the school back into the life of the city.

In 1998 Palermo was the only Italian city that had continued the project, which has been sponsored each year by Palermo Year One. During the academic year 1997–98 the pupils of 124 Palermo schools 'adopted' 121 monuments which were opened to the public during each of the four weekends in May along 13 different itineraries. Some took the form of guided walks through the old city of Palermo, others were coach tours outside the city boundaries, taking in eight or ten monuments along the way. At every stop, groups of pupils led visitors round the site, providing a historical, archeological or botanical description as appropriate. One of the properties on the itinerary, 'The Bourbon Parks', was the eighteenth-century Villa Savagnone which had been confiscated from a Mafia boss and assigned to the local community as a cultural centre and botanical garden under Law 109/96. It had been selected for the itinerary to illustrate the importance of the new law and because the villa had been neglected and abused over the years – the children who 'adopted' it gained a sense of indignation and a different perspective of the destructive force of the Mafia.

The business world has also played its part in the educational field by fostering collaboration between colleges in the south and business and industrial enterprises in the north. In the course of the academic year 1995–96, 400 post-school or post-diploma training schemes were provided within technical and professional institutes; in 1996 a collaborative project was set up between the Federation of Industrialists in the Emilia Romagna region and the Southern Industrial Association to offer young southerners with a school-leaving certificate in technical subjects or with an equivalent qualification concrete job opportunities. The Italian State Railways offered discounted tickets to help with travel costs and provided lodgings.

In Niscemi, a Sicilian town of 27 000 inhabitants, there was no elected town council from 1993–94 as it had been dissolved on grounds of Mafia infiltration. In the autumn of 1995 a new primary school had just been completed in a dilapidated part of the town without public lighting or asphalted roads, and the new administration, elected on a programme of honesty and reform, was concerned to prevent the newly-fitted wash basins, desks and radiators from being removed before the school had opened. From September until it was formally opened in November, the school was occupied day and night by relays of citizens including the mayor, local councillors, boy scouts and assorted volunteers. Gradually the school and the area around it became a focal point for civic activity as local people began to appreciate and 'own' the school's identity.

The extraordinary mobilization in the school community has provoked hostile reactions. Between October 1995 and February 1996 some 30 attacks were carried out on schools in the province of Caserta alone, although some were simple acts of vandalism and not necessarily Mafia-related.[37] The Giancarlo Siani school in Naples has suffered 11 arson attacks in addition to numerous acts of vandalism and theft. In February 1996 the scientific high school in Niscemi was scheduled to host an antimafia 'caravan' organized by *Libera* when intruders tried to set fire to the school's electrical circuit.

The antimafia awareness that has developed since 1992 has had one undeniable effect – there can be few, if any, schoolchildren in Italy who do not know who Giovanni Falcone and Paolo Borsellino were, what they stood for and why they were killed. The fight against the Mafia – which will undoubtedly continue for many decades more – may be led in the future by those who began to study the phenomenon in 1992.

The grassroots antimafia – a profile

The grassroots antimafia movement since 1992 is characterized first and foremost by apolitical and moral inspirations. The historian Salvatore Lupo has described this as 'the search for a new language [..] a new public ethic and a genuine collective reappropriation of the theme of legality'.[38] The apolitical aspect has been particularly apparent in Sicily, where disillusionment with clientilistic politics has been most evident and where, according to Lupo, given that the dominant party has been 'the single party of public spending', something new could only emerge in contraposition to the political parties, whether of government or of opposition. A broad spectrum of activities and a practical 'activist' approach have been other important features. Since 1992 the antimafia movement has been responsible for raising the number of cultural associations in southern Italy to levels similar to those in the centre and north: about 6400 associations, or three for every 10 000 inhabitants.[39]

Research carried out in 1995 into 80 antimafia associations in Italy's four southern regions divides them into two types – those founded with specific antimafia objectives and those founded to promote activities which include an antimafia component.[40] Membership tends to be well-educated and has a high level of female participation. Three-quarters of the 80 associations were founded after 1980, compared to less than 60 per cent in the case of other cultural associations. About one-third were formed after 1992, a figure which rose to three-quarters in the case of the specifically antimafia groups. A fifth of members were under age 20, and 85 per cent were under age 40. The leaders of the antimafia organizations were also relatively young (under 50 in almost 70 per cent of cases compared to barely 50 per cent in other cultural associations). The groups were relatively small (more than half had fewer than 50 members) and had modest funds (40 per cent were run on less than $3000 per year).

Of the members, 65 per cent had previously engaged in political activity. This share was highest (70 per cent) in the 40–50 age group. Within the general membership, 65 per cent considered themselves to be generically left of centre (compared to a 45 per cent average in voluntary associations). Political orientation was not generally reflected in party membership – only 21 per cent were card-carrying party members and only 27 per cent had been involved in political activities in the previous 12 months. Of the antimafia associations 50 per cent had contacts with parishes and with other religious groups; 34 per cent with trade unions and 34 per cent with political parties. Points of contact with the Greens, feminist groups and church-based groups were common.

The fact that southern Italy has shown itself capable of such widespread mobilization against organized crime marks an important break with tradition, and one not to be underestimated by those who have never lived in the *mezzogiorno*. In the early 1980s it was virtually impossible to buy books on the Mafia in Sicily; now the bookshops are laden and public debates on organized crime are held somewhere in southern Italy every week. In 1995 the Palermo branch of a national research institute set up an Internet web site in English and Italian to provide information on ongoing Mafia trials. In 1998 it had been accessed by 12 000 visitors.[41] The software was written by a Palermo researcher who is also a member of an antimafia association.

Conclusions – predictions

Unfortunately the future is not as rosy as the foregoing account might suggest. The prodigious efforts made by the grassroots antimafia movement have brought many positive improvements but inevitably they have been limited in scope and in geographical location. At the same time, economic progress has been slow. While the Italian economy as a whole has grown since 1992, the divergence between north and south has widened. In 1991 the GDP of southern Italy was 25.3 per cent of national GDP, in 1997 it had fallen to 24.2 per cent. Curiously, Palermo was among the top ten cities for consumption but in 80th place for income, and came last for services.

According to the Italian National Statistical Institute ISTAT, in 1997, 70 per cent of poor Italian families lived in the south;[42] in 1998 12.4 per cent of the national workforce was unemployed in comparison with 7.6 per cent in the centre-north and 22 per cent in the southern regions.

Unemployment in Campania was 25.5 per cent, in Calabria 25.2 per cent and in Sicily 23.5 per cent.[43] All over the south, youth unemployment levels are well over 50 per cent.

Businesses of all sizes in the south continue to be undermined by extortion demands of which relatively few are reported. Together with usury, it is one of the most ubiquitous examples of Mafia power. In 1989 Giovanni Falcone observed,

> It is one of the most delicate aspects of repression because very often there is a confusion between activities that are 'purely' Mafia and activities that are the result of intimidation by the Mafia. For example the businessman who is subject to protection by the Mafia very often gains some benefit from it. Then, being deemed trustworthy, he is used, for example to bid for public works contracts – because it's well known that they are a lucrative source of funds, and in this way he starts to draw some benefit from being in a state of subjection. To define the border between a victim of and a participant in Mafia activities is one of the most delicate problems that we have to deal with. Often we witness the process by which a businessman begins as the victim of the Mafia and then actually becomes a *mafioso* himself. [....][Extortions] are almost never reported of course, but on the other hand I don't see why they could or should be reported if to do so involves a whole series of reprisals which at the very least involves the cessation of the possibility of continuing to work. And that would be the best outcome ... The State simply does not have the capacity to guarantee comprehensively the safety of those who decide to collaborate. The State can only overcome this distrust by taking decisive action.[44]

Ten years on from this warning there has been little improvement, despite legislative interventions. A survey carried out by a business association indicated that in 1998, 70 per cent of shops in Reggio Calabria and four out of five shops in Palermo and Catania were extorted.[45] In 1997, after a trial in Palermo had concluded with 18 persons convicted of extorting businesses and hotels in central Palermo, not one of those who had been forced to pay had the courage to seek civil remedy through the courts.[46]

Palermo's Chief of Police believes that extortion serves as a cushion for organized crime at times of economic difficulty, a 'bread and butter' business which keeps the lower cadres employed and maintains the families of imprisoned *mafiosi*. 'Sometimes intimidation succeeds in a much "softer" way than we think. People who extort shops do not say, "You must give me half a million lire" [$300]. No, they say "there is a family suffering a great deal because the husband is in prison and they don't have enough to eat, so if you could give me a few hundred thousand lire for that family you would be making a contribution ..." The person knows that he has to pay up.'[47]

Cosa Nostra continues to exert considerable influence over Sicilian business practices. Documents found in the hideout of Mafia boss Giovanni Brusca after his arrest in May 1996 included letters from businessmen pleading for reductions in their regular payments and asking for his help in securing public works contracts, despite the fact that his capture was widely regarded as imminent.[48]

The Palermo constructor Enzo Lo Sicco admitted that between 1991 and 1996 his work in the Brancaccio district of Palermo was only tolerated by local bosses on condition that he make fictitious sales of apartments in the buildings he had constructed to persons whose names were given to him. After an initial blunder, he quickly learned the rules of the game: 'One: ask permission to do the work. Two: only go to "friendly" firms. Three: never take independent initiatives. Four: insert the cost of the Mafia presence into your balance sheet.' In January 1997 Lo Sicco found the courage to describe his working practices to the authorities but was obliged to leave Palermo for several months and to restructure his finances totally in order to keep his company afloat. On his return he was given bodyguard protection and a consultancy job in City Hall which finally allowed him 'to live and work in defiance of the Mafia rules to which I submitted for so many years'.[49]

Within the civic antimafia movement a certain weariness is apparent. Those with experiences pre-dating 1992 have a sensation of *déjà vu* with regard to a perceived superficiality and inconstancy in institutional antimafia efforts, and complain of the 'emotivity and discontinuity' of the grassroots movement.[50] There is bitterness that the periodic, emergency-driven revival of the antimafia impetus – in 1963, in 1982 and again in 1992 – has not called out a long-term commitment to ethical reform from those elements of society whose support is vital – the political and business classes. Too often, the grassroots antimafia has been left alone: voluntary interventions without proper coordination or systematic resourcing from public funds have been unsatisfactory, while the practice of delegating leadership in the antimafia fight to a small number of charismatic figureheads continues.

It is significant that these impressions are endorsed by those most aware of developing tendencies in criminality – juvenile court magistrates – who predict that unless much more sweeping reforms occur, the situation in southern Italy will not improve. In Naples, efforts to bring about a culture of legality through debates and meetings with experts and magistrates and to discourage pupils from dropping out of school have yielded poor results because of excessive bureaucracy and a lack of coordination, and because they have not been connected to any serious and coordinated initiatives for overcoming social or economic difficulties. Police efforts to prevent child labour and truancy are viewed as harassment by parents and young people, while criminal law reforms aimed at keeping minors out of the adult criminal circuit have created the expectation of impunity for minors and therefore an increase in incitement to crime on the part of adults.[51]

Calabria's problems are particularly intractable. Piero Gaeta, a prosecutor with over 15 years' experience in the field of juvenile crime, describes as a 'myth' the idea that social and economic decay are the factors that drive young Calabrians into crime. In his view this is a simplistic, convenient and fantastical interpretation because it suggests that by pouring in resources the problem can be solved. He believes that the youngster who enters the *'Ndrangheta* does not do so for reasons of economics but for psychological and existential survival.

The Mafia mentality is 'inside' the young Calabrian inasmuch as it reproduces matriarchal Calabrian society in the cultural sense of belonging to the group, the friendship which becomes private, rather than public virtue. Entry [into the *'Ndrangheta*] seals the meeting point between two intersecting domains – the Mafia structure and the Calabrian family, and the culture of the Mafia group and the world of the adolescent. Culturally, Calabrian society is without history, and thus without paternity. History has been replaced by folklore, tradition and myth, and this is fragile without the framework of history. Because Calabrians have taken their identity from myth and folklore rather than from history, they live inside a cultural vacuum. Tradition without history produces a crisis of identity. The authoritarian image of the Calabrian father is deceptive for this reason. The father figure transmits only dogma and authoritarianism and is incapable of mediating change or patterns of socialization. He organizes reality according to rigid schemes with diametrically opposed extremes, and sees transformation and change as negative and dangerous. [...] Growing up in a region without history or identity produces melancholy, boredom and tension. The boredom of isolation is a typical existential condition of young Calabrians, and is quite separate from solitude. [...] The Mafia

organization creates a cultural identity behind which the whole existential condition is concealed; the absence of history, the idealization
of tradition, authoritarian monism and the matriarchal family are all
mirrored in the common identity of organized crime. 'Belonging' to
the group is not really such but an affective dependency which takes
[an individual] from the family and replaces the maternal roles of care
and control. It provides protection and reinforces identity but at the
same time creates a dependency and an inability to go beyond.[...]
Committing crimes within a criminal group 'fits' with the existential
condition because crimes have a purely contingent purpose. All [the
individual] asks of the group is 'to do', and 'to obey'. [...] The quality
most prized in the group is loyalty, although less with regard to the
internal solidarity of the group and to a shared hostility and aggression
towards the world outside than to a loyalty in the sense of a dogmatic
acceptance of the model, a kind of loyalty to the *a priori* aspects of the
group's existence.[52]

Overcoming the attraction of the *sentire mafioso* – the attraction of the
Mafia identity – for the young southern male can only be a slow and
difficult process in a region where in early 1998 a football match was
preceded by a respectful minute's silence for a deceased *'Ndrangheta* boss,
and where the culture of *omertà* is so strong that in May, after the assassination in daylight of an eight-year-old girl and her grandfather while
they were driving through a busy square – by gunmen who mistook their
car for that of their enemies – not a single witness was prepared, even
anonymously, to report any details of the scene.
In Gaeta's view the most important tasks involve breaking down walls
of dogma and inflexibility and the attempt to bring private virtue into
the public domain.

There is a need to recognize that courage is not just the danger of
committing a murder, that friendship is not just complicity but can
be demonstrated publicly, that possibilities are less reassuring and
coherent than the certainties of a dogma, but that they can be accepted
without collapsing psychologically [...] Most of all, we need to offer
them doubts.

Meeting this challenge signifies overcoming the *anomie* of young southerners – expressed in their distrust, resignation and withdrawal – who long
for the 'Europeanization' of the *mezzogiorno* because 'Europe' conjures
up images of dynamism, modernity, efficiency and glamour, but who

doubt the State's ability or willingness to create the conditions within which this process can occur. A vicious circle must be broken. Investors will not risk capital in areas where local administrators and politicians are held to be corrupt, where the exercise of justice is compromised and where business integrity is not valued as a virtue. But in the absence of private investment, public spending will continue to be based on clientilistic practice which in the south means subject to the violence and intimidation of the Mafia clans. This in turn means that employment opportunities will continue to be mediated through a criminal filter, decided not on merit but on favours given and expected, with aspirations often going no higher than the security and guaranteed pension of a clerk's job in a public office.

Italy is often described as a country of variable legality, where respect for the law is a matter more of convenience than of principle. The natural propensity to delegate responsibility to a saviour figure who can redeem Italy's faults and misfortunes – what Santino calls a '*leader miracolatore*'[53] – is a legacy of religious tradition which has allowed Italians to delegate particularly difficult functions to idealized individuals from whom miracles are expected, and who in assuming their tasks on behalf of society, exonerate the majority from personal accountability. This practice was partially overcome by the grassroots antimafia movement, whose great achievements have been to show solidarity to the individuals most exposed on the antimafia front line, to take a public stance against corruption, ignorance and violence, to denounce the debilitating impact of the Mafia and to focus young people's energies on the construction of a better society through individual effort. These are forceful messages which must be maintained. The ideas of Giovanni Falcone and Paolo Borsellino should continue to walk on the legs of ordinary Italians – and of all good citizens. Defeating the Mafia is not just a matter of voting for honest politicians and rejecting overt violence, it calls for daily adherence to the 'Nine Uncomfortable Guidelines' which are valid wherever one happens to live. Then, as Giovanni Falcone wrote,

> [....] fortified by our experiences – both positive and negative – we must move forwards, but not with empty rhetoric, and no longer relying on the extraordinary commitment of a few but on the ordinary commitment of every one of us in a struggle which is, above all, one for a civilized society, and which can and must be won.[54]

6
The International Response

Introduction

The news of Giovanni Falcone's murder made headlines across the world. Foreign heads of state and government leaders paid fulsome tribute to his courage and dedication, and sent messages of condolence befitting the death of a statesman. Falcone had travelled widely in the course of his investigations throughout Europe and to North and South America, and had developed many personal contacts with attorneys and police officers. Former US attorneys Louis Freeh, Richard Martin and Rudolph Giuliani, who had worked closely with Falcone since 1984, expressed their grief at the loss of a close friend. The US government made an immediate offer to assist the Italian investigation, and within 48 hours of Falcone's death at Capaci, forensic scientists and explosives experts from the Federal Bureau of Investigation were on their way to Palermo. British law-enforcement officers were horrified by the ruthlessness and audacity of the attacks, and by the level at which the Mafia was prepared to strike. Their fears were aggravated by the implications for a post-1992, barrier-free Europe of an internationalized Italian Mafia with the capacity to challenge the sovereignty of an EU member state.

By the early 1990s investigations had shown that Italian Mafia groups were operating in every continent, and had begun to exploit the possibilities offered by the Single Market and the collapse of communism in Eastern Europe. The opening up of the former East bloc and the war in ex-Yugoslavia had created new drugs- and arms-trafficking routes between East and West. In June 1991 the Interior Minister of Czechoslovakia warned of 'numerous concrete indicators' that the Italian Mafia was trying to establish new centres of drug production in the USSR in collaboration with Soviet organized crime and said it was possible that the profits were being laundered in Czechoslovakia, where legislation did not permit the investigation of suspect bank accounts or financial transactions.[1]

West European countries had also become more alarmed about recent Mafia expansion. In the summer of 1992 there were around 70 Italian *mafiosi* in French prisons, most of whom had been arrested on the coast between Marseilles and the Italian border.[2] François D'Aubert, a deputy of the French centre-right party UDF, was one of several politicians who claimed that gambling, tourism and the construction industry had been heavily infiltrated by Italian criminality, and gave as an example the fact that Italian building firms in Nice were regularly undercutting French builders by as much as 30 per cent.[3] Members of the *Camorra* were reputed to be laundering drug profits on the Côte d'Azur, and in June 1991, had used front companies in Monte Carlo and in the French border town of Menton in an attempt to purchase the Menton casino – a bid thwarted at the last minute by a joint Franco–Italian police operation.

The absence of money laundering- and asset-tracing legislation had encouraged all four Italian crime groups to set up operations in Germany after 1982, when the *Rognoni–La Torre* law came into effect (see Chapter 2), while the fall of the Berlin Wall had opened up the possibility of new lucrative investments in the former East bloc, with Berlin as a convenient springboard. A senior Italian investigator recalls hearing an order being issued.

When the Berlin Wall fell we were intercepting the telephone line of an important *mafioso*. This *mafioso* received a telephone call from another in Germany, and said to him, 'Have you seen what's happened? Go off immediately and start buying.' He replied, 'But what should I buy?' 'Buy everything you can' was the answer. That's the Mafia for you, it goes wherever there's business to be done.[4]

The murder of Sicilian judge Rosario Livatino in September 1990 had been committed by two Sicilians employed in a pizzeria in Leverkusen, near Cologne, where they were arrested a month later. Four Sicilians had been arrested in April 1992 in Mannheim in connection with a series of murders committed in the southern Sicilian town of Palma di Montecchiaro on New Year's Eve 1991. Paolo Borsellino had been working closely with the German federal police investigation service, the *Bundeskriminalamt* (BKA) at the time of his murder – some 60 *mafiosi* had been arrested in Cologne and southern Germany in the previous few months. He had spent 6–10 July 1992 in Germany interrogating *Cosa Nostra* collaborators and told Italian colleagues of a 'decisive breakthrough' in his enquiries into the German branch of the Agrigento Mafia. He was intending to return to Germany in the last week of July.

With the North American market for cocaine apparently saturated, the Colombian cartels were focusing on Western Europe as a new growth market. A German intelligence report prepared for Chancellor Helmut Kohl at the end of 1991 (and leaked to the magazine *Der Spiegel*) described the power of the cartels as 'democratically uncontrollable', and warned that criminal organizations could make strategic use of illicit capital investments to manipulate party political funding, television and the print media, to acquire a share of the transportation sector and to destabilize the legitimate economies of western countries through the purchase of government-issued bonds, particularly those with large public-sector deficits such as Italy.

There were indications that *Cosa Nostra* was trying to gain the market position in cocaine that it had occupied in the early 1980s with heroin. An agreement between representatives of the Colombian Medellin cartel and the Galatolo and Madonia clans of *Cosa Nostra* had led to the shipment of 560 kilogrammes of pure cocaine to Sicily in early 1988 for onward distribution. It was intended as the first in a series of large consignments which, had details of the deal not been revealed a year later and had the Sicilians not defaulted on their agreed payment schedule, might have established the Palermo clans as principal importers of cocaine to Western Europe. Ten days before his murder, Giovanni Falcone referred to this case during a conference on drug trafficking, warning of the consequences of 'joint ventures in illicit activity at international level'. The Colombian–Sicilian deal had provided

> the proof of the beginning of direct contacts [which are] extremely dangerous for the possible risk of operational fusion between criminal organizations of considerable economic power and great operational capacity. [...] These links must be a source of concern, most of all because they are indicative of a trend that may lead to an increase in the dangerousness of these organizations through the development of a common strategy. It is precisely this common strategy which should be the inspirational goal for all the countermeasures to be taken.[5]

With these developments in mind, Chancellor Kohl had become one of the most determined proponents of a European police force, which he hoped – in contrast to many of his European colleagues at that time – would be endowed with wide-ranging operational powers to conduct cross-border operations. Some progress had been made in facilitating the identification, arrest and trial of criminal suspects through bilateral extradition and mutual legal assistance treaties, bilateral agreements on the transfer of evidence and by ratification by all the EU states of the 1988 United Nations Convention against Illicit Traffic in Narcotic Drugs and Psychotropic Substances, but the existence of juridical differences and the slowness of responses to rogatory letters (requests from one court to another to assist in evidence gathering) meant in practice that organized criminals were frequently able to evade justice for themselves and their ill-gotten gains even when, in principle, the country of sanctuary was well-disposed to assist a requesting nation. From the point of view of Italian investigators the absence from other European legislations of the offence of 'membership of a Mafia association' was a major obstacle to the arrest and extradition of Italian criminals abroad.

On 11 June 1992 the European Parliament in Strasbourg held a special commemorative session at which Giovanni Falcone was described as 'one of the most courageous combatants against organized crime' and his murderers 'vile assassins'. With 230 votes in favour and only two abstentions, a 14-point resolution was approved.[6] Describing the Mafia as a 'threat to the democratic state and to the physical and moral wellbeing of its citizens', it urged that:

- Italy and its democratic institutions should work to end the power of organized crime.
- Community legislation should be introduced to permit the creation of a European police force and the introduction of measures to combat Mafia-type organizations which would be applicable in all Member States.
- Political parties should expel anyone providing assistance to organized criminal groups.
- Specialized professional training should be provided for intelligence and investigative bodies.
- Magistrates should be provided with more resources and more specialized investigative tools.
- The independence of the judiciary from political power should be protected.
- The European Commission should ascertain the genuine willingness of the security and financial institutions in each country to combat money laundering.

On 29 July *Bundeskriminalamt* chief Hans-Ludwig Zachert paid tribute to judges Falcone and Borsellino, with whom he had worked closely, and called on the German Federal Parliament urgently to introduce more effective legislation against organized crime, in particular to permit electronic surveillance and telephone interception of those suspected of serious crime. In July 1992 a law on the protection of state's witnesses was passed with effect from the following January; in September money-laundering legislation came into force and shortly afterwards laws permitting electronic surveillance and the interception of telephone conversations were approved, although with significant restrictions. Public opinion had moved in favour of more rigorous legislation after the Palermo murders, and even more so in August following publication in *Der Spiegel*[7] of a 10-page dossier on the Mafia, citing a confidential 300-page BKA report on the activities of Italian organized crime in Germany between 1988 and 1991. A 27-page annex to the BKA report listed the principal Italian Mafia clans with the names of their corresponding 'families' resident in Germany. The BKA analysis summarized 88 investigations into Italian organized crime that had been conducted in Germany between 1989 and 1991. Of the cases where affiliation was clearly identified, 26 related to *Cosa Nostra*, 17 to the *Camorra*, 16 to the *'Ndrangheta* and 15 to the United Holy Crown.[8] Their activities included heroin and cocaine distribution, stolen vehicle trafficking, currency counterfeiting, extortion and money laundering. The chief prosecutor of Stuttgart, Helmut Krombacher, estimated that the *'Ndrangheta* had laundered over ten million Deutschmarks (approximately $6 million) in property and commercial investments in the *Land* of Swabia alone.

Countries outside the traditional cooperative framework began to take action against Italian fugitives: in early September, two *Cosa Nostra* members, Salvatore and Cesare Ciulla, were arrested in Chile; on 8 September, after repeated requests by the Italian authorities for the extradition from Venezuela of the brothers Paolo, Gaspare and Pasquale Cuntrera, wanted for years on charges of heroin trafficking and money laundering, they were arrested and sent back to Italy one week later. Three days before Falcone's murder, Venezuelan Justice Minister Mendoza Angulo had been in Rome for a meeting with Falcone and Claudio Martelli, his Italian counterpart, when the request had been repeated. The agreement to extradite may have been more than an act of contrition on the part of the Venezuelan authorities – after Borsellino's murder the US authorities had intimated that US extra-territorial legislation might be used in an operation to capture the brothers if Venezuela did not comply with the Italian request.[9]

On 18 September 1992 a meeting of Justice and Interior ministers was held under the auspices of the TREVI[a] Group in Brussels to discuss joint action against organized crime.The ministers agreed that the Mafia was a European and a global problem, and that there was an urgent need to approve measures against a range of activities such as money laundering. An Ad Hoc Working Group on Organized Crime was set up comprising representatives from law enforcement, the judiciary and the Justice and Home Affairs Ministries of the 12 Member States. The short-term aim was to reach bilateral agreements to facilitate mutual legal assistance and international collaboration such as had just been signed between France and Italy, whereby a judge from one country was seconded to the Justice Ministry of the other to assist in joint investigations.

The murders of the two Italian judges by no means marked the beginning of international collaboration against organized crime, but they served as a powerful catalyst which promoted it for the first time to a position of priority on many government agendas.

International action

The United Nations began to address issues of organized crime in September 1975 when the fifth United Nations Congress on the Prevention of Crime and the Treatment of Offenders, meeting in Geneva, discussed changes taking place in national and international criminality.[10] The dimension of 'crime as business' was recognized as a more serious form of threat than many traditional forms of crime. The sixth UN Congress, meeting in Caracas, Venezuela in 1980, added new elements to the international perception of organized crime with an emphasis on the abuse of power in political, social and economic sectors. The Seventh Congress, held in Milan in 1985, emphasized that multiple illicit operations carried out by international criminal networks represented a major challenge to national law enforcement and to international cooperation, against which national boundaries were ineffective. At this meeting the 'Milan Action Plan' was adopted. The Action Plan was intended as 'the collective endeavour of the international community to deal with a major problem whose disruptive and destabilizing impact on society is bound to increase unless concrete and constructive action is taken on an urgent and priority basis'. Meeting in 1990, the Eighth United Nations Congress studied the problem of organized crime in the

---

[a]   French acronym for Terrorism, Radicalism, Extremism and International Violence

light of the rapid political changes that had taken place and of the new dangers represented by the internationalization of criminality. Important new legal instruments were becoming available such as the 1988 United Nations Convention against Illicit Traffic in Narcotic Drugs and Psychtropic Substances, ratified in 1990, the Council of Europe Convention on Laundering, Search, Seizure and Confiscation of the Proceeds from Crime of 1990, the Model Treaty on Extradition and the Model Treaty on Mutual Assistance in Criminal Matters, also adopted by the United Nations General Assembly in 1990. As the name suggests, the model treaties were devised as blueprints for domestic legislation which any country could adapt according to the requirements of its legal traditions.

Three high-level meetings were convened in 1991, the Ad Hoc Expert Group Meeting on Strategies to Deal with Transnational Crime, held in May 1991 at Smolenice, an International Seminar on 'Practical Measures against Organized Crime' organized by the UN, Interpol and other agencies in Suzdal, the Russian Federation, in October and a Ministerial Meeting on the Creation of an Effective United Nations Crime Prevention and Criminal Justice Programme, convened in Versailles in November. The UN General Assembly of December 1991 adopted the proposed statement of principles and programme of action of the Versailles meeting and, with resolution 1992/1, established the Commission on Crime Prevention and Criminal Justice as a functional commission within the Economic and Social Council. At its first session the Commission requested the Secretary General to examine the possibility of coordinating multilateral efforts against laundering of the proceeds of crime and related offences and to propose means for providing technical assistance to requesting Member States in drafting legislation, training law-enforcement personnel, in developing regional, subregional and bilateral collaboration and in providing advice.

The decision to hold a World Ministerial Conference against Organized Transnational Crime was taken by the Economic and Social Council in 1993 at the recommendation of the Commission on Crime Prevention and Criminal Justice. Italy's proposal to host the event, which had been discussed and strongly supported by Falcone during his work with Justice Minister Claudio Martelli, was accepted. Its objective was to reach agreement on a series of measures against organized crime, including the establishment of a common perception of organized crime within the international community; the punishment, under national law, of participation in a criminal organization; confiscation of the proceeds of crime; the development of investigative methods to penetrate criminal organizations including specialized investigative units; the development of international agreements for extradition and mutual legal assistance and the practical improvement of existing model treaties in these fields; technical cooperation, including the international exchange of intelligence and the training of law-enforcement personnel; economic compensation for victims; and a study to assess the feasibility of elaborating international instruments, including conventions, against organized transnational crime. In anticipation of the ministerial conference a series of preparatory documents were drafted and high-level meetings held, including a conference on money laundering organized by the UN and the Italian government in June 1994 in the Italian town of Courmayeur. Conference participants identified seven areas as implementation priorities for an effective anti-money-laundering global strategy:

1. criminalization of the laundering of drug and non-drug criminal proceeds;
2. limitation of bank secrecy;
3. adherence to the 'know your customer' rule;
4. identification and reporting of suspicious transactions;
5. improved regulation of individuals involved in financial operations in a business or professional capacity;
6. asset confiscation;
7. workable international cooperation mechanisms.

The aim of an improved response to money laundering was to increase the risk of asset seizure and confiscation for the criminal and the criminal enterprise, and to raise the defences against crime for the legitimate economy.[11]

The World Ministerial Conference against Organized Transnational Crime, held in Naples from 21–23 November 1994, brought together 800 heads of government, ministers and high-level officials from 142 different countries to discuss the dangers posed by and the means of combating organized crime. Participants in the final plenary session voted unanimously in favour of a Political Declaration and a Global Action Plan designed to enhance international cooperation through a shared commitment to fighting a common enemy. The Declaration expressed 'deep concern' and 'alarm' about the 'dramatic growth' and 'global reach' of organized crime over the previous decade, which constituted 'a threat to the internal security and stability of sovereign States'. The signatories undertook on behalf of their governments to protect societies from organized crime 'through strict and effective legislative measures and operational instruments, always consistent with international human rights and fundamental freedoms'.

The Action Plan warned that countries must understand the nature and dynamics of criminal organizations in order to develop effective strategies against them, drawing on the knowledge of countries with experience in fighting organized crime. All countries should consider legislation which penalized criminal association or conspiracy, incorporating 'safeguards against corruption, intimidation and violence'. Substantive and procedural legislation should be aligned to permit international cooperation at investigative, prosecutorial and judicial levels; countries should introduce measures which 'encourage the cooperation and testimony of members of organized crime groups including adequate protection programmes for witnesses and their families' in order to overcome 'the criminal code of silence and intimidation'.

In a section entirely devoted to money laundering, effective legislation was recommended for countries where it was weak or lacking. Significantly, attention was not focused merely on reactive or repressive measures against the disguising of criminal profits but on preventive measures which would reinforce 'transparency and integrity' and rely on 'high ethical standards in public administration, the business sector, financial institutions and relevant professions'.

Education and training were given a high profile in the Action Plan, both at a general level, 'to create a culture of morality and legality and raise public awareness regarding the effects of organized crime', and also at investigative levels. The UN would assist by means of model legislation and by ensuring that developing countries were given financial and other forms of assistance.

Italy proposed the setting-up of a special task force in the form of a roving inspectorate to analyse the areas most vulnerable to international organized crime and to draw up a list of priorities for appropriate technical and legislative reform. The long-term Italian aim was the establishment of an antimafia college for the training of senior investigators, to be located in Palermo or Naples.

The Italian and Latin-American delegates to the Naples conference declared themselves in favour of an agreement in principle to draw up a new UN treaty against transnational organized crime, although this met with opposition from most of the industrialized countries, including Australia, the US and the UK, on grounds of excessive cost and dubious efficacy.

The General Assembly of the United Nations approved the Naples Political Declaration and Global Action Plan against Organized Transnational Crime with resolution 49/159 on 24 December 1994.

After Naples, the Crime Prevention and Criminal Justice Division of the UN (now called Centre for International Crime Prevention of the Office for Drug Control and Crime Prevention) began to develop a structured programme of activities to promote the full implementation of the Naples Political Declaration and Global Action Plan. The Centre collects and analyses information provided by Member States and relevant organizations; it provides assistance to countries with specific needs, ascertains the status of international cooperation in the field and encourages the strengthening of national criminal justice systems to deal with new and sophisticated forms of crime. A central repository of information on legislation, regulatory measures, organizational structures designed to prevent and monitor organized transnational crime, and bilateral and multilateral cooperation agreements was set up in 1997.[12]

Member States' views on the desirability and feasibility of a UN convention against organized crime were formally sought. The most problematic issues concerned agreement on an appropriate definition of organized crime, the list of offences that would be included and finding the resources to draw up and implement the convention. The text of a draft framework convention was presented by Poland at the 51st session of the General Assembly in 1996 and this was followed up by high-level meetings in Palermo in April 1997, Warsaw in February 1998, Buenos Aires in September 1998 and Vienna in January 1999, which further elaborated on the draft convention and its additional protocols. Delegates to the Palermo conference stated:

> With respect to the effectiveness and scope of such a convention, a clear and specific definition of organized crime would be essential. The definition could consist of two parts. The first part could address the special features of organized crime that made it a particularly dangerous form of crime and differentiated it from other types of criminal activity. [...] the second part of the definition could reflect the types of criminal activity and the fact that those crimes, when committed by organized criminal groups, were more serious and therefore warranted the priority attention of the international community. [...] the definition would increase in importance if an obligation to criminalize organized crime was provided for by the convention.[13]

The types of criminal activity to be considered for inclusion were:

(a)   fraud, including advance fee fraud;
(b)   money laundering;
(c)   extortion and usury;
(d)   kidnapping;
(e)   crime involving computer or other technology;
(f)   illicit trafficking in children;
(g)   murder and infliction of injury;
(h)   trafficking in illegal immigrants.

The intergovernmental group meeting in Warsaw in February 1998 moved the process a step further: 'There was broad consensus on the desirability of a convention against transnational organized crime. [...] There was unreserved confirmation of the commitment of the international community to devote priority attention to developing such a convention and ensuring its full implementation.'[14]

There were two possible ways in which the criminal offences to be covered by the convention could be approached. One was to list all the possible criminal activities in which criminal organizations were likely to engage. This was considered rather restrictive in scope and might exclude emerging forms of criminality, although the need to deal with specific offences could be dealt with by additional protocols which could be negotiated separately without affecting the overall effectiveness of the convention. An alternative approach was to consider the seriousness of the offence on the basis of the penalty foreseen. It was agreed that the convention should include practical measures concerning judicial co-operation, mutual assistance in criminal matters, extradition, law-enforcement cooperation, witness protection and technical assistance. It should expand the predicate offences for money laundering and should include provisions concerning the obligations of states to confiscate illicitly acquired assets and regulate bank secrecy. There was strong opposition to a 'serious crimes convention' as opposed to an instrument focused on organized crime.

The working definition of organized crime was that proposed in Article 1 of the draft text presented by Poland:[15] 'group activities of three or more persons, with hierarchical links or personal relationships, which permit their leaders to earn profits or control territories or markets, internal or foreign, by means of violence, intimidation or corruption, both in furtherance of criminal activity and to infiltrate the legitimate economy, in particular by [...] ' followed by a list of 'typical' activities.

Closely linked to the possible efficacy of a UN convention against organized crime is the issue of extradition. The Intergovernmental Expert Group on Extradition, set up to monitor the relevance and applicability of the UN Model Treaty on Extradition, reported on progress in that field in December 1996.[16] The meeting was hosted by the International Institute of Higher Studies in Criminal Sciences in Siracusa, Sicily, which in October 1998 was chosen by the DNA *(Direzione Nazionale Antimafia)*, the antimafia prosecution service, as its scientific partner in matters relating to international cooperation in the fight against organized crime. The report concluded that the principal obstacles to extradition arose from: clarity (or lack of it) in procedures; problems relating to dual criminality (when a crime in one jurisdiction is not defined as a crime in another); the political offence exception (when a country refuses to extradite on the grounds that the crime for which the requesting country seeks extradition was committed for political motives); conflicting claims of jurisdictions (several countries may seek extradition of the same individual); non-extradition of nationals (countries refuse to extradite their own citizens whatever the crime); differences in evidentiary standards and burdens.

The problem of organized criminality has continued to feature prominently on the agenda of the United Nations and of the political summits of the most industrialized nations. The declared goal of all international initiatives is to 'equalize the risks' to criminal organizations across countries and regions such that eventually there are no safe havens in which criminals can enjoy impunity. In 1995 Cambodia was described as one such sanctuary, where, because of the lack of extradition treaties with other countries, between 150 and 300 of the 2000 most wanted criminals sought through Interpol were thought to be residing.[17]

The Group of Seven most industrialized countries (now G8 including the Russian Federation) set up a Financial Action Task Force in 1989 to encourage and monitor progress in anti-money-laundering procedures. FATF published a list of 40 Recommendations the following year which, with some updating, have remained the text book on regulatory controls to facilitate the identification, seizing and confiscation of criminal assets. The 40 Recommendations complement the money-laundering provisions contained in the 1988 Vienna Convention and those in the 1988 Declaration of Principles formulated by the Basle Committee on Banking Regulations and Supervisory Practices. FATF is now a part of OECD and comprises 26 countries, plus the EU and the Cooperation Council of the Gulf States.

In 1995, the Group of Seven meeting in Halifax, Canada, agreed that 'transnational criminal organizations are a growing threat to the security of our nations. They undermine the integrity of financial systems, breed corruption and weaken emerging democracies and developing countries around the world.' A Senior Experts Group on Transnational Organized Crime set up by the G-7 has met regularly since 1995 to examine issues relating to international action against organized crime and to identify the optimum investigative tools to tackle its most dangerous aspects such as money laundering, arms trafficking and illegal immigrant smuggling. The Senior Experts Group developed a series of 40 Recommendations along the lines of the FATF recommendations, which were endorsed by the G-8 summit held in Lyons, France, in 1996. They deal with the problems of international cooperation – judicial collaboration, extradition, cooperation between police forces and money laundering. Specifically, they underline the need to promote:

- international agreements to protect state's witnesses or other persons at risk;
- the use of international agreements on liaison officers, facilitating their insertion into host police forces;
- international collaboration in investigations involving electronic surveillance, controlled deliveries and undercover agents;
- the extension of the offence of money laundering to a greater number of predicate crimes and the establishment of agreements which allow the exchange of information in this area at international level;
- establishment of arrangements to monitor financial flows and to identify suspicious transactions, and to permit the exchange of information thus acquired at international level.[18]

The Senior Experts Group prepared an inventory of conventions concerned with specific forms of criminality and on mutual legal assistance, as well as an inventory of international organizations dealing with transnational crime. An extensive questionnaire asked for information on each Member's domestic legislation concerning organized crime.

The G-8 leaders meeting in Birmingham, England, in May 1998 promised support for efforts to negotiate a UN convention by the year 2000. They also backed a ten-point plan relating to international organized crime, including Internet-based crime, money laundering (with improved regulation of offshore centres), asset confiscation, corruption, the illegal manufacture and trafficking of firearms, the smuggling of human beings and environmental crime. Agreement would be sought on a legal framework for obtaining, presenting and preserving electronic data as evidence and on sharing such evidence with international partners, while maintaining appropriate privacy protection.[19]

Regional action – Europe

The European Union

The Ad Hoc Working Group on Organized Crime

The TREVI Group, comprising the Justice and Interior Ministers of the European Community, set up the Ad Hoc Working Group on Organized Crime in September 1992 as a direct response to the murders of judges Falcone and Borsellino. The Group prepared two reports – in May and in November 1993 – which reviewed available information on the extent and nature of organized crime within the Community. A mechanism for collecting and analysing information relating to organized crime was adopted by the Council in November 1993.[20] It was agreed that for a criminal group to fall into the category of 'organized crime' at least six of the following characteristics should be present, the first three in all circumstances:

1. collaboration between two or more people;
2. suspected of having committed serious penal offences;
3. operates for profit and/or power;
4. operates over a fairly long or indefinite time period;
5. has some form of discipline or control;
6. specific tasks are assigned to each individual;
7. operates on an international scale;
8. resorts to violence or other means of intimidation;
9. utilizes commercial or commercial-style structures;
10. engages in money laundering;
11. exercises influence over political circles, the media, public administration, the judiciary or the economy.

The Ad Hoc Working Group made a series of recommendations for further action.[21] They included calls for:

- an annual report to be prepared on the level of and trends in organized crime;

- greater use of non-criminal measures such as controls over the financial sector;
- greater cooperation on extradition;
- greater support to non-Member States;
- greater exchanges of information and personnel to increase knowledge of other Member States' systems;
- progress towards the establishment of Europol, the European Information System and the Customs Information System and to identifying opportunities for more formal police and customs co-operation;
- the inclusion in all Member States' criminal legislation and judicial procedures of specific provisions, including measures relating to criminal sanctions, confiscation and prosecution time limits;
- regular exchange of information on the effectiveness of relevant national laws;
- further study of ways of improving measures against money laundering and of the effects of new technology on interception of communications;
- exchange of experience on protection of witnesses and others involved in the administration of justice.

Following on from the work of the Ad Hoc Working Group on Organized Crime, a conference was held under the auspices of the European Union on drugs and organized crime with countries of Eastern and Central Europe (Bulgaria, Poland, Romania, Czech Republic, Slovakia, Hungary) in Berlin in September 1994 during the German presidency of the EU. By the final Declaration of the conference, ministers from EU and non-EU states committed themselves to closer cooperation, exchanges of liaison officers and experts, accession to key international conventions and to the examination of particular difficulties arising in respect of drug trafficking, trade in nuclear material, traffic in people and cross-border theft.[22] As part of the ongoing process of cooperation, Central and Eastern European ministers have continued to meet their EU counterparts and a pre-accession pact on a common approach to organized crime has been drawn up with EU applicant countries.

Europol

Under the terms of the Maastricht Treaty, signed in 1992 and ratified the following year, more emphasis was given to formal structures for co-operation between Member States of the European Union in the Third 'Pillar' or Title VI of the Treaty, covering matters of Justice and Home

Affairs. One of the new structures created under article K1 of the Title VI process was the Europol Drugs Unit (EDU), which began to operate on 1 January 1994 on a limited basis of bilateral exchanges of information and intelligence. With the entry into force of the Europol Convention on 1 October 1998, Europol has been empowered to:

- exchange operational information and intelligence between two or more Member States;
- make operational and strategic analyses;
- support operational law-enforcement activities such as controlled deliveries and give other forms of support to the Member States such as training;
- draft strategic reports.

Europol's brief covers illicit drug trafficking; illegal immigration; trafficking in human beings; illicit trafficking in vehicles; trafficking in radioactive and nuclear substances; and money-laundering activities relating to the foregoing. Terrorism is to be added from October 2000. Important modifications to Europol's sphere of operations were envisaged in the Amsterdam Treaty, which came into force on 1 May 1999. Title VI of the Treaty, article 30, section 2, states that the Council of the European Union shall promote cooperation through Europol and shall, in particular, within a period of five years after the date of entry into force of the Treaty:

(a) Enable Europol to facilitate and support the preparation, and to encourage the coordination and carrying out, of specific investigative actions by the competent authorities in the Member States, including operational actions of joint teams comprising representatives of Europol in a support capacity;

(b) Adopt measures allowing Europol to ask the competent authorities of the Member States to conduct and coordinate their investigations in specific cases and to develop specific expertise which may be put at the disposal of Member States to assist them in investigating cases of organized crime;

(c) Promote liaison arrangements between prosecuting/investigating officials specializing in the fight against organized crime in close cooperation with Europol;

(d) Establish a research, documentation and statistical network on cross-border crime.

To what extent Europol will assume these tasks and obligations was not certain in mid-1999 – these powers would come close to endowing it with the operational capacity which some EU members, including the UK, have hitherto rejected, and would involve modifications to the Europol Convention and a reconsideration of the immunity protocol which functionaries currently enjoy.

The EU Action Plan to Combat Organized Crime

The need to undertake concrete action against organized crime at Community level was reaffirmed during the EU summit in Dublin in December 1996 which tasked a High-Level Group with responsibility for drafting an Action Plan against organized crime. The High-Level Group completed its work in April 1997 with the elaboration of 15 Political Guidelines and 30 Specific Recommendations, together with a proposed timetable for each. The Guidelines and Recommendations in this document, JAI 14 of 28 April 1997, address the full range of organized criminal activity in the EU (see Annex). They derive from two fundamental premises – that judicial cooperation needs to be brought up to a level comparable with police cooperation and that the driving force behind organized crime is the pursuit of financial gain. Among the more innovative proposals are the setting-up of a judicial network for exchanges of information, the creation of the offence of participation in a criminal organization, the development of procedures to prevent members or associates of organized crime groups from participating in public tenders or from receiving public grants or subsidies and the development of evaluation mechanisms for measures undertaken. Rapid completion of the texts of new draft conventions on mutual legal assistance and on corruption was urged. A Multidisciplinary Working Group was set up to oversee implementation of the initiatives.

Progress on the 30-point plan has been made, although at a pace considerably slower than the time-scale contained in the recommendations. A draft Joint Action was adopted by the Council of the European Union in March 1998 which, subject to parliamentary scrutiny in each Member State, must be implemented. This requires Member States to make it an offence 'for a person, present in its territory, to participate in a criminal organization, irrespective of the location in the Union where the organization is concentrated or is carrying out its criminal activity'. A criminal organization was defined (article 1) as

a lasting, structured association of more than two persons, acting in concert with a view to committing crimes or other offences which are punishable by deprivation of liberty or a detention order of a maximum of at least four years or a more serious penalty, whether such crimes or offences are an end in themselves or a means of obtaining material benefits and, if necessary, of improperly influencing the operation of public authorities.

According to the original timetable, the Joint Action should have been adopted by the Council before the end of 1997; the deadline was extended to the end of March 1998 but in November 1998 no Member State had taken concrete action to modify its domestic laws as a direct consequence. Progress towards the signing of an EU Convention on Mutual Assistance in Criminal Matters was slow and there was no immediate prospect of its coming into force. A detailed questionnaire on the efficacy of Member States' anti-money-laundering measures prepared by the Multidisciplinary Group on Organized Crime in November 1997 had not been circulated to Member States for completion.[23]

The Schengen Convention

The Schengen Convention was drawn up in 1985 by Germany, France, the Benelux countries, Portugal, Italy and Spain, but only came into effect in 1995. Italy became a full member in April 1998. Participating countries have abolished internal border controls and, in compensation, have imposed stronger controls at external frontiers. A Schengen Information System based in Strasbourg keeps a record of 'undesirable aliens' who are barred from entry to the countries in the group. It also stores information on refugees, asylum seekers, crime, firearms and people under surveillance. Provisional arrest and extradition procedures between Schengen countries partially circumvent the rigidity of those based on an exchange of rogatory letters. Within specific limits, law-enforcement officers are permitted to cross borders in 'hot pursuit' and in surveillance of suspected criminals.

Italy – bilateral agreements and initiatives

From the autumn of 1992 onwards Italy intensified collaboration against organized crime with existing partners and opened up to new inter-locutors; by 1994 there were 30 bilateral agreements with 25 countries on organized crime. Since the DIA's inception in 1992 the most prolific international contacts for Italian law enforcement have been with the German BKA – in 1995 it accounted for 33 per cent of all international exchanges of information, followed by US law-enforcement bodies at

24.3 per cent. Overall, European contacts amounted to 64 per cent of all exchanges, North America 28 per cent and the rest of the world 8 per cent. Between 1994 and 1995 cooperation rose by 51.6 per cent with Europe, 25.4 per cent with North America and 9.6 per cent with the rest of the world.[24] The following examples of bilateral collaboration are by no means exhaustive, but are among the most important.

North America

Historically, the most intense form of Italian bilateral collaboration – against crime and against organized crime – has been with the United States of America. An Italian–American Working Group on Organized Crime set up in 1984 to coordinate investigations into Mafia activities spanning both countries contributed to the successful prosecution of Italian and US *mafiosi* in the Pizza Connection trial of 1985. Since then, four technical groups have developed a strategic programme which defines the procedures for judicial collaboration and police cooperation, sets guidelines for the exchange of information and intelligence and works to improve procedures on extradition, the application of confiscation orders and access to collaborators.[25] A crucial factor has been the existence of similar laws to deal with organized crime in both countries. The US Racketeer Influenced and Corrupt Organizations law (RICO) makes it an offence for a person to participate in the affairs of an enterprise through a pattern of racketeering activity, a term which in practice can be applied to virtually all serious criminal activity. The provisions of the Italian *Rognoni–La Torre* law of 1982 were modelled directly on this statute. Italy's laws on witness protection and collaboration were also borrowed from the United States, and several Italian collaborators who had given evidence in US trials and for whom Italy was considered too dangerous were taken into the US protection service. The sense of greater security that Italian collaborators have under US protection has facilitated a more continuous form of collaboration.

After the Palermo murders, the FBI Director at the time, William Sessions, and his successor Louis Freeh, made various forms of assistance available to the Italian authorities, from technology to training. Italy regularly sends officers to the FBI and to the Drug Enforcement Administration to follow joint cases.

One of the most important joint collaborative projects since 1992 has been developed between the DIA and the US Immigration and Naturalization Service, known as Project INSIDIA. Its aim is to study the records of any Italians who have committed crimes against US immigration laws, to establish whether any have been reported, charged with or convicted of crimes relating to Mafia association. By 1994, 1469 names of offending Italians had emerged, although it was thought the number could rise to a total of 60 000.[26] Of those identified, 20 had a criminal record in Italy, of whom 10 had been reported for Mafia association. Among the 20, 12 were fugitives from Italian justice.[27]

Other joint DIA–INS projects include: a study of all prisoners of Italian nationality awaiting deportation, known as IHP (International Hearing Program), from which an initial batch of 80 names was given to the DIA from New York prisons; a project to study the threat from the Apulian Mafia, the United Holy Crown, in the USA;[28] and an investigation into a group of Calabrians linked to the *'Ndrangheta* who had opened a chain of pizzerias in New York State with the presumed aim of laundering money behind an apparently legitimate front.[29]

Collaboration between the DIA and the FBI is more extensive and involves a constant exchange of information about the strategies and activities of the principal Mafia families on both sides of the Atlantic. Joint meetings are held on a regular basis in Rome, while the DIA has a permanent representative at FBI headquarters in Washington DC. The international money-laundering investigation known as 'Operation Green Ice' which culminated in September 1992 (see Chapter 4) was a direct result of close Italo–American cooperation. Information gained in the USA also contributed to the arrest of *Cosa Nostra* leader Leoluca Bagarella in 1995.[30] A project called GIANO has been set up to assess the extent of Italian criminality in the USA, in particular with regard to money-laundering and drug-trafficking activities. From an examination of 42 088 Italians with a criminal record in the United States, it transpired that 211 had been reported in Italy for crimes of association, and of these, 7 for Mafia association. Of the 211, 50 were fugitives from Italian justice.[31]

The Drug Enforcement Administration has provided training on data analysis for intelligence purposes for DIA officers and, together with the DIA and with the Italian Central Antidrugs Directorate, has been involved in many joint investigations. 'Operation Dinero' was set up by the DEA in 1992 to trace new drug and money-laundering routes from Colombia through North America, Spain and Italy, and involved the setting-up of a bogus bank in the British dependent territory of Anguilla. It led to the arrest of more than a hundred suspected traffickers in Spain, the US and Italy in December 1994 and the seizure of $33 million-worth of assets, nine metric tons of cocaine, several tons of cannabis and a freightload of arms destined for Croatia. A more recent focus of DEA/DIA collaboration has consisted of studying large groups of *Camorra* affiliates involved in money-laundering operations between Italy and Guatemala.[32]

The US Customs Service has collaborated with the DIA in money-laundering investigations concerning the *Camorra* and the United Holy Crown in Los Angeles and other major US cities. It has also helped the DIA with an investigation into a large sum which had been illicitly obtained from the Sicilian Region and invested in the US by individuals contiguous with organized crime.[33] The Customs Service was also helping with Italian enquiries into the death of Italian banker Roberto Calvi.[34] Finally, the DIA has worked with the US Secret Service on the involvement of the Italian Mafia in the counterfeiting and global distribution of counterfeit dollar banknotes.[35]

Several Italo–US investigations into Mafia activities abroad have extended beyond the national frontiers of the two countries, such as the 'Siderno Group' project, which involves collaboration between the FBI, the INS, the DEA, the US Customs Service, the Royal Canadian Mounted Police (RCMP) and the Australian Federal Police (AFP). The Siderno group – so named for its origins in the Calabrian town of Siderno – has been involved in extensive drug and money-laundering operations in the US, Canada and Australia.[36] Periodic meetings take place of Siderno group investigators, and while the Italian side of operations has been virtually wound up, work continues in Canada to trace and seize the assets of the group members and to identify possible investments in the Canadian economy. At the end of 1997 a joint investigation was studying the case of three Calabrians murdered in Canada in the previous 12 months, and the possible responsibility of three suspects, also Calabrian. A DIA agent was seconded to the RCMP to help in this investigation.[37]

Australia

The Italian authorities collaborate closely with Australian counterparts, especially in investigations into 'Ndrangheta members suspected of drug trafficking and money laundering. The Australian financial crimes unit *Austrac* has made an important contribution to the identification of illicit financial transaction routes. There have also been contacts and agreements to exchange information with the National Crime Authority (NCA), which has the task of coordinating all organized crime investigations in Australia. In 1994 the NCA asked the DIA to send officers who could be used as undercover agents, and this invitation was being studied for its legal implications.[38] A joint Italo–Australian project called AUXILIA carried out with the NCA, AFP and DIA revealed the presence in Australia of around 3000 Italians who had faced criminal charges. Among them 52 had a criminal record of Mafia association and 20 had been charged with association to commit a crime. Three were fugitives from Italian justice. A further 1749 names supplied by the AFP underwent a similar process of cross-checking, and the project concluded at the end of 1997.

South America

The countries of South America were for many years a sanctuary and operational base for prominent Italian *mafiosi*, but since 1992 the situation has improved significantly, with numerous suspected criminals being returned to Italian jurisdiction. In addition to the three Cuntrera brothers, arrested and extradited in September 1992 after their Venezuelan citizenship proved to have been obtained under false pretences, the Venezuelan authorities arrested *Camorra* member Giuseppe Autorino, held to be a dangerous fugitive on the run from arms and murder charges, in July 1994. In mid-1997 some 30 requests for the arrest of Italian criminal suspects were awaiting Venezuelan approval. The suspected *Cosa Nostra* affiliate Gaetano Giuseppe Santangelo was arrested in Brazil on charges of drug-money laundering in early 1995. He had escaped from Italy after being found guilty of murder in 1976. A key member of the Siderno Group, Roberto Pannunzi, was arrested in the Colombian city of Medellin in 1994 and was extradited a year later; a leader of the powerful Nirta family of the *'Ndrangheta* was extradited from Bogotà in 1998.

In October 1995 a bilateral agreement to cooperate against organized crime, terrorism and drug trafficking was ratified between Italy and Chile, following discussions begun at a meeting in October 1992. A bilateral committee was set up, comprising representatives from the Foreign Affairs and Interior Ministries and from law-enforcement bodies. In January 1996 a similar agreement to cooperate in the fight against terrorism, drug trafficking and organized crime was ratified between the governments of Italy and Argentina. This too was the conclusion of an agreement formulated at a meeting in October 1992 in the aftermath of the Palermo atrocities.

Eastern Europe

Italy has had a bilateral cooperation agreement with Russia on organized crime since September 1993. At the signing meeting in Moscow between Italian Interior Minister Nicola Mancino and his counterpart Victor Erin, it was acknowledged that there were contacts between criminal organizations in both countries. A cooperation agreement was formalized in May 1993 between the Interior Ministers of Italy and Ukraine to regularize counterpart arrangements between police forces. In 1996 agreements were signed between Italy and Eastern and Central European countries and with the Baltic states to collaborate on organized crime, the Balkan and Baltic zones being important bridges between the Mafias of East and West. Hungarian and Romanian police have also assisted the Italian authorities in identifying and subsequently arresting wanted criminals.

Western Europe

Germany

German investigations into organized crime have multiplied in recent years. In 1994, BKA investigations into organized crime involved 85 different nationalities, with Germans accounting for only 40 per cent of the total. Estimated annual turnover from organized criminal activities in that year was estimated to be around DM3.5 billion (around $2 billion).[39] In 1996 German law-enforcement authorities conducted 845 investigations into organized crime, of which 489 had been initiated in the current year. For almost 50 000 criminal offences 3000 arrests were made.[40]

A DIA–BKA Working Group known as AGIG has had as its objective the collection and exchange of information on Italian organized crime in Germany. A study was made of the judicial positions of all Italian nationals resident in Germany with a criminal record – a total of 34 963. Of these, 528 had been reported in Italy for Mafia-type association; 120 were considered to be of 'extreme interest' to the authorities from the point of view of their contacts and activities, while 24 had been the object of restrictive measures decreed by judicial authorities and transmitted via international arrest warrants. The 120 were the subject of detailed investigations, with reference to the individual's position within the organization, the clan to which he belonged and its past activities, his tax position and whether his name had ever been notified in other police enquiries. All these data were cross-referenced in the search for connections between Italians resident in Germany and criminal partnerships in Italy. The results of the research provided definitive proof of the extensive penetration of Mafia-type groups in Germany.[41] A second stage has begun to identify and seize Italian Mafia assets in Germany.

Collaboration between the DIA and the BKA since 1992, supported by input from the police forces of the German *Länder*, has revealed *Cosa Nostra* activities in Mainz, Koblenz, Freiburg, Esslingen, Metzingen, Ludwigshafen, Frankfurt, Kassel and Heidelberg. *Camorra* members from Quindici, near Avellino, were identified in Stuttgart and others in Wiesbaden and Düsseldorf.[42] Several arrests of the Calabrian Latella clan, fugitives from Italian justice, were also due to a joint BKA–DIA operation.

According to the DIA, the *'Ndrangheta* has built up an economic empire in Germany, with its members well integrated into middle-class German life and with political contacts developed in the adopted country.

An intelligence group was established in July 1994 at BKA headquarters in Wiesbaden comprising representatives of the BKA, DIA, FBI, RMCP and the Russian Interior Ministry division against organized crime, HVOK, later called GUOP. A dedicated encrypted fax line was set up linking Washington, Rome, Wiesbaden and Moscow. From 1995 the Group has included the UK's National Criminal Intelligence Service (NCIS). The Six Nation Group was formed as a response to the expansion of Russian criminal groups in North America and Western Europe, with the aim of sharing information on specific criminals and criminal groups. Collaboration has led to the dismantling by the BKA of an organization operating at international level in the smuggling of drugs, cigarettes and alcohol, and the arrest of one of its operatives in Italy who was subsequently extradited to Germany.[43]

Belgium

The Belgian authorities have collaborated with Italian counterparts since the late 1980s, when it was discovered that a restored castle in Charleroi owned by *Cosa Nostra* boss Pasquale Cuntrera was being used as an organizational base by *Cosa Nostra* and the *Camorra* to move large numbers of illegal African immigrants into Belgium and northern France.[44] A consignment of 600 kilogrammes of cocaine seized near the French town of Perpignan in September 1992 destined for Milan was sent by a Brussels-based branch of *Cosa Nostra*. Since that time, a project named BICO, similar to the AGIG group in Germany, has identified 25 665 Italians responsible for committing crimes in Belgium, including a 'significant presence' of Italians linked to 'a vast criminal organization connected to members of the United Holy Crown who had been murdered in Taranto'.[45] A joint investigation into money laundering in Belgium has also been set up.

France

France was one of three countries – with the Netherlands and the UK – to set up a parliamentary commission of enquiry into organized crime after the events of 1992. The French Antimafia Commission was created on 7 August 1992 and consisted of 25 deputies and 25 senators. Its findings were published in a report prepared by the Commission chairman, François D'Aubert, which was approved unanimously on 26 January 1993.[46] According to the French law-enforcement officers who gave evidence to the Commission, 'organized crime' in France was 'disorganized' and, with the exception of Corsica, the Paris suburbs, the Marseilles area and to a lesser degree around Bordeaux, there existed only isolated and occasional cases. An Italian state's witness had said there existed a *Cosa Nostra decina* (group of ten 'men of honour') in Grenoble which was linked to the Sommatino clan in Caltanissetta. Most of the Italians resident in France – 294 000, of which 37 900 Sicilian – were held to be extremely well-integrated and law-abiding. Of the Italian fugitives in France, *Camorra* boss Michele Zaza was the most notorious. Zaza had served a three-year prison sentence for cigarette smuggling and then was freed by the French authorities with the requirement to report each day at police headquarters in the provençal town of Villneuve-Loubet where he lived. He had been convicted in his absence on 13 different counts in Italy but could not be extradited because it had not been proved that he had participated in a criminal band (an *association des malfaiteurs*) in France, and, because the offence of Mafia association contained in the Italian request did not exist under French law, there was no dual criminality. The Commission noted that Zaza had set up some 30 companies in Europe, the US, Panama and the Franco-Dutch dependency of Saint Martin. He had bought up five container and transportation companies in Marseilles from individuals on the verge of bankruptcy and was thought to own several shipping companies including the Dutch registered Nordana Lines (which was still functioning). According to the Commission,

> The Mafia periodically tries to establish bridgeheads in France. [...] Michele Zaza is perhaps the best example of these attempts at colonization. Indeed, Zaza has tried to create along the *Côte d'Azur* a veritable criminal organization employing the Mafia techniques of corrupting public officials and taking control of financial intermediaries, without however going to the lengths of assassination.

Camorra families linked to Zaza were thought to be laundering profits by means of investments in private health clinics and through casinos on the Côte d'Azur, where 85 per cent of takings were of Italian origin (Italian cheques could be changed directly into chips). Further organized crime involvement was suspected in the areas of golf-course construction, property agencies, public works, waste disposal, slot machines, construction and a variety of other activities involving high cash turnover.

Concern was expressed at the existence of tax havens in territory under French influence – Monaco, where France shared authority with the

Principality – Andorra – shared with the Spanish – and the island of Saint Martin where, it was alleged, the Dutch imposed no financial regulations whatsoever.

The Commission studied the difficulties under French law of extraditing wanted *mafiosi* to Italy. Articles 265 and 266 of the French penal code punished the *association des malfaiteurs* when it was directed at the preparation of any crime against persons or things and involved a number of specific crimes which included drug trafficking, but excluded most types of financial crime. Since the adoption of a new penal code on 1 September 1993, the *association des malfaiteurs* is 'constituted by any group, formed or agreed to be established with the aim of the preparation, characterized by one or several material facts, of one or several offences or by one or several crimes punishable with 10 years of imprisonment'.

The association has three elements: firstly, the agreement (*entente*) between several persons to form an association to engage in illicit activities. This requires overt acts of preparation, for example a meeting – 'the things that must be in place before the crime can be committed'. The second element is the purpose (*but*) of the association, the aim of committing crimes (of an unspecified nature) which carry a penalty of (at least) ten years. The third element – the existence of a general intention (*élément intentionnel*) – does not require that every member knows about or takes part in every criminal activity, but that an individual who participates in the association is fully aware of its purpose and of the fact that illicit activities are being undertaken.

The Commission decided not to press for a change of the law and concluded that there was no need for the adoption of special antimafia legislation in France. Nonetheless, it was necessary to maintain constant vigilance since the Mafia

> [...] is a model for organized crime of the future. [...] France enjoys no immunity with regard to Mafia organizations even if the strength of the State and the civilization of its people have until now limited the enterprises of the multinationals of crime. There is no part of our territory or of our economic life that may not be of some interest to such versatile organizations.

Cooperation between France and Italy in Mafia investigations deepened after 1992. 'Ndrangheta member Domenico Libri was arrested in September 1992 in Marseilles and was subsequently extradited to Italy. He had formed a series of front companies in the form of estate agencies and service companies which had been used to purchase land in the Finistère area of north-west France and, allegedly, to launder illicit profits. In March 1993 Michele Zaza was rearrested and a year later was finally extradited to prison in Italy, where in July 1994 he died of a heart attack. In May 1993 a joint police operation entitled 'Green Sea' led to the arrest of 27 *Camorra* members accused of taking part in an international wholesale meat conspiracy involving France, Belgium and Italy. The network used the services of an import–export agency opened up in Menton, allegedly run by Zaza's collaborator in the attempted Menton casino takeover, who was rearrested.

In March 1994 a meeting was held in Aix en Provence between French and Italian antimafia judges to discuss Mafia penetration of Corsica, the Côte d'Azur and the department of Rhône Alpes. The Italians warned that the Mafia was still expanding on the Côte d'Azur and that, despite successes against the military strength of *Cosa Nostra*, its wealth was still substantially intact. It was agreed at the meeting to intensify coopera-tion, particularly on money laundering. France, like Italy, had extended the range of predicate crimes for money laundering in 1993 in line with European treaty recommendations. Since then, collaboration in asset-tracing investigations concerning Italians in the South of France has been pursued through *Tracfin*, the French financial crime investigation unit, and UCRAM, the Coordination Unit of Research into the Mafia, set up in December 1992. At a meeting between DIA and *Tracfin* representa-tives in March 1996, a comprehensive project was begun to identify the channels used for money laundering by Mafia groups in France. *Tracfin* agreed to give DIA details of suspicious disclosures in order to verify these connections.[47] Several Catania members of *Cosa Nostra* were investigated for involvement in complex financial money-laundering operations in France and in Monaco. Other investigations were under way into Mafia activities in Nice and other cities operating with groups from inside Italy.[48] In December 1997 a powerful *'Ndrangheta* boss, Natale Rosmini, was arrested in the Côte d'Azur resort of Juan les Pins.

Spain

Collaboration between Italian and Spanish police forces against organized crime is long-established, particularly in the area of drug traf-ficking, since considerable quantities of cocaine and cannabis resin have been distributed to Italy through Spain using Spanish-based Italian networks. Numerous Italian fugitives have been arrested and extradited to Italy, a procedure which has been simplified under the terms of the Schengen Convention.

Austria

Joint investigations carried out since 1992 by the DIA and the Austrian criminal police, EDOK, helped to identify a 'vast settlement' of Italians suspected of using Austria as a base for developing illicit trade with the Czech Republic. Out of more than 200 Italians resident in Austria with a criminal record, some were identified as Mafia suspects and two were arrested for trading in false bank certificates.[49] In 1993, Austria introduced a series of offences relating to the founding of, participation in and laundering the proceeds of criminal organizations.

Antimafia efforts in the UK since 1992

Increased concern in the United Kingdom after the 1992 Palermo murders and, more especially, about the influx of criminality from Eastern Europe, caused the House of Commons Home Affairs Committee to set up a formal inquiry in 1993. Its purpose was[50]

> to examine the extent of the threat within the United Kingdom from organized crime, including drug trafficking and related crime. [The Committee] will seek to establish the distinguishing features of organized crime and to ascertain the extent to which the problem can be tackled (a) by amendment of the law in the criminal, company and taxation and other fields, (b) by new or improved structures for the police and prosecuting and other authorities and (c) by other means. The Committee will examine the international aspect of organized crime and, in particular, how cooperation both between the Twelve and more widely might be improved.

The Committee sought evidence from representatives of official bodies and from academic experts in the UK, and visited Bonn, Amsterdam, the Hague and Rome to hear evidence from other European governments and police representatives.

Evidence presented to the Committee indicated that criminal activity in the UK was not dominated by large organized crime groups such as the Mafia, and that crime by such groups did not originate in the UK, but instead represented the 'tentacles' of organized crime overseas. The level of organized crime in the UK was judged to be 'relatively low' and did not display characteristics of the more sophisticated type 'such as power seeking, influence and corruption'. Nonetheless British drug traffickers had links to organized crime, and police evidence suggested that some 50–60 per cent of crime was drug-related. There was agreement that a significant share of the more organized criminal activity in the UK was linked to ethnic minority groups. The Italian Mafia was not thought to use the UK as a major base for operations, but it was active in a wide range of criminal activities such as money laundering in which London could be a significant centre.

Although there was little concrete evidence of a growth of organized criminal activity linked to Eastern Europe and the former Soviet Union, witnesses warned that the example of Germany had shown how quickly a situation could deteriorate. During 1993, the financial intelligence unit of the National Criminal Intelligence Service – the recipient body for suspicious disclosures – had identified 200 money-laundering cases which had Russian connections. Generally, it was felt that the UK was a target for international organized crime because of its sophisticated and stable financial institutions and that it was open to the risk of economic crime and fraud.

The British Bankers' Association had declined to comment on the possible amount of money laundered through UK banks. The National Criminal Intelligence Service referred to sums of £2.4 billion laundered per annum through the UK of which £1.75 billion went through the financial sector. Other sources gave the figure of criminally-generated money from both domestic and foreign criminality as between £2.5 billion and £4 billion.[51]

The effectiveness of the UK anti-money-laundering procedures was studied. Of the annual total of around 15 000 suspicious disclosures, some 5 per cent of reports generated new cases which could not have been generated without disclosure; a further 10–15 per cent added to pre-existing intelligence; 30 per cent were written off as unconnected to crime, leaving 50 per cent which related to funds the origin of which could not be determined. Taking into account the fact that not all arrests led to trials and convictions, it was suggested that it might take 1000 disclosures to convict a trafficker. A 'fast track' procedure to filter the most important disclosures had been established in the UK in the autumn of 1994. In the period up to 1992–93, the total sum of assets actually confiscated in a given year in relation to the sums ordered to be confiscated over a similar period was slightly over 30 per cent; in 1994–95 this had risen to nearer 60 per cent.

The Director of the National Criminal Intelligence Service described international cooperation against organized crime in 1994–95 as 'very slow' and 'extremely time-consuming'.[52] Two-thirds of all requests from abroad received by the UK Central Authority (the Home Office Unit responsible for coordinating incoming and outgoing requests for assistance) took over three months to process; of requests to foreign countries made by the UK, more than three-quarters took more than three months.[53] One of the most useful elements for police and customs cooperation was the drug liaison officer (DLO) scheme and this was particularly the case in Rome, where the DLO was also responsible for joint organized crime investigations.

The Committee noted an anomaly whereby the interception of mail or of telephone conversations required a warrant from the Home Secretary, whereas authority for electronic surveillance could be given by a Chief Constable. The situation changed from January 1999 when, according to Part III of the Police Act 1997, six commissioners for England and Wales were given responsibility for authorizing certain levels of intrusive surveillance (different legislation applies in Scotland). The authority of the Home Secretary remains necessary for the interception of communications. In neither case can the information acquired be used as evidence in court. From a prosecution point of view, this remains a major problem which law-enforcement officers hope will be resolved through a change in the law.

The Metropolitan Police Criminal Justice Protection Unit, responsible for the protection of witnesses who may be at risk, had dealt with fewer than ten cases in the period 1988–92, but protection had been sought for 45 persons in 1993 and 81 in the period from February to June 1994. Police officers and their families had also been threatened.

On the question of introducing the crime of participation in a criminal association into British legislation, police officers reported to the Home Affairs Committee that they sometimes found difficulty in instituting conspiracy proceedings against key organized crime figures who distanced themselves from the criminal activities carried out by junior members, but nonetheless enjoyed the profits from those crimes. It was thought this might be overcome by criminalizing the association between key figures and other members of a criminal enterprise, especially if it was coupled with indications of wealth without an apparent source of income. Under current legislation these indications fell short of supporting proceedings for conspiracy or other substantive offences.[54] In contrast, the Crown Prosecution Service felt that the laws on conspiracy were adequate for dealing with organized crime and that they knew of no case where a prosecution could not proceed because of the non-existence of such an offence.

The Home Affairs Committee completed its report with a series of recommendations, most of which were limited to the reinforcement of existing measures. It concluded, while the level of [organized] crime in the UK may be lower than in some other countries, it is nevertheless substantial and is probably growing [...] It must be understood that we are today faced with organized crime resourced to an hitherto unimaginable extent. So it must be recognized that organized crime can – by using these resources to internationalize its activities and to exploit every weakness in the system, and by using intimidation – take advantage of a criminal justice system which has evolved to meet the challenges of a lower level of essentially localized crime. If it should become apparent that serious and organized crime continues to grow and to threaten the very fabric of British society [...] Parliament would have to introduce stronger measures.

Three years on from these conclusions, several steps had been taken to strengthen the UK response to organized crime, in particular through the creation of the National Crime Squad (see below). But in the view of senior British investigators, there was no immediate prospect of the UK introducing the offence of participation in a criminal organization, despite the EU Joint Action, nor was the British Government likely to approve the increased powers for Europol envisaged in the Amsterdam Treaty.

The most radical legislative innovation being considered in 1999 was the introduction of wider civil forfeiture powers, which would enable a court to order the confiscation of the instruments or proceeds of crime on the balance of probabilities (the civil burden of proof) without the necessity of a criminal conviction. Discussion of civil forfeiture powers had arisen from one of the recommendations of the Home Affairs Committee, namely that confiscation order recovery rates should be studied in order to understand the difficulties in realizing the sums ordered to be confiscated. The results of this research were published by the Home Office Working Group on Confiscation in November 1998.[55] Over the period 1987 to 1996, criminal confiscation orders issued had amounted to £105 762 828 (approximately $176 million) – a sum which, after appeals and other considerations, was reduced to £92 853 828 ($155 million). The amounts actually confiscated had totalled £37 261 600 ($62 million), or 40 per cent. It was noted that large numbers of persons were convicted who had insufficient assets to justify a confiscation order being made, but that relatively few confiscation orders were made against major criminals with substantial assets. The Working Group Report recommended that consideration be given to the extension of current civil forfeiture provisions – whereby cash sums of £10 000 or more ($16 700) can be seized on import or export if there are reasonable grounds to suspect that they relate to drug trafficking – to cases where there was strong circumstantial evidence of the criminal origins of assets, but insufficient evidence for a criminal prosecution of the owner. Various options for extending the provisions of civil forfeiture were elaborated and were awaiting further discussion in 1999.

UK structures to combat organized crime

Several bodies within British law enforcement have responsibility for organized crime. The Metropolitan Police Joint Action Group on Organized Crime was established in 1992 and meets quarterly to share intelligence on criminal activity, individual criminals and criminal groups, and to facilitate action against them by the relevant agencies. It brings together representatives of 25 different bodies – the Metropolitan Police, the City of London Police, the Royal Ulster Constabulary; the National Criminal Intelligence Service, the Crown Prosecution Service, the Home Office, the Northern Ireland Office, the Foreign and Commonwealth Office, HM Customs & Excise; HM Immigration and Nationality Department; the UK Passport Agency; Inland Revenue, HM Treasury; the Department of Social Security; the Department of Trade and Industry; the Bank of England; the Serious Fraud Office; the Attorney General's Chambers of Guernsey, Jersey and the Isle of Man; the Securities and Investment Board, the Financial Fraud Information Network (FFIN); the Post Office Investigation Department; the Gaming Board for Great Britain; and the Credit Industry Fraud Avoidance Scheme (CIFAS).

The National Criminal Intelligence Service (NCIS) has an Organized Crime Unit within its Specialist and Organized Crime Branch which provides an intelligence-based consultancy and advisory service on organized crime as it affects UK interests. It is responsible for providing strategic overviews on specific areas of organized crime and for identifying possible attempts to infiltrate the British gaming industry. Its main concerns have been Triads, Vietnamese and Far Eastern crime groups; the Italian Mafia and US *La Cosa Nostra*; criminal motorcycle gangs; Eastern European organized crime; South American groups; white-collar fraud and infiltration of the gaming sector.[56]

Joint Anglo–Italian law-enforcement efforts are conducted primarily through NCIS and the DIA, and specifically through liaison officers in the respective capitals. There has been a constant exchange of information on the extent of Mafia penetration of the UK, and, potentially connected with this, on the circumstances in which Italian banker Roberto Calvi died in 1982. A project named DIANA has been set up to identify Mafia-linked individuals in the UK and their contacts. The starting point was an analysis of Italians involved in UK criminal proceedings to establish any possible Mafia connections. From this 20 063 names emerged, of whom 172 had previous charges of Mafia association and 115 were fugitives from Italian justice.[57]

Since the end of the Cold War, the UK intelligence services MI5 and MI6 have gradually taken over a role in combating organized crime at home and overseas respectively. The Secret Intelligence Service (MI6) has a 'Global Issues Controllerate' which includes officers working on organized crime, while for some years the Government Communications Headquarters at Cheltenham has provided assistance in the tracking and surveillance of drug traffickers and their vessels.[58] The Security Service (MI5) was given official authorization under the 1996 Security Services Act to act in the UK 'in support of the activities of the police and other law enforcement agencies in the prevention and detection of serious crime', that is, any offence carrying a sentence of three years or more on first conviction. Police officers have been helping to train MI5 colleagues in assembling evidence which can be used in prosecution cases. Warrants for interception or for interference with property sought by the Security Service in support of the police against serious crime must have the support of the relevant Chief Officer of Police or equivalent and all operations are tasked through NCIS.[59]

Among the most important recommendations of the 1995 Home Affairs Committee Report was that the existing structure of separate Regional Crime Squads be replaced by a nationally coordinated structure with a central executive direction in which serious crime investigations could be concentrated. On 1 April 1998 this recommendation was brought into force with the creation of the National Crime Squad of England and Wales (NCS) as a statutory police organization, operating under the authority of the Home Secretary, a Service Authority (composed of 17 members) and a Director General. Composed of 1450 detectives seconded from their previous posts to 44 locations in England and Wales, its task is 'to provide leadership and expertise to combat serious and organized crime nationally and internationally'. It has three strategic aims:[60]

- to concentrate effort on successfully bringing to justice and/or disrupting those responsible for serious and organized crime;
- to provide appropriate support to police forces and other law-enforcement agencies in relation to serious and organized crime;
- to create and maintain a recognized, robust, professional and ethical national organization staffed by people with integrity, ability and commitment.

Importantly, the remit of NCS is to target serious and organized crime proactively without being distracted by having to investigate committed crime reactively.

Evaluation – international collaboration since 1992

In terms of intellectual input and dedication of effort, great progress has been made in the fight against organized crime since 1992. The reluctance expressed by many nations in Naples in 1994 to elaborate a United Nations convention against organized crime has been replaced by the endeavour to have such a convention ready for signature by the year 2000. Considerable resources have been invested by the international community into the search for and agreement on the cardinal points of the fight against transnational organized crime. The principal areas of criminal operation – drugs and arms trafficking, corruption, fraud and money laundering, extortion, trafficking of women and children – have been identified and instruments and methodologies for tackling them have been drawn up. Hostility within EU Member States to a quasi-operational Europol – as opposed to a body with research and intelligence functions only – seems to have been overcome in principle, if not in fact, and law-enforcement cooperation has reached unprecedented levels. Why then, despite these efforts, do criminal organizations seem to be in continuous expansion?

Several explanations are possible. Firstly, it is premature to evaluate the results of such recent commitment and legislation. The transmission of paper resolutions and recommendations through intergovernmental and domestic bureaucracy into concrete implementation takes time. Within the European Union, all Third Pillar proposals (those concerning Justice and Home Affairs) have to be considered at five different levels: Working Group; one of three Steering Groups; the K4 Group of senior officials (established under article K4 of Title VI of the Treaty on European Union); COREPER (Committee of Permanent Representatives at the Council of Ministers); and the Council of Justice and Home Affairs Ministers. Moreover agreement has to be unanimous – the Third Pillar is intergovernmental and not Commission-led, and so there is no routine provision for majority voting.[61] At global level the decision-making process is correspondingly more protracted – if a United Nations convention against organized crime is indeed ready for signature by the year 2000 it will have taken six years to prepare, and several more will be necessary before it comes into force.

Secondly, in any confrontation between a democratic society and organized crime, the latter has the advantage – organized crime is better resourced; it moves faster and with greater flexibility (while parliaments discuss, organized crime plans counter-tactics); it disregards laws and frontiers and operates on the sole principles of profit and power. In comparison, democracies move slowly and reactively; they have many priorities and their continuing legitimacy rests on respect for due process and the rule of law.

Thirdly, there are objective difficulties involved in overcoming juridical discrepancies between countries, and these are aggravated by concerns for national sovereignty. A nation's criminal justice system is the product of its history, the national characteristics of its citizens and their perceptions of crime and security. To make compromises in this area can be considered an erosion of a nation's integrity and individuality.

Fourthly, if international cooperation against organized crime is in its infancy, cooperation between organized crime groups has come of age. There is evidence to show that, whereas in the past criminals used the trust deriving from shared ethnicity and blood ties as the basis for the transfer of illegal goods and services from one continent to another, post-Communist organized crime collaborates on the principle of 'strategic partnerships' – business alliances between criminal groups of different nationalities which are reasonably stable in time and are established on the premiss of congruent goals. These partnerships have the same function as their counterpart agreements in legitimate business – to spread and reduce risk and to gain market access.

It is generally believed in police and intelligence circles that a series of meetings between the major criminal groups took place in Warsaw in 1991, Prague in 1992 and Berlin in 1993.[62] French intelligence monitored a high-level 'business' meeting in a hotel in the French Burgundy town of Beaune in November 1994 between representatives of the Italo-American Gambino family, the Japanese Yakuza and Colombian, Russian and Chinese crime bosses.[63] The apparent purpose of the meeting was to subdivide Western Europe for drugs, prostitution, smuggling and extortion rackets. Police think that groups now liaise to ensure that individual drug routes are not over-utilized, to agree the amounts of drugs that each organization can bring into different countries, and to discuss the sharing of equipment such as vehicles and arms and the hiring of specialists in technologically sophisticated areas such as computer crime. Since the Beaune meeting, senior intelligence sources in Europe and the USA believe that two further meetings have taken place on chartered yachts in the Mediterranean.

The relative paucity of results in the fight against organized crime can be attributed to other factors, of which the most important concern the supposed spearhead of the antimafia fight – money-laundering legislation. The effectiveness of money-laundering legislation depends upon every country adopting it, but states where such laws are non-existent, weak or are not applied far outnumber those which deter the money launderer by their severity. The problems in prosecuting money laundering were described from an Italian perspective in Chapter 4, but – with variations – they are the same as those faced in every country: the complexity and technical difficulty of investigations; the degree of specialization required (and rarely found) in police and judicial investigators; the inexperience of banking personnel in dealing with the phenomenon; the reluctance of the financial sector to police itself; the flexibility and speed with which criminals identify new methods of laundering; the gaps in the system such as anonymous bank accounts and offshore havens; and difficulties in reconciling the requirements of law enforcement with those of financial deregulation and globalization.

Whereas the police and judiciary have had to adapt their professional skills as best they can, their traditional training leaves them greatly disadvantaged compared to organized criminals who can afford to hire the best tax consultants, lawyers and accountants that money can buy. Money-laundering investigations involve time-consuming, painstaking office-based work which conflicts with the conventional law-enforcement tradition of seeking fast results. A single money-laundering operation which takes two and a half seconds to perform may take an investigator the same number of years to pursue – by which time the assets may well have been removed or transformed.

There is an urgent need for mechanisms to evaluate existing policies – little information on effectiveness is available at national or international level. The only international body that has undertaken any systematic process of evaluation is the Financial Action Task Force, but its 26 members represent a small proportion of the world's nations. In November 1998 a questionnaire on anti-money-laundering practices drawn up a year earlier by the EU's Multidisciplinary Group on Organized Crime had not been circulated to Member States for completion. The suspicion-based reporting system on which many countries' legislation is based is judged to be ineffective by European investigators: several German public prosecutors stated in March 1997 that, given the results of the legislation, it did not justify the cost of the paper it was printed on. This view was endorsed by representatives of other countries.[64] Beside the most conservative estimates of criminal proceeds, the magnitude of seized criminal assets pales into insignificance, as was seen in Chapter 4. A European money-laundering research unit has calculated that the percentage of frozen assets which are confiscated varies from 25 per cent in the USA to an average of 10–15 per cent elsewhere. This means that between 75 and 90 per cent of any seized assets are dissequestered and returned for lack of evidence linking the beneficiary with the assets and a specific crime.[65] The Europol official responsible for money-laundering issues believes that the cases of international cooperation within the EU to seize and confiscate illegal proceeds are 'almost as rare as a kingfisher in Amsterdam', and that 'unless international judicial cooperation at global level is improved in a dramatic way, efforts to combat money laundering and consequently organized crime are doomed'.[66]

Shortcomings in this area are due in part to a lack of political will. A senior British investigator considers that Austria and Greece 'do nothing' against money laundering; in March 1998, five EU countries – Spain, Germany, Greece, Portugal and Luxembourg – had not formally ratified the Council of Europe Convention on the Laundering, Search, Seizure and Confiscation of the Proceeds from Crime eight years after its adoption. A plea by law-enforcement experts to the European Central Bank not to issue the 500 Euro note on the grounds that it will attract money launderers seems to have been ignored. With a face value much higher than any US dollar bill, the 500 Euro note is set to become the money launderers' 'bill of choice', inasmuch as currency smugglers will be able to carry a million dollars-worth of Euros in an ordinary handbag. The arrest of a gang and the seizure of Euro counterfeiting equipment in Sicily in February 1999 suggested that three years ahead of time, the Mafia was already making provision for the Euro becoming legal tender.

A crucial role in money laundering is played by offshore centres. The geographical size and relatively remote location of many of these havens belies their central function within the international financial system. The International Monetary Fund estimated in 1994 that more than half the world's stock of money passes through offshore centres, around 20 per cent of total private wealth is invested in them and around 75 per cent of the captive insurance industry is located offshore.[67] Some, such as the Isle of Man, implement a full range of anti-money-laundering procedures but others pay little more than lip service. In many cases their existence provides a screen behind which funds from tax avoidance, tax evasion, corruption and capital in flight to a secure haven are indistinguishable from profits laundered from drugs and arms trafficking. They can only operate with the acquiescence of the former colonial powers on which they are or were dependent, and with the participation of the international financial and business community for which they generate valuable profits.

Any possible benefit to society of such centres is offset by the fact that almost every international money-laundering investigation is hindered, if not brought to a halt, by the corporate and banking anonymity that characterizes them. In the view of Palermo chief prosecutor Gian Carlo Caselli,

> As long as these centres exist the fight against money laundering is a fight of words, not of deeds, because although you may have one or two successful operations, for every one you win, you lose another ten or a hundred cases. Just try to find the *mafioso* who is so stupid that he doesn't put his money in an offshore centre to avoid investigation! Offshore centres are an insurmountable brick wall, an abyss that engulfs our investigations.[68]

Conclusions – international cooperation

Italy has won general approbation for its efforts to lead by example in the fight against organized crime at international level. Italian judges and police officers have impressed their foreign counterparts by the humility, courage and dedication with which they have undertaken the long uphill struggle from 1992. 'Admiration' was the most commonly mentioned word during the research for this book, although doubts remained over the capacity and the will of the Italian political class to rid itself entirely of the Mafia. Italy's partners in the Schengen Group were also sceptical about whether the country's porous maritime borders and ambiguous immigration laws were an effective barrier against organized illegal alien smuggling.

At a wider European level international collaboration has progressed significantly, but many problems remain. According to the deputy director of Europol, the principal obstacle to obtaining preventive intelligence on criminal suspects is the absence of any clear defining norms and the different concept of 'intelligence' in each country. The distinction between suspicion-based intelligence and information usable as evidence varies considerably. With regard to crimes committed, the slowness of official channels of mutual assistance such as rogatory letters is a major impediment: Schengen has improved matters for participating states but more is expected of the EU Convention on Mutual Assistance in Criminal Matters. Progress is largely the result of personal contacts and trust built up over years between police officers, but there is a danger that the informality of these exchanges takes them beyond correct legal and professional limits, and ultimately renders the substance of the exchange unusable, for example in a court of law.[69]

A limited survey of opinions among senior British and Italian law-enforcement officials revealed the following as the most important elements in international police cooperation, in descending order: a similar perception of threat level or urgency of problem; similar legal systems, and the existence of formal cooperation agreements (of equal importance); continuous, direct and personal contact; political–institutional will; a shared language; shared borders.

The future

On current evidence, there is every likelihood that organized crime will continue to expand its activities, both in the provision of 'underworld' goods and services and by penetration of 'upperworld' markets through domestic and international financial fraud and money laundering, facilitated by 'off-planet' financial services on the Internet. Globalization has eroded not only the power of nation states to regulate commerce and finance, but the power of nation states to enforce their own laws. The American criminal law expert Jack Blum has coined the term 'international interspace' to describe the gaps in the legal and regulatory jurisdiction of nation states when transactions involve many countries.[70] These are present particularly in the areas of taxation, securities and bank regulation, and in application of the criminal law.

It must be acknowledged that the liberalization and globalization of financial markets have been encouraged to the detriment of responsibility and oversight – the examples of the Bank of Credit and Commerce International and Barings Bank are cases in point. Liberalization policies which involve less state responsibility in critical sectors of the economy run directly contrary to the requirements of strategies against organized crime, which call for more. Too much emphasis has been given to goals of profitability and the laws of the market-place and not enough to ethical standards, which western democracies should promulgate by example. As one observer has commented, 'when greed is enshrined as ideology, the unfettered pursuit of self-interest becomes the socially sanctioned goal for all of us'.[71]

It is to be hoped that a better understanding of the threat of organized crime to the legal economy, together with the repercussions of the financial crises in Asia, Russia and Latin America in the late 1990s, will encourage governments to reconsider the guiding principles of financial market operations. At the same time, democratic accountability must be the defining characteristic of all the institutions which represent the public interest in matters of law enforcement. There is a growing body of opinion among law-abiding European citizens that the electorally popular campaign against organized crime – the new 'evil empire' which has replaced the Communist threat – has driven policing towards intolerable violations of personal privacy, and that law-enforcement agencies exaggerate the threat in order to win more resources and greater autonomy. There is considerable resistance in many of the EU Member States to the intelligence-led aspects – and therefore 'clandestinization' – of law enforcement, which by definition make it less accountable. Organized crime is international and requires a coordinated international response, but it must not be used as a smokescreen for the proliferation of secretive, inadequately regulated transnational investigation agencies, nor must it become a rhetorical tool for winning votes or populist scaremongering. Quite simply, the threat to democracy is too serious.

ANNEX

The Multi-Disciplinary Working Group on Organized Crime set up by order of the Council of the European Union elaborated an Action Plan and 30 Recommendations. The Recommendations deal with:

- Coordination at national level of the fight against organized crime
- Collection and analysis of data on organized crime activity
- Pre-accession pact with the EU on cooperation against crime for the countries of Central and Eastern Europe and the Baltic States
- Development of closer relationships in the fight against organized crime between EU and other third countries and international organizations
- Study on high-technology crime
- Development of comprehensive policy against corruption
- Tighter control over the participation in public tender procedures
- Greater protection of 'legal persons'
- Use of structural funds to combat organized crime
- Fraud against the Community Budget
- Multi-annual programme to combat organized crime
- Prevention of exploitation of vulnerable professions by organized crime
- Early ratification of relevant conventions
- Ratification of relevant EU conventions by given dates

- Development of evaluation mechanism
- Work on draft Convention on Mutual Assistance in Criminal Matters
- Creation of offence of participating in a criminal association
- Follow-up on measures agreed by the Council in 1993
- Central national contact points to facilitate information exchange
- Establishment of multi-disciplinary teams
- European network for judicial cooperation
- Re-organization of Third Pillar working group structure
- Ratification of Europol Convention
- Europol's relations with third countries and international organizations in fight against organized crime
- Europol's role in the fight against organized crime
- Measures against money laundering
- Measures against money laundering for potential members of EU
- Study of existing legislation for tracing and seizing criminal proceeds
- Measures against fiscal fraud
- Measures dealing with off-shore centres

7
War ... and Peace?

The Mafia response to the Antimafia

The January 1992 verdict of the Supreme Court came as no surprise to *Cosa Nostra,* but was seen as the last in a series of failures by those who had done a deal with the organization on the basis of reciprocal advantages to keep their side of the bargain. There had been several indications during the previous 12 months of a greater commitment to combat organized crime, against which *Cosa Nostra*'s former protectors had shown themselves unwilling or unable to act. Judicial impunity – on which the equilibrium of cohabitation between State and Mafia had rested throughout the entire Cold War period – had definitively collapsed, and with it a consolidated system of alliances and clientilistic exchanges that had outlived its usefulness. *Cosa Nostra*'s response was a tactical one, calculated to sweep away the past and open up new channels of political–institutional mediation with interlocutors unconnected to the old regime. The principal points of contact in the Mafia–institutional interface, Salvo Lima and Ignazio Salvo, were murdered in March and September 1992 respectively; Giovanni Falcone and Paolo Borsellino, the 'historic memory' of the antimafia fight and *Cosa Nostra*'s most determined opponents, were eliminated in May and July. Their death sentences had been pronounced some ten years previously but suspended until such time as circumstances made them necessary.

From the summer of 1992 onwards, legislative innovations such as the introduction of the 41 *bis* prison regime, the provision of new investigative procedures and of incentives to collaboration moved the strategy

200

into a second phase. On the one hand *Cosa Nostra* tried to bully the Italian state into submission and on the other it offered sweeteners to potential partners through promises of protection and advancement. In effect, a war of attrition had begun in the spring of 1992 in which, to differing degrees, all four criminal organizations participated. An important indicator was the sharp rise in arms seizures throughout 1993. In January investigators discovered 26 rockets with relative propulsion charges and eight missile warheads, each containing 800 grams of TNT, near Catania. In early April, *carabinieri* raiding a luxury villa near Palermo found four charges for missile launchers and 600 grammes of Semtex explosive, fuses and detonators, all of East European provenance. Two weeks later, 11 kilogrammes of dynamite were found buried on the coastline near Palermo. In July police stopped a car near Salerno, in Campania, and found four bazookas loaded with Soviet-made anti-tank missiles. In December, a shipment of arms was seized on its way to the 'Ndrangheta which included two sub-machine guns, an anti-aircraft machine gun capable of firing up to 1500 shots per minute with a range of up to 3500 metres, a high-precision rifle with telescopic sight and silencer and large quantities of the relevant munitions. Some of the weapons were thought to be intended for use against judges and other representatives of law enforcement, while other evidence indicated that the 'Ndrangheta was becoming a major player in the international illicit arms traffic. In the course of 1993, over 13 000 weapons, 3000 bombs and 138 000 kilogrammes of explosives were seized in Italy. Calabria was the region with the highest number of seizures – 9.25 seizures per 10 000 inhabitants, compared to a national average of 4.1.[1]

Senior politicians and law-enforcement figures received constant threats in early 1993, as experts predicted that *Cosa Nostra* was preparing to strike again, a view supported by Mafia collaborators living under protection in the United States. The capture of Totò Riina in January had dealt *Cosa Nostra* a symbolic blow to which, it was felt, the organization would feel obliged to respond. There was considerable unrest among prisoners subject to the 41 *bis* regime, who for the first time had difficulty in maintaining contacts with the outside world, in particular the approximately 200 who were held in the island prisons of Pianosa, in the Tuscan archipelago, and Asinara, near Sardinia.

In April 1993 a plan to kill 14 prison guards at Pianosa was discovered. An intercepted telephone conversation between two *mafiosi* revealed the intention to torture one of the guards – a Sicilian – before killing him, in order to make an example of him and punish him for not showing 'due respect' to the prisoners.[2]

Observers speculated as to whether Riina's capture would destabilize the hegemony of the *Corleonesi* (the families from the town of Corleone) and provoke a battle for succession, but his first court appearance dispelled any doubts as to his continuing authority. Behind an apparent deference to the President of the Court and to the lawyers and prosecutor who questioned him, Riina alternated a succession of carefully framed threats and messages with protestations of injured innocence.

The car bomb campaign of 1993

At 21.40 on 14 May 1993, on the eve of a three-day international conference organized by the Antimafia Commission to commemorate the first anniversary of the Palermo murders, a car bomb exploded in via Fauro, near a theatre in the fashionable Parioli district of Rome where television presenter Maurizio Costanzo had just finished recording his daily chat show. Costanzo's regular chauffeur had taken the day off and he and his wife were being driven home in a rented Mercedes when a Fiat Uno, packed with 120 kilos of explosive, blew up. The car bomb caused extensive damage to the surrounding buildings but neither the Costanzos nor any bystanders were seriously hurt.

Shortly after 1a.m. on 27 May, a Fiat Fiorino van exploded in via dei Georgofili in Florence, close to the Uffizi Galleries. The explosion caused the thirteenth-century Pulci Tower to collapse over Italy's oldest agri-cultural institute, the Georgofili Academy, killing the Academy's custodian, his wife and two young children who were asleep in the building. In the fire that broke out a student living in an adjacent block died and 30 others were injured. Serious harm was done to the structure and the interior of the Galleries and numerous paintings were damaged, some irreparably. The nearby church of Santo Stefano and the History of Science Museum were also damaged in the blast.

On 2 June, anniversary of the proclamation of the Italian Republic, a Fiat 500 car bomb was discovered and defused in a Rome side street near the prime minister's official residence, Palazzo Chigi. In contrast to the previous two car bombs in which plastic explosive was used, the device was of a rudimentary type and in fact, could not have exploded.

Three car bombs exploded in the space of a single hour during the night of 27–28 July. A pedestrian in via Palestro, Milan, close to the Gallery of Modern Art, noticed smoke coming from a parked Fiat Uno and alerted a police patrol which in turn summoned the fire brigade. The car bomb exploded at 23.15, killing a policeman, three firemen and a Moroccan who was sleeping rough on a park bench nearby. Fiat Unos were also used for the other car bombs, both in Rome – the first exploded two minutes before midnight beside the wall of the Basilica of St John Lateran and the second, four minutes later, destroyed the portico of the seventh-century St George, Velabro, in the heart of the city. Although the damage to the buildings was severe in both cases and destroyed cars parked in the area, neither caused injury to persons. Throughout the night of 27–28 July, all the telephones in the prime minister's official residence were mysteriously out of action.

The country was profoundly shaken by the sequence of mainland bombs and by the deaths of ten innocent people, including two children. Apprehension was all the greater given Italy's history of indiscriminate bombings, the worst of which, in Bologna station in August 1980, had caused 85 deaths and 200 injuries. While these had been attributed to extremist right-wing groups, court proceedings had failed to establish unequivocally the guilt of all those responsible. Only for the last of the attacks – a bomb placed on a Naples–Milan express train just before Christmas 1984 – had the Supreme Court reached a final verdict. The bombing had been ordered by *Cosa Nostra* and materially carried out by a group of Mafia hirelings in Naples with the aim of distracting the attention of police and judiciary from Sicily, where the revelations of the first collaborators were leading to hundreds of arrests and the severe disruption of Mafia activities.[3]

With the exception of the car bomb found near the prime minister's residence – an anomaly in every respect when compared with the others – there was general agreement that the only criminal organization capable of setting up such a well-coordinated series of attacks was *Cosa Nostra*. Nonetheless the choice and location of targets, all on the mainland and all but one (Costanzo) at sites of historical or cultural importance, led to the widespread impression that the bombs were the work of 'the Mafia, but not only the Mafia'. Faced with the evident inability of the intelligence services to prevent the attacks and amid speculation that the Palazzo Chigi car bomb was a provocation by disaffected intelligence agents, Prime Minister Carlo Azeglio Ciampi sacked the director of the domestic security service, SISDE.

In August 1993 the director of the *Direzione Investigativa Antimafia* (DIA), Gianni De Gennaro, presented Ciampi with the antimafia police agency's report on the five car bomb explosions in Rome, Florence and Milan. The sequence of attacks was attributable to *Cosa Nostra* as part of a long-term criminal strategy that had begun with the murder of Salvo Lima in March 1992. The aim of the strategy was to frighten the general public and to pressurize the government into slowing the pace of antimafia efforts rather than continuing to reinforce countermeasures beyond the emergency situation that had been created by the 1992 attacks. The report stressed the likelihood that other subversive elements had been working alongside *Cosa Nostra*, as had happened in the past. The bombs were a survival strategy, an 'authentic campaign of Mafia terrorism decided not just by the top echelons of *Cosa Nostra* but by other exponents of a broader occult criminal power'.[4]

The investigations moved swiftly, in the first place to establish a common matrix for the attacks (the Palazzo Chigi car bomb was omitted from the series and investigated separately).

In four out of the five cases a Fiat Uno had been used, on each occasion stolen within 24 hours of the attack, while in the case of the largest bomb – in via dei Georgofili – a Fiat Fiorino van had been used. In all five attacks the explosive had been packed in the rear of the vehicle. The particular mix of seven explosive materials, including TNT, Semtex and blasting gelatine, was common not only to all five bombs but had been present in the car bomb which had killed Paolo Borsellino and his bodyguards, and also in the bomb which had exploded in 1984 on the Naples–Milan express.

The investigation drew on three major sources – scientific analysis, a study of mobile-phone and human traffic during the period, and the testimonies of state's witnesses. The DIA checked hotel registers for all persons who had stayed in Milan, Rome and Florence during the period immediately prior to the attacks, who had rented cars in those cities and who had flown between Sicily and the target cities at what would have been the crucial stages of preparation and execution. *Telecom* provided lists of all phone calls made in the period between mobile phones in the cities concerned. Eyewitnesses had contributed to the construction of several identikit pictures which were matched with Mafia suspects. Suspicion fell on the Madonia clan of the Resuttana district of Palermo, known for its recourse to terrorist-type tactics. The brothers Filippo and Giuseppe Graviano of the Palermo Brancaccio clan were recognized as having been present in Florence, indicating that allies of Totò Riina's *Corleonesi* were involved.[5] It would later emerge that the organizers of the Florence bomb had stayed the night of the attack in a hotel in the city centre and had stolen the van from a nearby street. Once the common matrix of all five bombs had been established, the investigation was centralized under the DDA (district antimafia prosecution office) in Florence, led until his appointment as national antimafia prosecutor in December 1996 by Pier Luigi Vigna.

The logic behind the Costanzo attack was the most straightforward. His nightly programme, the *Maurizio Costanzo Show*, recorded mid-evening in the Parioli Theatre and transmitted two hours later, had frequently dealt with the subject of the Mafia through on-stage interviews with judges, politicians, Mafia victims or their families, and on one occasion the wife of an imprisoned *mafioso*. Shortly after the murder of Palermo businessman Libero Grassi in August 1991 Costanzo had run a special 'two-hander' programme linking up with a colleague on a rival television channel as a gesture of unity and of protest at the assassination. He had produced a TV commercial which encouraged viewers to take a stand against the Mafia and report suspicions of Mafia-type activity, and had commented favourably on the arrest of Totò Riina. During the trial it emerged that the final decision to kill him had been taken after a discussion during the programme about Mafia bosses who had had themselves admitted to hospital under false pretences. Costanzo had expressed the hope that, if hospitalized boss Francesco Madonia were not already suffering from a tumour, one would soon develop.

The *Maurizio Costanzo Show* attracts a broad cross-section of the population and has several million viewers on an average evening. In the view of a Mafia state's witness who gave evidence in the trial, the murder of the popular chat-show host would have aroused horror and fear in the general public and would have proved that *Cosa Nostra* could silence anyone who spoke out against it. He revealed that the attack had been planned for the previous day, 13 May, but that the detonating mechanism had failed; it missed its target on the 14th because Costanzo was travelling in a different car, causing the bomber a moment's hesitation before he detonated the charge.

As state's witnesses would later explain, the 'monument' attacks were a protest against the laws on collaboration and against the 41 *bis* regime introduced by Law Decree 306 of June 1992.[6] The 41 *bis* rules which prevented *mafiosi* from having contact either with each other or with the outside world reduced their power of command and consequently their personal prestige. The state of physical and psychological isolation compromised the decision-making process of the organization and most seriously of all, favoured collaboration with the authorities. On 20 July 1993 the article 41 *bis* provisions had been extended for a further year – the bombing campaign recommenced exactly one week later.

The collaborator Filippo Malvagna told prosecutors he had heard from a relative, a member of a powerful Catania clan, that an important meeting had been held near the Sicilian town of Enna towards the end of 1991. At that meeting Riina had said that pressure was building up on

Cosa Nostra and that the 'traditional alliances with elements of the State were no longer working'. Because of this *Cosa Nostra* was without the protection on which it habitually relied. Riina had explained the need to launch an all-out attack on the State with a series of murders and actions in- and outside Sicily which 'would have all the appearance of terrorist actions'. He had justified this course of action on the grounds that 'you have to make war in order to negotiate peace'.[7] Salvatore Annacondia, a collaborator from the United Holy Crown but also affiliated to *Cosa Nostra,* testified that he had learned in September 1992, before he turned state's witness, of a plan to carry out large-scale attacks in the two regions where the island prisons were located, Tuscany and Sardinia, and that if the 41 *bis* regime were not abrogated on 20 July 'major havoc' could be expected.[8] Salvatore Cancemi stated that for the *Cosa Nostra* leaders, every attack from the Falcone murder onwards was an attempt to stop the wave of collaboration. He recalled a conversation between Riina and three others during which it was agreed that collaboration was destroying *Cosa Nostra*, and that there was a need to discredit state's witnesses and try to have the legislation repealed. Riina would have 'given his right arm' to have these laws abolished.[9]

State's witness Maurizio Avola testified that, around September 1992, he had learned that Riina wanted to plant bombs to hit institutional targets and wished to create a new political party in which he could place *Cosa Nostra* members without a criminal record who could take direct charge of the organization's interests. Riina had asked Catania boss Nitto Santapaola to indicate suitable individuals. The party was to be launched with the image of a complete break with political tradition and therefore it was necessary to chose candidates as far removed as possible from the old political world. The most important task for the new party would be to modify the antimafia legislation.[10] Giving evidence in court in Florence in 1997, Avola stated that the new party to which he had referred was Silvio Berlusconi's *Forza Italia.*[a] He also said that *Cosa Nostra* had agreed in September–October 1992 to kill the anti-corruption judge Antonio Di Pietro, 'to do a favour to people at that time who could be useful later' in setting up the new party. Had the attack taken place, it would have been carried out by members of the Catania Santapaola clan.[11] Filippo Malvagna told judges he had been reassured that from 1995 things would start to get better, and that privileges would again be extended to Mafia prisoners. Cancemi confirmed the mood of optimism, and said that Riina

---

[a]   At time of writing there was no evidence to support the impression given by Avola that *Forza Italia* was the 'creation' of Totò Riina.

had reported having new political contacts through whom things would improve. He recalled a conversation between Riina and two others in which they appeared to have found political contacts who could be persuaded to change the legislation. He had also been told in January and in July 1993 by Bernardo Provenzano, another *Corleonese* patriarch, that political contacts had been made.

The attacks on St George, Velabro and on St John Lateran – the Cathedral of Rome and therefore the highest symbol of papal authority in Italy – were carried out within the same overall strategy, but investigators believe that they were also intended as a reprisal for the exhortations against the Mafia made by Pope John Paul II during his trips to Sicily, and as a warning to Church leaders to give up their antimafia commitment. In particular, the Pope's message of May 1993 in the Valley of the Temples at Agrigento had strengthened the position of priests like Father Puglisi in Palermo who were actively engaged in encouraging young people to turn against the Mafia and to have respect for the law (see Chapter 5).

The car bomb attacks effectively carried out in 1993 were not the only terrorist tactics to be considered by *Cosa Nostra*, as collaborators later revealed. In one case, only chance prevented the deaths of up to 60 *carabinieri*, when a car bomb parked close to a stationary police van at the entrance to Rome's Olympic football stadium failed to explode. Other murder attacks were planned down to the last detail but were deferred for reasons of tactical expediency, excessive risk or because arrests of key figures prevented their implementation. Intended victims included former Justice Minister Claudio Martelli, a judge in the Palermo maxi-trial, Piero Grasso, and Giulio Andreotti's son, selected because unlike the real target, his closely-guarded father, he had no bodyguard protection.

Giovanni Brusca, boss of the town of San Giuseppe Jato and one of the most powerful *Cosa Nostra* leaders between Riina's arrest in 1993 and his own in 1996,[b] told the Florence court that a campaign of terror had been launched with the explicit aims of causing panic in the general public and the collapse of tourism in Italy. The original plan had involved the poisoning of pre-packaged supermarket snacks of the type consumed by schoolchildren in their mid-morning break and the strewing of syringes

[b] Brusca was not granted the status of full collaborator until February 1999, despite having confessed to a long series of murders and other criminal activities and having given evidence against others which was judged to be credible. Suspicions remained that his evidence might have been part of a strategy to pervert the course of justice.

filled with HIV-infected blood on public beaches along the Adriatic coast. These were envisaged as demonstrative actions, and would have been followed up immediately by telephone calls. According to Brusca the idea came from reading about the Japanese sect whose members had released nerve gas in the Tokyo underground system.[12] He stated that the decision to concentrate on monuments came later, and was suggested to *Cosa Nostra* by a prison cellmate of *mafioso* Antonino Gioè, a neo-fascist called Paolo Bellini. Bellini is thought to have been set up by the *Carabinieri* to negotiate a deal with *Cosa Nostra* by which precious works of art in *Cosa Nostra*'s possession would be returned to the State and, in exchange, a number of imprisoned *mafiosi* would be given house arrest or admitted to hospital. The deal did not go ahead.[13] A *Cosa Nostra* collaborator told prosecutors about a conversation, also with Gioè (who later committed suicide in prison), shortly after the failed assassination attempt on Maurizio Costanzo, at which Gioè had said, 'What would you think if you woke up one morning and the Leaning Tower of Pisa wasn't there any more?' The logic behind this, the collaborator assumed, was that individual roles could always be filled, whereas monuments or works of art were irreplaceable, and the symbolic impact of their loss was greater.[14]

The material executors of the five car bomb attacks were identified, arrested and charged, and came to trial in the Florence Court of Assizes in November 1996. The trial ended in June 1998 with guilty verdicts for 24 out of the 26 defendants and 14 sentences of life imprisonment. The contribution made by state's witnesses was recognized, and had been corroborated with sufficient independent evidence to be regarded as valid. Sentencing was weighted by the aggravating factor that the attacks had been perpetrated with the 'objective of terrorism and subversion of the constitutional order', as had been the case for the bombing of the Naples–Milan express in December 1984. No verdict was pronounced on Totò Riina or Giuseppe Graviano, whose responsibilities formed part of a separate investigation. This second line of enquiry continues, and concerns those whom national antimafia prosecutor Pier Luigi Vigna calls 'the instigators with hidden faces' – the shady figures external to *Cosa Nostra* whose interests may have converged with and been served by the atrocities committed.

Integrated criminal power structure?

According to Vigna, the 1993 attacks in mainland Italy revealed the existence of an 'integrated criminal power structure' in which *Cosa Nostra*, the *'Ndrangheta* and the *Camorra* had become increasingly close partners. On the one hand the attacks demonstrated 'the certainty of *Cosa Nostra*'s involvement' but on the other a degree of 'wisdom' in the way they had been managed.

> [...] the subtle evaluation of the effects of a terrorist campaign and the exploitation of the resultant psychological state do not seem to be the simple product of a common criminal mind, albeit *mafioso*: in these operations of analysis and evaluation, a familiarity with the dynamics of terrorism and with the mechanisms of mass-media communication can be distinguished, and also a capacity to sound out political opinions and interpret the signals. One could think of an aggregation of a horizontal type in which each component is a bearer of particular interests which can be pursued in the context of a more complex project in which objectives converge. [...] Developments in the judicial response to the repression of Mafia-type criminality and to corruption, with the well-known disruptive effects on political parties, could have produced a convergence of the interests of *Cosa Nostra* with those of other sectors under investigation: sectors of corrupt politics and of right-wing subversion; secret Masonic lodges; maverick businessmen and financiers; individuals or 'little groups' of disloyal state officials. The existence of this composite but converging set of 'entities', each bearing its corresponding set of interests, is supported by investigative analysis.

Recalling that the vast turnover of business undertaken by criminal organizations generated large sums of money which required laundering and reinvesting in apparently licit activities, Vigna pointed out that this necessitated the penetration of economic sectors such as that of public-sector financing and, therefore, of public-sector bureaucracy.

> The result has been that for a long time *Cosa Nostra* has favoured the rise to power or permanence in power of certain politicians [...] in a sort of exchange from which each group has drawn its own benefits: the politicians the advantage of holding convenient electoral seats with a mass of consensus such as to guarantee a significant role within the party [...] and the *mafiosi* that of gaining useful support for the management of their business affairs and for the solution of their various problems.

Secret Masonic lodges were a particular focus for this type of associa-tion, in which, according to Vigna, the traditions of confidentiality and solidarity had created a 'privileged meeting ground for dialogue and inter-action between Mafia criminality and that sector of politico-institutional life which had to be penetrated and controlled'.[15]

Mafia–Freemasonry

The hypothesis that an ' integrated criminal power structure' was respon-sible for the car bombs is substantiated by circumstantial evidence which, it should be stressed, had not been judicially ascertained at the time of writing. Links between Italian Mafia groups and occult Freemasonry go back many years. The collaborator Tommaso Buscetta has said that they date at least from the late 1960s, and that *Cosa Nostra*'s support was sought in two projected *coups d'état* in which Freemasonry was implicated, in 1970 – when supporters of a right-wing coup planned by Prince Valerio Borghese asked *Cosa Nostra* to assume temporary control of Sicily during an interim period – and again in 1974. The strategic decision to reinforce the link between the two secret fraternities is thought to have been taken around 1976–77, when a Sicilian lodge invited *Cosa Nostra* to enrol two members for each province of Sicily. It appears that this was done and that, from then on, all the members of the 'Commission' became Freemasons. By 1986 there were 4600 Freemasons in Sicily divided among 113 separate lodges, of whom a significant proportion had joined in the years 1976–80. Police investigations revealed that many affiliates had a criminal record of Mafia association.[16] The benefits to *Cosa Nostra* derived from the secrecy of membership and from the existence of an élite, discreet forum where deals with legitimate sectors of the political and business world could be done and where judges who were Masons could be 'approached'.[17] The type of contact is illustrated by the case of Totò Riina's accountant Giuseppe Mandalari, convicted of Mafia association in 1997, who apparently used his Masonic rank to persuade fellow Masons to vote for candidates of the centre-right coalition in 1994 elections.

Cosa Nostra gained its first access to international financial circuits through a Freemason, Sicilian banker Michele Sindona, a member of the Propaganda 2 (P2) lodge who was sheltered in Sicily between August and October 1979 while a fugitive from Italian and US justice – Sindona's activities and his connection with Giulio Andreotti are discussed below. Another prominent P2 member whose name has been linked to *Cosa Nostra* was Roberto Calvi, chairman of the *Banco Ambrosiano*, found hanging under Blackfriars Bridge in London in June 1982 shortly after the bank had been taken into compulsory liquidation. Investigations into Calvi's death were continuing, but suggest that he may have been murdered on the orders of *Cosa Nostra*'s principal treasurer, Pippo Calò, as punishment for careless handling of Mafia funds.

Judicial investigations in Calabria have revealed close links between secret Masonic lodges in Vibo Valentia, Catanzaro and Reggio Calabria and the criminal activities of the dominant clans in those areas. According to collaborators, a truce reached between warring factions of the 'Ndrangheta in 1991 was mediated by, among others, a lawyer who was a serving member of Parliament and a Mason. A Calabrian collaborator has talked of a meeting held in 1992 at which a representative of Tuscan Freemasonry asked *Cosa Nostra* to carry out a series of demonstrative actions in retaliation for the numerous investigations being undertaken into the criminal activities of Calabrian Freemasonry. According to this interpretation there was a common 'Masonic' denominator in three mainland bombs of 1993 – the excommunication of Masons had been declared in the church of St John Lateran in the nineteenth century; the villa housing the Gallery of Modern Art in Milan had been a meeting place for Masons during the Five Days Revolt in 1848 and the Academy of the Georgofili in Florence was considered a stronghold of Tuscan Freemasonry.[18]

Mafia–terrorism

From 1970 onwards there has been evidence of contacts between the 'Ndrangheta and right-wing subversion. Similarly, links between *Cosa Nostra* boss Pippo Calò, right-wing terrorists and elements of the 'Magliana band' – a Rome-based criminal group thought to include disaffected members of the intelligence services – emerged in the trial for the 1984 bomb on the Naples–Milan express train at which Calò received a life sentence. The explosives expert charged with constructing the train bomb was an Austrian citizen, Friedrich Schaudinn, who evaded house arrest before his conviction *in absentia* and fled to Croatia, where members of *Cosa Nostra* were also operating. It was from Schaudinn that *Cosa Nostra* learned its more sophisticated bomb-making techniques.

Mafia–corrupt intelligence agents

Italian intelligence officials were implicated to varying degrees in all the indiscriminate bomb attacks attributed to the far Right in Italy from 1969 onwards. Collusion between the security services and organized crime has also emerged. In 1993 the Palermo prosecution office intercepted a telephone conversation between two *mafiosi* in Mazaro del Vallo in the province of Trapani in which there was an explicit reference to the intelligence services, to their link with Masonic and judicial circles, and to the intention of using these links to have trials 'adjusted'. The most serious case was that of Bruno Contrada, former head of the Palermo Flying Squad and former deputy head of the domestic security service, SISDE, in Sicily, sentenced to ten years imprisonment in April 1996 for collusion with the Mafia (see Chapter 4).

The collaborator Salvatore Cancemi told prosecutors that, with the exception of Maurizio Costanzo, the choice of mainland targets had been 'suggested' to *Cosa Nostra* since the organization did not possess sufficient 'refinement' to select them autonomously, and said that Riina and others had implied they had support from individuals inside the State.[19] Giovanni Brusca told the Florence court that Riina had had meetings with someone in authority after the 1992 killings of Falcone and Borsellino, and said that the 1993 bomb targets had not been chosen by *Cosa Nostra*. He claimed that Riina had presented a *papello* – Sicilian dialect for a list, or an account to be paid – to someone in authority, and that he expected some gains in return.[20] He did not know to whom the *papello* had been presented but thought it might have been prepared by Riina's doctor, Antonino Cinà, who was arrested shortly after Riina and was a high-ranking 'man of honour' himself. According to Brusca, discussions were under way to have the 41 *bis* modified but they needed an extra 'push' to reach a conclusion. For this reason there were plans to recommence attacks on institutional figures. A meeting to discuss this was scheduled for 15 January, the day of Riina's arrest.[21]

Cosa Nostra–Bribesville

At the time of writing no connection had been proven between companies or individuals within the Italian business sector, the 'Bribesville' investigations and the 1992–93 bombings. Nonetheless, judicial investigation of the 'grey area' of cohabitation/collusion between political, business and Mafia circles in Sicily has begun to expose layers of white-collar corruption that may yet prove to be relevant.

In July 1997 a *Cosa Nostra* affiliated entrepreneur named Angelo Siino, imprisoned under the 41 *bis* regulations, began to collaborate with the authorities. His role and that of another Sicilian businessman, Filippo Salamone, have emerged as central to the interface between the criminal and legitimate sectors of the Sicilian economy. From the evidence given by Siino and others in the second half of 1997, national antimafia prosecutor Pier Luigi Vigna concluded that there had been 'total control of the system of public works contracts' in Sicily between 1985 and 1993 by *Cosa Nostra*, including those assigned to large companies based in the centre and north of Italy.[22] Contracts were allocated according to prior agreements made by 'business committees' at which the Mafia, politicians and the business community were represented. From 1988 until 1991 all tenders for public works contracts over the value of 5 billion lire ($3 million) were mediated through Filippo Salamone. Companies wishing to participate in a public works tender had to pay a kickback of 2.5 per cent to Salamone, to be used for the financing of political parties. All parties, including the PCI-backed cooperatives, were allegedly party to the arrangements. According to Siino and to Rino Nicolosi, five-times DC president of the Sicilian Region from 1984 to 1991, who was arrested in 1994 on corruption charges, contacts with *Cosa Nostra* were handled by business managers rather than the politicians, who used Salamone as their principal intermediary. A payment of 0.8 per cent of all the kickbacks relating to the contracts assigned through Salamone went directly to Riina; a further 3 per cent was paid by construction site managers to the clans who controlled a given area to obtain their permission for the organization of the site and to keep it 'peaceful'; the site manager would also receive from these clans the names of the local firms to whom subcontracts were to be distributed, for example for the supply of raw materials. The monopoly of extortion payments to ensure ongoing protection went to the Brusca clan of San Giuseppe Jato, which, according to Siino, amounted to $120 000 per month.[23] A further 6 per cent of the contract went to ensure that public officials falsified documents and balance sheets. Pre-existing agreements on a rotation system would normally dictate who would win the contract but if the 'wrong' company won – one that did not belong to the business committee – a series of intimidating messages followed by attacks would force it to withdraw. Riina had opposed the rotation system to start with, but changed his mind at the prospect of taking a regular 0.8 per cent on every contract.[24]

Many of the contracts went to companies indicated directly by *Cosa Nostra*, and of these a significant share was allocated to Calcestruzzi Spa – the Sicilian division of the huge Ferruzzi Group led by Ravenna entrepreneur Raul Gardini – which allegedly sub-contracted work to Mafia-affiliated companies. Siino has testified that the chairman of the Ferruzzi Group, Raul Gardini, met representatives of the Brusca clan on several occasions; Giovanni Brusca has said that *Cosa Nostra* intended to use Gardini to make contact with Claudio Martelli, who throughout the 1980s was a close aide of Socialist Party Secretary Bettino Craxi. Contacts between *Cosa Nostra* and Calcestruzzi were apparently maintained on the company's side by Managing Director Giovanni Bini, and on the Mafia's side by Antonino Buscemi, boss of the Boccadifalco district on the periphery of Palermo. Calcestruzzi chairman Lorenzo

Panzavolta, Bini, Buscemi and Filippo Salamone were all under arrest in October 1997.

In February 1991, a report requested by Giovanni Falcone on *Cosa Nostra*'s infiltration of public works contracts in Sicily had just been completed by the ROS unit of the *Carabinieri* in Palermo. In circumstances that remain obscure, *Cosa Nostra* obtained a copy – presumably from someone working in, or closely with, the prosecution office. After Falcone's departure for Rome the Mafia–public works report was not followed up but according to Giovanni Brusca, *Cosa Nostra* acted on it by replacing the front company used by Riina for his business operations in the construction sector with a 'clean' company recently acquired on his behalf, and by substituting the principal intermediaries who had been compromised by the report.[25] The report is thought to contain the first evidence of links between Mafia-owned companies and the Ferruzzi Group. Raul Gardini committed suicide in July 1993, on the day when he would almost certainly have been arrested in a corruption scandal concerning the merger between the Ferruzzi company Montedison and the state holding company ENI.[26] It has been suggested that Gardini was trying to cover up the serious losses being made by Mafia companies working for Calcestruzzi and that there were hints of this in the 1991 *carabinieri* report. Shortly before his death, Falcone warned that the Mafia had 'gone on to the Stock Exchange', a statement which, according to Siino, caused alarm in *Cosa Nostra* as it indicated that Falcone knew about the connection with Ferruzzi; this had accelerated the decision to kill him. This might also explain *Cosa Nostra*'s projected assassination of judge Antonio Di Pietro, who was investigating Ferruzzi in Milan.

After the Capaci attack, Paolo Borsellino decided to reopen the Mafia–public works enquiry in strictest secrecy, with two trusted colleagues from the *Carabinieri* ROS division but without the knowledge of chief prosecutor Giammanco, who had shelved it 18 months before. In the course of 1999 there was mounting evidence that Borsellino's decision to pursue this investigation was a precipitating factor in *Cosa Nostra*'s decision to murder him. Otherwise it is hard to imagine why the organization would have invited further repression during the very period that Parliament was debating (and subsequently reinforced) Law Decree 306.

Political objectives

The extent to which a dialogue was opened with individuals in positions of institutional or political power before, during or after the bombings was still under investigation. There is certainly evidence to suggest that *Cosa Nostra* hoped for and expected to receive benefits from the electoral success of the Freedom Alliance in 1994 and that it urged its members to vote accordingly. Although several *Forza Italia* deputies appointed to senior positions in the Berlusconi administration publicly opposed part of the more stringent antimafia legislation there is no proof that this opposition derived from sympathy with the Mafia or that the individuals concerned personally increased their votes because of it. Concerning Sicilian representatives of *Forza Italia*, the situation is less clear. Three prominent *Forza Italia* members in Sicily were under suspicion of collusion with *Cosa Nostra* in the late 1990s: the lawyer Francesco Musotto, arrested in November 1995, forced to resign as president of the province of Palermo and immediately re-elected after his acquittal in April 1998 (the Palermo prosecution office has lodged an appeal against the acquittal); national *Forza Italia* deputy Marcello Dell'Utri, whose trial for Mafia collusion began in November 1997 and was continuing; and another national deputy, Gaspare Giudice, whom the Palermo prosecutors described as 'organic' to *Cosa Nostra* and whose trial began in June 1999. Only definitive judicial verdicts on these individuals will provide an answer to whether an exchange of favours between *Cosa Nostra* and representatives of *Forza Italia* took place.

Another theory holds that *Cosa Nostra*'s political aspirations in the early 1990s were directed at the federal division of Italy into three self-governing regions. By this rationale a bombing campaign by the Mafia would have accelerated the desire by northern Italians to rid themselves of the problems of the south. Judge Carmelo Petralia, prosecutor in the appeal trial for the Borsellino attack, stated in 1997 that there was mounting evidence that *Cosa Nostra* had received a mandate from 'other entities' for the terrorist campaign of 1992 onwards, and associated this with *Cosa Nostra*'s separatist aspirations:

> [...] it was the time when the idea of a Europe no longer of nations but of little states was being envisaged [...] The idea of macro-regions is attractive to *Cosa Nostra*: it would mean having Sicily run exclusively by Sicilian ministers and politicians.[...] *Cosa Nostra* was undergoing a profound crisis with the old system as early as 1991. Moreover its primary role as a bulwark against Communism had disappeared. For this reason too it might have been in favour of separatism, while not neglecting a dialogue with the new political forces capable of ensuring the status quo.[27]

By drawing together the various theories discussed above, some tentative conclusions can be made. The car bomb attacks were functional to an overall strategy which *Cosa Nostra* adopted after the Supreme Court verdict of January 1992. The aim was to remove obstacles to the operational capacity and security of the organization and to influence the Government's criminal law policies. In this sense the 1993 attacks were 'bombs of dialogue', not intended to cause loss of life – although that eventuality was necessarily part of the equation – but to weaken Italy's antimafia resolve by demonstrating that *Cosa Nostra* could strike where and whom it wished. The 'message' of the bombs was directed at specific groups or individuals considered capable of interpreting the signals and whose actions could influence political or legislative antimafia policies directly or indirectly. These included politicians, investigators (police and judiciary), opinion leaders, church leaders, state's witnesses, and individuals external to the Mafia who had moved from a position of compliance to defiance *vis à vis Cosa Nostra*. Implicit in the message was the invitation to mediate or to retract, with the threat of more precisely targeted violence in the future were the invitation declined.

The threat to judges, collaborators and the judicial process continued: projects to murder antimafia judges in Palermo, Messina, Reggio Calabria, Turin, Venice and Florence were revealed; in Milan a plan to kill three antimafia prosecutors, one of whom was to be killed with a bazooka as he entered a Milan prison, was thwarted. Missile launchers were to be used in an attack on a judge in Catania. Plans to kill retired judge Antonino Caponnetto and Palermo chief prosecutor Gian Carlo Caselli were exposed. The trial for the attempted murder of *Cosa Nostra* boss Gerlando Alberti had to be abandoned for a month in March 1994 when five members of the jury resigned after intimidation. In July of the same year a bomb was found in a rubbish container outside the courthouse in the Sicilian town of Siracusa; had it exploded as intended in the middle of the morning, it would have killed a large number of people.

In December 1995 a prison guard at Palermo's Ucciardone prison was assassinated. Mafia prisoners encouraged non-*mafioso* convicts to make official complaints of maltreatment in order to attract the attention of parliamentarians who had criticized the 41 *bis* regime, since to make a formal complaint was beneath the dignity of 'men of honour'.[28]

Numerous attempts were made on the lives of state's witnesses, including three in the space of a single week in April 1994: a powerful bomb was discovered – apparently by chance – at the roadside close to the secret hideout near Rome of one of the earliest *Cosa Nostra* collaborators, Salvatore Contorno; there was an attempt to murder United Holy Crown collaborator Salvatore Annacondia; and a distant relative of key *Camorra* collaborator Carmine Alfieri was assassinated. On 16 July 1994 the wife and the mother-in-law of a collaborator were killed in Catania. The 13-year-old son of state's witness Santo Di Matteo – giving vital evidence in the Falcone investigation – was kidnapped in 1993 and held prisoner for 28 months in an attempt to make his father retract his testimony. Giovanni Brusca had him strangled and dissolved his body in acid. The father of another state's witness, Gioacchino La Barbera, was killed by hanging in a mock suicide scenario in June 1994. By creating a climate of insecurity among collaborators it was hoped they would distrust the State's ability to protect them and their families, retract their test-imonies and deter others from becoming state's witnesses.

Political opponents of the Mafia were also targeted. During the period of the general election and European election campaigns in the spring of 1994, some 20 attacks were carried out against members of the Progressive or centre-left coalition in Sicily. These took the form of fire-bombing of property or of vehicles, the poisoning of animals, and macabre threats such as a cow's head impaled on a post outside the target's home or bullets sent through the post. In the final hours of the European election campaign there were five such attacks.

The politicians most at risk were those who had begun to oppose *Cosa Nostra* after accepting the benefits of its support. Collaborators confirmed that the murder of Salvo Lima had been a warning to Giulio Andreotti and a deliberate attempt to block his chances of becoming president. Riina had been heard to say that Andreotti should 'carry Lima's death on his conscience'.[29]

Giulio Andreotti – victim or accomplice?

Senator Giulio Andreotti, born in Rome in 1919, seven times Prime Minister, and a government minister in another 19 governments between 1948 and 1992, once remarked that he was 'a truly Italian product – Roman, Romanesque, untranslatable and non-exportable'. The descrip-tion is an apt one. Throughout Andreotti's long political career his formidable reputation for emerging unscathed from almost every major scandal in Italy earned him the nicknames 'the Fox' and 'Beelzebub'. Andreotti is a politician of the Macchiavellian school and regards political ideals and grand plans for changing society with suspicion, preferring to adapt his own position to the requirements of the moment. He refined intellectual detachment and pragmatic cynicism into a consummate, vote-winning art which appealed to the innate pessimism of the Italians, deeply mistrustful of grandiose promises – however eloquent – made by their political representatives. Being *furbo* (cunning) and always appearing cynically cheerful endeared him to large sectors of the Italian people for whom his most memorable remark remains, 'Power wears down those who do not possess it.'

Until 1993, when the Italian Parliament modified the system of parliamentary immunity from prosecution, lengthy procedures were involved in making Italian parliamentarians accountable for their actions. In practice few ever saw the criminal law courts, although Giulio Andreotti came closer than most: 26 requests to incriminate him were received by the Parliamentary Commission of Investigation, of which only two were passed on for parliamentary discussion. In the first, Andreotti was accused of perjury in the trial for a right-wing bomb attack in Milan – the majority voted in his favour. The second occasion concerned the propriety of Andreotti's appointment as head of the Finance Police of General Raffaele Giudice, who was later convicted and imprisoned for fraudulent transactions in the oil industry. Again Andreotti escaped, thanks to a surprise vote in his favour by the Communist Party.

Andreotti–Sindona

A virtue which Andreotti undoubtedly possesses is loyalty to his friends, many of whom he would have been advised to jettison before they dragged his reputation down with their own. One of these was the banker Michele Sindona, Sicilian-born proprietor of the *Banca Privata Italiana* and prominent member of the P2 Masonic lodge. Sindona's career began in 1943 when he obtained a truck seized from its previous owners by the US occupying forces and began to haul grain from the Sicilian interior.[30] By the end of the war he had accumulated enough profits from the lucrative black market to set himself up as a financial consultant, first in Messina and then in Milan, where he moved in 1946. From the acquisition of the *Banca Privata Finanziaria* (renamed *Italiana*) in 1960, he constructed a constantly expanding empire of financial holdings, banks and property companies. Vatican connections enabled him to buy into an international financial market protected by banking secrecy and in 1969 he bought over the Vatican's huge property company, *Generale Immobiliare* in partnership with the UK merchant bankers, Hambros. Sindona's unorthodox financial methods caused Hambros to pull out of the partnership but he continued to enlarge his financial interests, taking over the nineteenth largest bank in the United States, the Franklin National Bank. Sindona's career peaked in 1973, when it was estimated that on an average day his companies accounted for up to 40 per cent of the dealings on the Milan stock exchange. During a period of financial instability and currency speculation in that year (later believed at least in part to have been provoked by Sindona himself), he was hailed by Andreotti as 'the saviour of the lira'. Soon afterwards Sindona was in financial difficulties and needed to raise capital. His plan to increase the capital of one of his small companies in order to take over two others needed approval from the Parliamentary Credit Committee. He tried to buy the support of the DC by donating two billion lire ($1.2 million) to support the party's campaign against the divorce law in 1974 but the Treasury Minister of the day, Republican Ugo La Malfa, refused to allow the capital-raising venture to go ahead. In the autumn of 1974 his financial empire crashed on both sides of the Atlantic, taking with it over one hundred million dollars-worth of savings. Sindona was charged with fraudulent bankruptcy in Italy, and on 99 counts of fraud, embezzlement, bribery, perjury and corruption in the US, for which he was given a 25-year prison sentence. He devised a salvage plan for the *Banca Privata Italiana* for which his political friends, including Giulio Andreotti, assiduously lobbied the Bank of Italy. During the period 1978–79, when Andreotti was Prime Minister and Sindona was living in the United States as a fugitive from Italian justice, indicted, but not yet convicted in the US, the two men met at least once and Andreotti had ten meetings with Sindona's defence lawyer. In the attempt to avoid extradition for trial in Italy Sindona presented an *affidavit* to the US authorities signed by leading politicians, the Procurator General of Rome, the Grandmaster of the P2 lodge and a number of prominent Milanese financiers who swore to Sindona's integrity and supported his conviction that he was being pursued in Italy for his anti-communist beliefs and consequently would not receive a fair trial.

When this failed, Sindona faked his own kidnap and fled to Sicily, where he was protected by *Cosa Nostra* for a period of three months. The Bontate faction of *Cosa Nostra* had entrusted large sums of money to him and he was under pressure to return them. From his 'captivity' Sindona wrote a series of letters to his lawyer in Rome warning that he might be forced to reveal embarrassing details about the financial arrangements of 500 politicians, bankers and other influential figures who had illegally exported capital to Switzerland. The blackmail attempt also failed, and Sindona officially reappeared in the US – after several days as guest of a member of the New York Gambino family of *La Cosa Nostra*. When his kidnap story broke down he claimed he had gone to Sicily to raise support for its eventual secession from Italy and its annexation to the United States.

The official receiver of the *Banca Privata Italiana*, Georgio Ambrosoli, had begun to unravel the illegal transactions and money-laundering operations which Sindona had undertaken for *Cosa Nostra* with the assistance of the head of the Palermo Flying Squad, Boris Giuliano. Both men were murdered in July 1979. In 1986 Sindona was convicted of ordering the Ambrosoli killing and was sentenced to life imprisonment. The prosecuting magistrate concluded,

> The most serious matter in our view [...] is the support given to the salvage plan – an outright attempt to defraud the Bank of Italy and thus the whole nation – by the most senior political figures, amongst them the then Prime Minister, Giulio Andreotti. [...] Without Andreotti and the protection given to Sindona between 1974 and 1979, the Ambrosoli murder would never have taken place.[31]

A few days after the verdict, Sindona died in a top-security prison after drinking a cup of poisoned coffee.

Andreotti–Salvo Lima

Another friendship to which Andreotti has remained loyal and which led directly to his committal for trial in Palermo on charges of Mafia association is that with Salvo Lima, his Sicilian 'ambassador'. Andreotti's name was explicitly linked through Lima to *Cosa Nostra* for the first time in August 1992 by the collaborator Leonardo Messina, a boss from San Cataldo, near Caltanissetta. Messina told investigators that Andreotti was 'the contact with Salvo Lima for all the things that interested *Cosa Nostra*', and said that he and other *mafiosi* habitually referred to Andreotti as 'uncle' to protect his identity. The collaborator Gaspare Mutolo, from the Mafia family of Partanna-Mondello near Palermo, stated that Andreotti was 'precisely the person to whom the Hon. Salvo Lima turned constantly for the decisions to be taken in Rome that involved the interests of *Cosa Nostra*'. After Messina, a further 23 state's witnesses added to the prosecution's case until, on 27 March 1993, the Palermo prosecution office requested permission from the Senate Procedures Committee to continue investigations. According to the 246-page document,

> In the light of the most recent acquisition of evidence and the logical and historical deductions to be made therefrom, elements of proof have emerged such as to permit the identification of Senator Andreotti as the point of reference in Rome for *Cosa Nostra*, that is, within a contextual relationship established in a form neither casual nor occasional, at least since 1968 and certainly until 1982, with connotations from which the crime of complicity in Mafia association can be inferred. [...] So far, the

elements of proof hitherto acquired lead to the belief, not that Senator Andreotti has ever assumed formal membership of the Mafia association known as *Cosa Nostra*, but rather that his actions and behaviour have made a positive contribution to the protection of the interests and to the realization of the goals of the organization.[32]

The elements on which the prosecution case was based were separated into different strands, based on presumed relationships of different types with the following: Salvo Lima; Nino and Ignazio Salvo; judge Corrado Carnevale; the banker Michele Sindona; General Carlo Alberto Dalla Chiesa; the journalist Mino Pecorelli; on Andreotti's actions during the kidnap of Aldo Moro in 1978; and on his alleged meetings with *Cosa Nostra* members.

The prosecution case can be summed up as follows:[33]

Salvo Lima was the son of *mafioso* Vincenzo Lima, although was probably not a sworn 'man of honour' himself. Lima's election as mayor of Palermo between 1958 and 1964 was supported by the La Barbera clan, according to a *carabinieri* report. In 1968, Lima agreed to take over the Andreotti faction of the Christian Democratic Party which until that time had drawn most of its support from the Rome area. Lima continued to enjoy electoral backing from *Cosa Nostra* and from the head of the Commission, Stefano Bontate, and was closely allied to the influential Salvo cousins. Under Lima's leadership, the Sicilian share of Andreotti's national vote rose from 2 to 10 per cent. In 1976 Andreotti accepted the offer of further support from another former DC mayor, Vito Ciancimino, who in turn was supported by the *Corleonesi* faction of *Cosa Nostra*. The pact was formalized in the Prime Minister's official residence in Rome, in the presence of Andreotti, Ciancimino, Lima, and two other national deputies from Sicily. This agreement continued at least until the regional conference of the DC held in Agrigento in 1983.

At the end of the 1970s Andreotti began to make specific use of *Cosa Nostra* support. In the early days of the kidnap of DC President Aldo Moro in March 1978 by the Red Brigades (BR), Stefano Bontate was asked to help to locate Moro's prison. Tommaso Buscetta, an influential *mafioso* at that time being held in the top security prison of Cuneo, was requested to make contact with BR leaders in prison. To do this he requested a transfer to prison in Turin, where the BR were on trial. Buscetta's transfer was to be facilitated by a friend of Andreotti, Rome prosecutor Claudio Vitalone. But Buscetta was not transferred and he subsequently discovered that Bontate's offer to help had been coun-termanded because Andreotti did not want Moro's prison to be found. Andreotti had learned that in the course of his interrogations by the Red Brigades, Moro had been giving information away which would discredit him. After Moro had been murdered, Andreotti learned that two men had copies of Moro's statements under interrogation, *cara-binieri* General Carlo Alberto Dalla Chiesa and an astute but unscrupulous journalist, Mino Pecorelli, whose weekly paper OP was considered close to the security services. Pecorelli had continuously attacked Andreotti in his paper, had hinted at what he knew of the Moro case, and in January 1979 was set to publish an article linking Andreotti to a series of irregular financial manoeuvres that had been carried out by company director Nino Rovelli. In the course of a dinner in a Rome restaurant, Pecorelli was given 30 million lire ($18 000) not to publish the story. Pecorelli was murdered in March 1979 by members of the Magliana band together with *Cosa Nostra*. The killing was ordered by Stefano Bontate who had been requested by the Salvo cousins to 'do a favour' for Andreotti.

Between the end of 1978 and spring 1979 Andreotti met Michele Sindona, a banker who had laundered money for the Bontate faction of *Cosa Nostra,* during the period when Sindona was a fugitive from Italian justice. Sindona was protected by *Cosa Nostra* during his fake kidnap later that year.

In the course of 1979, a number of Sicilian politicians tried to withdraw from *Cosa Nostra*'s influence and began to combat it with determination. The Secretary of the Palermo DC, Michele Reina, was assassinated in March 1979. After this Andreotti went to Sicily where he met Catania boss Nitto Santapaola together with Salvo Lima, their presence confirmed by the owner of the hotel where they met. The DC President of the Sicilian Region, Piersanti Mattarella, was murdered in January 1980. In February Andreotti flew secretly to Sicily in a private plane provided by the Salvos, where he had a meeting with Bontate and other members of the Commission at which he protested at the killings. Bontate warned him, ' We command in Sicily and if you don't want the DC to disappear completely you'll have to do as we say. Otherwise we'll take away not only your votes in Sicily but the votes in Reggio Calabria and the whole of the south of Italy as well. You'll have to make do with the votes in the north where everyone votes Communist.'

A few months later, war between the Bontate faction and the *Corleonesi* escalated; Bontate was murdered and his faction of *Cosa*

Nostra virtually annihilated. All Bontate's political contacts were taken over by the *Corleonesi* (Ciancimino having been politically discredited), while the Salvo cousins and Salvo Lima survived the conflict because they were the principal link with Andreotti.

In the spring of 1982, following the assassination of PCI regional secretary Pio La Torre, General Dalla Chiesa was appointed Prefect of Palermo. Dalla Chiesa was invited to a meeting by Andreotti before taking up his post, at which he told Andreotti that he would have 'no respect for the most corrupted faction on the island'. In his private diary Dalla Chiesa wrote that the Andreotti faction in Sicily was 'in it up to their necks'. Dalla Chiesa did not obtain the institutional support and the special powers requested by him to deal with the Mafia and in September 1982 he was murdered together with his wife. According to Tommaso Buscetta, the Pecorelli and Dalla Chiesa murders were linked: in 1979 Buscetta had been asked on behalf of a 'political entity' (whom he later named as Andreotti) to sound out the Red Brigades' willingness to claim responsibility for the murder of Dalla Chiesa if carried out in any part of Italy. He was told that the BR would only agree if one of their members participated in the attack, and the plan was dropped. Buscetta was with fellow *mafioso* Gaetano Badalamenti in Brazil when he heard the news of Dalla Chiesa's murder, when Badalamenti commented that Dalla Chiesa had been sent to Palermo deliberately so that he could be assassinated. Pecorelli and Dalla Chiesa were both murdered because they represented a threat to Andreotti.

In August 1985 Andreotti visited the Sicilian town of Mazaro del Vallo, officially to inspect the naval fleet, and the same day had a series of private meetings in a seaside hotel with local politicians. One of his meetings – a discreet encounter over which the mayor of the town stood guard – was with an important *mafioso* of the area. The meeting had been noted by a police superintendent, whose filed report came to light during the judicial investigation.

Cosa Nostra had traditionally voted for the DC because it was the party which gave the best guarantees for the organization's interests, in particular through influence over court trials in Palermo and the Supreme Court in Rome. At Lima's request, Andreotti had intervened in a Supreme Court verdict in 1981. A meeting was held in Rome between Mafia boss Gaetano Badalamenti, one of the Salvo cousins and Andreotti to discuss the Court's verdict on Badalamenti's brother-in law, Filippo Rimi. Although Rimi had been given a life sentence, the Supreme Court annulled the verdict. The Supreme Court also annulled three life sentences handed out for the 1980 murder of police captain

Emanuele Basile, despite overwhelming evidence of the defendants' guilt, on the grounds that one of the defence lawyers had not been informed of the date the jury was to be selected. Carnevale had a 'special personal relationship' with Andreotti and had 'always been approachable' by *Cosa Nostra*. According to one collaborator, he 'constituted a guarantee and certainly not just for his juridical ideas'.

Cosa Nostra felt that Andreotti was not doing enough to influence the maxi-trial in its favour. The attempts made by lawyers to block the trial – by challenging the President of the Court and by trying to have all the trial documents read out in court – had failed. As a warning to Lima and Andreotti to do more, votes were shifted in the 1987 general election to the Socialist Party and to the Radicals. Andreotti had a further meeting with *Cosa Nostra* leaders on 20 September 1987 at the Palermo home of Ignazio Salvo, who at that time was under house arrest and on trial for Mafia association. Totò Riina and Salvo Lima were also present. When Andreotti entered he and Riina kissed on both cheeks. By this stage Andreotti was so deeply compromised with *Cosa Nostra* that he could not withdraw – he was obliged to attend the meeting to save Lima's life and safeguard his party's electoral support.

From 1987 the Supreme Court began the process of dismantling the prosecution's case in the maxi-trial through repeated annulment of convictions. Retrials continued until the spring of 1991 when judge Corrado Carnevale indicated the composition of the Supreme Court section that would pass final judgement. However the President of the Supreme Court decided in October to appoint Arnaldo Valente to preside over the hearing rather than Carnevale.

Senator Andreotti has denied all the charges made against him, the substance of his defence being as follows:

- His movements in Sicily were always fully accounted for, he has never met any of the Mafia figures mentioned, and never knowingly met either Nino or Ignazio Salvo. He was never directly involved in Sicilian politics and left all such matters to Salvo Lima. Lima was not a devil amongst angels and had great organizational and political skills.
- There were two Michele Sindonas – 1 and 2. He knew only Michele Sindona 1, whom half of Italy had hailed as the saviour of the lira.
- Everything possible was done to obtain Aldo Moro's release without compromising national security. He and General Dalla Chiesa had great mutual respect and their relationship was always cordial.

- On no occasion did he interfere with court trials. He led a government which from 1989 to 1992 had passed some of the most severe antimafia legislation to date.

At Giulio Andreotti's own wish, on 10 June 1993 the Senate Procedures Committee authorized the Palermo prosecution service to continue its investigation. The charges of complicity in murder and of Mafia association were split into two separate court proceedings because a co-defendant in the Pecorelli murder trial, Claudio Vitalone, had been a public prosecutor in Rome at the time of the murder, and thus responsibility for investigating the murder could not be given to his former office but was transferred to Perugia. The request to commit Andreotti and Vitalone for trial for complicity in the murder of Mino Pecorelli was made on 20 July 1995; the trial began the following November and was continuing. After more than a year of investigations, the antimafia prosecution office in Palermo requested that Giulio Andreotti be committed for trial. The weight of evidence against him had increased such that the original charge of *concorso esterno* or 'favouring from outside' was altered to formal participation in an association of a Mafia kind – *associazione a delinquere di stampo mafioso*.

The request for committal was evaluated by the judge for preliminary enquiries, Agostino Gristina, in January 1995. The primary aim of Andreotti's defence lawyers was to have the charges dismissed completely, but failing that, they hoped to have the trial proceedings transferred from Palermo to Rome. If it could be proved that the charges related to Andreotti's role as a government minister then he could be tried by a Court of Ministers rather than an ordinary court. On 2 March judge Gristina accepted the prosecution's case almost in its entirety and committed Andreotti for trial. He ordered that it should take place in Palermo since the charges by their very nature related to Sicily, *Cosa Nostra*'s operational centre. They did not fall within the competence of the Court of Ministers because there was no indication that *Cosa Nostra* had made use of Andreotti's role or abilities as minister or as prime minister; rather, 'the contribution that Giulio Andreotti offered *Cosa Nostra* derived from the concentration of powers in the hands of the defendant as leader of the national party faction and as a person of undeniable prestige'.[34]

On hearing the decision Andreotti commented, 'I feel bitter about this injustice [...] I bear no ill will towards procurator Caselli, he found the stew already cooked, but I will prove that there are paid witnesses.'[35] On 26 September 1995 the trial began, with 401 witnesses summoned for the prosecution and 128 for the defence, including former UN Secretary-General Xavier Perez de Cuellar, the former German Foreign Minister Hans Dietrich Genscher and a former US ambassador to Italy, Peter Secchia.

The accusations made against Giulio Andreotti had not been judicially verified at the time of writing. They rely to a considerable extent upon eyewitness accounts and testimonies of lifelong criminals whose motives for collaboration are questionable. The circumstances of the two meetings between Andreotti and Stefano Bontate were described by the collaborator Francesco Marino Mannoia, a member of Bontate's 'family' of Santa Maria de Gesù in Palermo, during an interrogation in the United States in April 1993. Tommaso Buscetta broke his silence on Mafia–political links that same month, talking to investigators about his friendship with Salvo Lima and the Salvo cousins, and about Andreotti's position with regard to the Moro kidnap and Mino Pecorelli. Andreotti's meeting with Totò Riina in 1987 was recounted by Baldassare Di Maggio, whose information had led to Riina's arrest in January 1993.

An important question is why Tommaso Buscetta, who had begun to collaborate with the authorities in 1984 and who had built up a relationship of trust with judge Falcone, always refused to discuss with him the political links with *Cosa Nostra* which he confirmed after Falcone's death. For an explanation, the Palermo prosecutors referred to the transcription of an interrogation of Buscetta by Falcone in February 1988:

I have warned you on several occasions that I would only speak about Mafia and politics if and when the time is right. From what I have seen so far I must point out with a certain bitterness that the lack of any serious will on the part of the State to fight the Mafia phenomenon persists; [...] I would be most ill-advised to speak about this, the real nub of the Mafia problem, when the people I would have to talk about have not yet left active public life.[36]

Buscetta had referred to the same difficulty in 1985, during an interrogation by the US attorney Richard Martin, public prosecutor in the 'Pizza Connection' heroin trial in New York. In July 1996 Martin stated under oath that Buscetta, when asked to clarify his objections to revealing Mafia–political links, had replied with the single word, 'Andreotti'.

Strategies for survival

The harsh measures introduced in 1992 and the social isolation that followed the attacks of 1992–93 forced a number of structural changes on *Cosa Nostra*. The organization has become less hierarchical and more impermeable with smaller, tightly structured cells whose membership is unknown to all but a few. The 'ground rules' have changed – there are no more grand initiation ceremonies or rituals, instead there is greater internal secrecy and more careful selectivity in recruitment. There is an increased tendency to recruit family members on the presumption that collaboration with the authorities is less likely. In this sense *Cosa Nostra* has moved more towards the structure of the *'Ndrangheta*. Potential members do not go through a long period of assessment as was once the case, and senior positions are reached at a younger age, with relative novices increasingly taking over the functions of their imprisoned fathers. At the same time a new generation of *Cosa Nostra* membership seems to have developed – a white-collar Mafia, not formally affiliated – whose aim is to get rid of the *Corleonesi* and the strategies of open confrontation with the State, and to return to a 'live and let live' situation of reciprocal tolerance. There have been several signs of dissent from Riina's methods, including an attack in December 1995 on the country house owned by his defence lawyer, Nino Fileccia, and the information from a collabora-tor that a plan was under way to kidnap Riina's 18-year-old son Giovanni. The capture in April 1998 of one of Riina's closest allies, Vito Vitale, boss of the town of Partinico, west of Palermo, was considered by observers to be another important defeat for the militarist strategy.

While the perennial goals of profit making and power seeking have continued, constant pressure from law enforcement has caused *Cosa Nostra* to concentrate attention on reimposing control over local territory and on activities with which collaborators are unfamiliar, such as expansion outside the traditional areas and into new sectors of operation.

Involvement in the politics, administration and economic life of a locality is fundamental for *Cosa Nostra's* control of territory and conse-quently for its potency as a criminal force. Survival for a socially integrated criminal organization depends at least as much upon protection and *omertà* from below as from above. Thus even in the early 1980s, when the principal heroin-trafficking clans in Palermo were making annual profits of around $600 million per annum, activities such as door-to-door extortions of shops and small businesses never ceased – they are a means of social control as well as a source of revenue for the lower cadres of the organization. When life becomes more difficult for the Mafia, as it has done since 1992, these more 'primitive' criminal activities take on greater importance. This explains why, although most forms of violent crime have dropped in the four southern regions, extortion and loan-sharking have been either stable or rising.

Another consequence of increased law-enforcement pressure in the southern regions has been that *Cosa Nostra* and its sister organizations have moved outside their traditional areas of operation. The coastal zones of Liguria, Tuscany and Emilia Romagna have attracted investments in tourism and leisure-related activities; north-eastern Italy serves as a corridor for drugs and arms trafficking. Milan has become the primary centre for heroin and cocaine distribution and for money laundering. In 1996 the Interior Ministry estimated that 104 organized crime families were operating in northern Italy; in the three years to October 1997 the Milan antimafia prosecution office issued arrest warrants for more than 2500 members of the *'Ndrangheta,* although investigators had no illusions that they had dismantled the criminal structures in Lombardy.[37] In the Milan area an estimated 10 per cent of commercial businesses pay up in order to operate in peace; in 1996 the north accounted for 31 per cent of all reported extortion attempts in Italy (this could of course indicate less fear on the part of those making the reports).

The development of international political, police and judicial collaboration against organized crime was discussed in Chapter 6. Geo-political changes such as the Single European Market and the end of the Cold War have encouraged international criminal mobility and cooperation, to which a multilateral response has been framed. For Italian criminality, overseas expansion has not only offered economic benefits but has become an important means of avoiding arrest and imprisonment in Italy. All four organized crime groups have operated in Eastern Europe and Russia since the early 1990s, initially with the aim of laundering illicit profits but also for trafficking in drugs, arms and in counterfeit currency. Italian criminals are thought to have provided expertise and distribution networks to help Russian *maffiya* groups extend their illicit activities throughout Russia, Poland, the Czech Republic, Bulgaria and Romania. A 1993 investigation showed that Calabrian clans from Locri and Gioia Tauro had purchased large sums of roubles with which to invest in a bank, a steel works and a chemical plant near St Petersburg. A network of contacts had been established between Italian criminals and prominent public officials and private individuals connected to the Russian Defence Ministry. The same network was thought to have been used for the acquisition and importation of arms and explosives into Italy. Calabrian clans were working with criminals in Romania to exploit the privatization process through criminal joint ventures; members of the United Holy Crown have relocated to Montenegro where they operate arms and cigarette smuggling rings.

There has been an increasing tendency for all four Mafia groups – in particular when operating outside their own home regions – to cooperate in federative arrangements at home and abroad, according to geographical area and sector of competence, the aim being to reduce conflict and maintain competitiveness in global illicit markets. Arrests of major drug-trafficking rings in Italy invariably reveal mixed networks comprising all four Italian groups and frequently include non-Italian nationals. In 1997, 195 Colombians were being investigated for drug-trafficking offences in Italy.

Factional conflicts have diminished, in particular between the *'Ndrangheta* clans. A six-year war between the Di Stefano and Imerti factions was concluded with a truce in 1991, since when a horizontally-structured 'council' of *'Ndrangheta* leaders meets regularly to resolve disputes and discuss strategy. The *'Ndrangheta*, less prone to the phenomenon of collaboration because of its biological family-based structure, is probably the most robust of all the Italian criminal organizations and has taken precedence over *Cosa Nostra* in the arms, heroin and cocaine markets.

The most fluid situation remains in Campania, where the collapse of institutional protection and the arrests – often followed by collaboration – or natural deaths of virtually all the 'historic' leaders have decimated the *Camorra*. In the absence of strong leadership the resulting situation is one of anarchic, unfocused violence as newcomers fight for entry into drug distribution, cigarette smuggling and the territorial control of illicit markets and public works contracts in Naples and its hinterland.

One of the most important new sectors of Italian criminal activity, and one in which the *Camorra* has taken a dominant role, is environmental crime, in particular the illicit disposal of toxic and industrial waste. In 1995 the Environment Ministry reported that of 22.3 million tonnes of annual industrial waste, only 14 million had been recycled in authorized centres, and that of 26 million tonnes of solid waste, only 19 million had been disposed of officially.[38] In other words, around 15 million tonnes of waste are being recycled illegally each year, an activity which brings in an estimated volume of business for the criminal organizations of \$3–3.6 billion.[39] By April 1997 the threat had become so serious that a parliamentary commission of enquiry was set up to investigate the infiltration of the waste disposal sector by organized crime and to recommend appropriate measures to overcome the problem.

The greatest single danger in this sector is the involvement of organized crime in the illegal traffic of radioactive materials. In 1996 over one hundred seizures of such material had been made and 75 individuals were under investigation.[40] While all the seizures made until recently have involved the recycling of spent fuel, in March 1998 there was proof for the first time that the Mafia was dealing in weapons-grade material. A sting operation led to the seizure of a bar of enriched uranium, part of a consignment of nine units for which *Cosa Nostra*, together with the Magliana band and the *'Ndrangheta,* were apparently seeking purchasers.[41]

The role of women

One of the consequences of law-enforcement efforts against Italian criminality since 1992 has been a partial redefinition of the role of women. Traditionally kept on the margins of criminal activity, the women of *Cosa Nostra* saw and heard everything but were excluded from decision making, from the direct exercise of power and from carrying out acts of violence. A woman's principal functions were to serve as a bridge by which the power of two Mafia families could be reinforced through marriage, and to rear children, preferably sons. The participation of women in illegal operations was often limited to the preparation of drug consignments or to a role as courier or intermediary. If their menfolk were arrested, they became vital messengers between prison and the outside world. The essence of the Mafia code of honour – *omertà*, or silence – literally means 'the ability to be a man' and calls for 'self control, a negation of sentiment in oneself and in others and the rejection of any "feminine" qualities in other men'.[42] Women were not generally trusted to fulfil these requirements.

The role of women within the *anti*mafia movement was described in Chapter 5. While a significant number of women have broken free of the subordination of *Cosa Nostra*, it should be pointed out that they are the exception rather than the rule. Women have on occasions influenced their partner's choice to become a state's witness but many are unwilling to sacrifice the status and respect that a boss's wife commands, and have reacted negatively to a decision to collaborate. The wife of one collaborator set fire to his house and to that of her parents-in-law and refused all offers of state protection, despite having two young children. When brothers Emanuele and Pasquale Di Filippo decided to collaborate, their mother, sister and wives disowned them. Their sister Agata announced 'I want people to know that I, my mother and my father dissociate ourselves totally from the decision taken by my brothers, rather by my ex-brothers, they are infamous traitors [...] we cannot open our shutters for the shame of it.' Both wives would have preferred their husbands dead than collaborators, and one commented, 'for the children he is dead, it's as if they never had a father'.[43] In another case a collaborator's wife who had taken a lover was absolved from blame as it had exposed him to further ignominy.

With the arrest of so many of their menfolk – and perhaps independently, in a process of natural evolution – Mafia women have begun to take charge of specific sectors of illicit activity. Even though the woman who contributes to the associative force of the Mafia organization through violence or intimidation is still rare, economic and financial operations including money laundering are increasingly dominated by women. To use a division of roles invented by Alan Block,[44] women have entered the 'enterprise syndicate' but not the 'power syndicate' of organized crime. The statistics reflect the growing but still exiguous level of female involvement in reported cases of Mafia association.

Table 7.1 Incidence of reported cases of Mafia-type association, 1990–95

	1990	1991	1992	1993	1994	1995
Men	80	132	215	232	1214	1888
Women	1	1	10	9	16	89
Total	81	133	225	241	1230	1977

Source: Ministero di Grazie e Giustizia. Elaboration by DIA 1995.

After the war, peace?

This chapter has described the Mafia's response to the antimafia efforts made since 1992 and the consequences of that response. But to complete the analysis we must return to the reason given by Totò Riina for launching a terrorist campaign against the State – 'you have to wage war in order to negotiate peace'. There can be no doubt that the war was waged, but has peace been negotiated, and if so, on what terms? What objectives, if any, did *Cosa Nostra* achieve through its twin-track strategy of terror and dialogue?

In most respects the bombing campaign of 1992 and 1993 was a complete failure for *Cosa Nostra*. Those materially responsible for the Falcone and Borsellino killings and for the five car bomb attacks were identified, arrested and convicted. Arrests for membership of a Mafia-type organization increased from 874 in 1991 to a record high of 2136 in 1994 and were still high at 1324 in 1997. Of the known *Cosa Nostra* leadership, most of the key operatives were in prison with the exception of *Corleonese* boss Bernardo Provenzano and his sidekick Matteo Messina Denaro. The perpetrators of the attacks did not bomb or talk their way to impunity nor was the legislation passed in 1992 withdrawn. The 41 *bis* regime remains in force – despite attenuation – at least until the end of 1999. Attempts to assassinate and to discredit the collaborators did not stem the tide of *Cosa Nostra* members willing to betray the organization. In a period of five years from 1993 there were no massacres and no murders of state representatives, although two parish priests were assassinated for their antimafia commitment. The intensity with which Italian society as a whole pursued antimafia efforts after 1992 created a powerful movement which removed a layer of consensus and left *Cosa Nostra* more exposed.

Future court trials will examine whether any dialogue was opened up between elements of *Cosa Nostra* and political or institutional figures, and if so, whether any criminal responsibilities derive from them. But a number of circumstances – suggesting that some form of 'peace negotiation' was opened with the State – may have been deliberately obscured at institutional level. These concern the sequence of events leading to Totò Riina's arrest in January 1993. Baldassare Di Maggio, whose information led directly to Riina's capture, was arrested only one week earlier, on 8 January, at a routine police road block in Piedmont, when he was found to be carrying a gun without authorization. Apparently, within hours of his arrest, Di Maggio asked to speak to a *Carabinieri* official whom he had known and trusted in the past, General Francesco Delfino[c] and decided to collaborate because, after beginning an affair with a woman from his home town of San Giuseppe Jato, his life was in danger from the rival Brusca family. Di Maggio indicated to *Carabinieri* the zone of Palermo in which he believed Riina was living, and a few days later, on 12 January, he was consigned to the custody of ROS, the special *carabinieri* antimafia group, in Palermo. The Uditore area of the city was kept under continuous surveillance by ROS until 14 January when a woman was filmed leaving an apartment building in via Bernini. Di Maggio recognized her as Riina's wife, Ninetta Bagarella. The next morning, Di Maggio and ROS agents were waiting in vehicles at a road junction a short distance from via Bernini when a car with Riina and driver Salvatore Biondino drew up to the junction. They surrendered without a struggle. After the arrests, which took place around 8.30a.m., ROS officials requested the magistrates in charge of the investigation, including the newly arrived chief prosecutor, Gian Carlo Caselli, not to raid the apartment but to place it

---

[c]   General Delfino was arrested and indicted for extorting money in a kidnap case in 1998.

under surveillance in the hope of making more arrests. This was approved, after assurances were given that ROS had sufficient men and resources for the task. In fact, the apartment in via Bernini was watched for only six hours, after which all surveillance was abandoned. The Palermo prosecution office was informed eighteen days later that there had been a 'misunderstanding' over the surveillance and that, in the intervening period, every item of furniture down to the last picture hook had been removed and the apartment had been completely repainted, leaving no fingerprints or any other trace of its former occupants.

It has been suggested that some kind of deal was negotiated, not on the basis of the *papello* or written list of requests which, according to Brusca, was presented by Totò Riina, but with, or on behalf of, the other Corleone godfather Bernardo Provenzano, more sceptical about the 1993 bombing campaign, who may have 'sold' Riina in exchange for the opportunity to acquire an archive of valuable and compromising material which Riina held in the via Bernini apartment.[45] This version of Riina's arrest has been denied by ROS commander General Mario Mori, but he has confirmed that channels of communication were opened with *Cosa Nostra* through a former mayor of Palermo, Vito Ciancimino, known to be close to the *Corleonesi*. Ciancimino had been prepared to cooperate in the hope of being exempted from serving the residual portion of a ten-year sentence for Mafia association for which he was convicted in 1992.

In an interview of November 1997 Mori admitted, 'It's true we were very active in 1992. We wanted to capture Riina and we wanted to put an end to the massacres. We rolled up our sleeves and got to work as we knew how.'[46] In January 1998 he confirmed his account in court in Florence – 'We had to make the attempt and Vito Ciancimino in certain respects was blackmailable.'[47] To sound out the willingness of *Cosa Nostra* to talk, Ciancimino had used Riina's doctor, Antonino Cinà, as intermediary. A reply had come back suggesting a meeting outside Italy and asking to know on whose behalf discussions were being sought. When Mori told Ciancimino that the aim was the capture of Riina, he protested that his life would be in danger and seemed unwilling to continue. After some weeks he had apparently changed his mind and asked for a detailed map of the Uditore zone of Palermo. At this point – January 1993 – the arrest of Di Maggio brought matters to a rapid conclusion.

General Mori's version of 'negotiations' with *Cosa Nostra* differs in one significant respect from that of Mafia boss Giovanni Brusca – the *carabinieri* officer's account makes no reference to the *papello* thought by Brusca to have been written by Antonino Cinà. Mori has denied the existence of such a list, saying he would have seized it in evidence had it been presented. Giovanni Brusca remains convinced that Baldassare Di Maggio, who knew the proprietor of the apartment in which Riina and his family had lived since 1987, could have led authorities directly to it, allowing Riina to be arrested in his sleep rather than risking a bloodbath in the street, and that some deal was mediated through the *Carabinieri*. Several well-placed observers in Palermo are inclined to agree.

Given the circumstances that prevailed in 1992–93 in Italy, one should not be too surprised if some form of compromise was reached with the less violent wing of *Cosa Nostra*. Governments in many countries, including that of the United Kingdom, have reluctantly sat down to talk with murderers or their protectors in the interests of peace. But if such a deal was made, it might be in the general interest for the Italian authorities to give public account of their actions as soon as possible, in order to avoid political blackmail and the risk of more violence in the future.

Conclusion

Italy stands at a crossroads in the antimafia fight. Outstanding results have been achieved in the seven years since 1992 but the political battle against organized crime is in limbo. Sadly, without the spectacle of 'illustrious corpses' there is little political capital in maintaining a rigorous antimafia front. Industrialists, bankers, politicians and all those anxious to promote Italy's investment potential do not want to be reminded that the Mafia still exists, that it is far from defeated and that some areas of the country remain under the effective control of organized crime. But only continuity and constant alertness to the developments of the Mafia phenomenon will prevent it from regaining the ground wrested from it by the Antimafia. The Sicilian proverb *'Calati iunco ca passa la china'* meaning, 'lie low until the floodwater has subsided ' has served the Mafia well for decades and could do so in the future.

Independently of whether any compromise was reached with elements of *Cosa Nostra*, Italy is in a position to prove by the operation of its democratic institutions, and in particular through its criminal justice and social policies, that there will be no going back on the determination to defeat the Mafia which united Italian society and set an inspiring example to the rest of the world. Continuing law-enforcement efforts are necessary, but policies should focus at least as much on the antimafia of prevention as on the antimafia of repression: tolerance of a 50 per cent unemployment rate among young people in traditionally Mafia-dominated regions is a sign of unforgivable neglect.

The most important challenge facing the Italian political class in the antimafia struggle is identical to that which it confronts in the wider sphere – that of relegitimizing the exercise of public power by example, of leading Italians towards a faith in public authority and institutions and reversing the common view of the State as a hostile force to be distrusted to one which recognizes it as guardian of the collective good. If successive Italian parliaments have the wisdom to pursue the antimafia struggle by ensuring that, in Paolo Borsellino's words, the State 'works' throughout Italy, there is a real chance that the criminal phenomenon which has so tragically depleted the extraordinary people and land of Italy's *mezzogiorno* will wither and fade away. There could be no greater gain for Italy, and for Europe, in the new millennium.

Remember to remember

those who fell
struggling to build
another history
and another land

remember them one by one
so that silence
does not close for ever
the mouths of the dead
and where justice has not arrived
let there be memory
and let it be stronger
than dust
and complicity[48]

Notes

Introduction

1. G. Falcone, in collaboration with M. Padovani, *Cose di Cosa Nostra*. (Milan: Rizzoli, 1991) p. 71.
2. *Ibid.*, p. 171.
3. Confirmed by Paolo Borsellino, speaking at a conference held by the magazine *Micromega* in Palermo on 25 June 1992.
4. In conversation with the author, Palermo, 3 June 1998.
5. In conversation with the author, Palermo, 30 March 1989.
6. Interview by the author with Giovanni Falcone, Rome, 28 February 1989.
7. P. Borsellino writing in *Secolo d'Italia*, 18 January 1989.
8. A. Blok, *The Mafia of a Sicilian Village 1860–1960*, (first published Harper & Row, 1974); with foreword by Charles Tilly, Cambridge: Polity Press, 1988 p. xxi.

1 The significance of 1992

1. U. Santino, *Oltre La Legalità*, (Palermo, Centro Siciliano di Documentazione, Appunti 6, 1997) p. 36.
2. G. Falcone, in collaboration with M. Padovani, *Cose di Cosa Nostra*, (Milan: Rizzoli, 1991) p. 83.
3. Interrogation of Leonardo Messina by Palermo prosecution office on 8 January 1993, cited in request for authorization to proceed against Giulio Andreotti, Procura della Repubblica presso il Tribunale di Palermo, Direzione Distrettuale Antimafia, 27 March 1993.
4. *Il Mondo*, 9–16 March 1992.
5. Interrogation of Gaspare Mutolo by Caltanissetta prosecution office, cited in *Delitto Lima, L'Atto di Accusa dei Giudici di Palermo*, (Agrigento: Suddovest, 1992) p. 15.
6. Interrogation of Gaspare Mutolo by Caltanissetta prosecution office, *op. cit.* p. 19.
7. Statement made in court in the trial of Giulio Andreotti for Mafia association by state's witness Angelo Siino, Rome, 18 December 1997.

2 The Mafia–Antimafia seesaw

1. Commissione Parlamentare Antimafia, VI Legislatura, *Disegni di Legge e Relazioni, Documenti*, vol. XXXVI, no. XXXIII-2, (Rome, 1976) p. 97. Henceforth called Antimafia Commission 1976.
2. P. Ivaldi, *Narcomafie*, Turin, October 1995.

3. This clarification was first provided by the collaborator Tommaso Buscetta during his interrogations by judge Giovanni Falcone in 1984.
4. L. Franchetti and S. Sonnino, *Inchiesta in Sicilia, vol. I, Condizioni Politiche e Amministrative della Sicilia* (1877), (Florence: Vallecchi, 1974).
5. J. Schneider and P. Schneider, 'Mafia, Antimafia e la Questione della <<Cultura>>' in *La Mafia, le Mafie*, (eds) G. Fiandaca and S. Costantino (Bari: Laterza, 1994) p. 299.
6. Antimafia Commission 1976, p. 109.
7. *Ibid.*, p. 118.
8. *Ibid.*, p.1121.
9. *Ibid.*, p. 35.
10. *Ibid.*, p. 44.
11. S. Lupo, *Storia della Mafia*, (Rome: Donzelli, 1996) p. 247.
12. C.A. Dalla Chiesa, *In Nome del Popolo Italiano*, autobiography edited by N. Dalla Chiesa, (Milan: Rizzoli, 1997) p. 151.
13. Antimafia Commission 1976, p. 165.
14. *Ibid.*, p. 108.
15. Antimafia Commission 1976, Final majority report, p. 54.
16. Intervention during discussion of draft Final Report in Antimafia Commission, 16 July 1975, in *Cesare Terranova In Memoria*, (privately published) Palermo, 1982.
17. Antimafia Commission 1976, Final minority report, p. 581.
18. Intervention during declaration of vote on the Final Report in Antimafia Commission, 5 January 1976, in *Cesare Terranova in Memoria, op. cit.*
19. P. Arlacchi, *Mafia Business*, (Oxford: Oxford University Press, 1988), p. 207.
20. D. Dalla Porta, M. Rossi, *Cifre Crudeli*, (Bologna: Istituto di Studi e Ricerche Carlo Cattaneo) 1984) Tab. 5 p. 35.
21. Statement made to the Parliamentary Antimafia Commission, (XI Legislature) by collaborator Leonardo Messina, 4 December 1992.
22. Interview with Giorgio Bocca in *La Repubblica*, 10 August 1982.
23. 'Direzione Nazionale Antimafia', undated document, Rome.
24. G.M. Flick, 'L'Associazione a Delinquere di Tipo Mafioso. Interrogativi e Riflessioni sui Problemi Proposti dall'Art. 416 bis C.P.', *Rivista Italiana di Diritto e Procedura Penale*, Anno XXXI-Fasc.3, (1988) 849–66.
25. Commissioners Elkan and Assennato, cited in G. Di Lello, *Giudici*, (Palermo: Sellerio, 1994) p. 137.
26. Author's interview with Luciano Violante, published in *Scotland on Sunday*, 23 May 1993.
27. G. Chinnici, U. Santino, *La Violenza Programmata*, (Milan: Franco Angeli, 1989) p. 257.
28. U. Santino, 'Mafia e Lotta alla Mafia: Materiali per un Bilancio e Nuove Ipotesi di Lavoro', in *L'Antimafia Difficile* (ed.) U. Santino, (Palermo: Centro Siciliano di documentazione Giuseppe Impastato, CSD Quaderni, 1989) p. 28.
29. *Commissione Parlamentare d'Inchiesta sul Fenomeno della Mafia e sulle altre Associazioni criminali similari*, X Legislatura, Relazione di minoranza, 24 January 1990, p. 40.
30. G. Falcone, in collaboration with M. Padovani, *Cose di Cosa Nostra* (Milan: Rizzoli, 1991) p. 65.
31. Open letter to CSM, published in *Corriere della Sera*, 31 July 1988.

32. Giovanni Falcone's sister Maria, in conversation with the author, Palermo, 27 May 1998.
33. S. Lodato, *Dieci Anni di Mafia*, (Milan: Rizzoli, 1990) p. 276.
34. Judge Luca Tescaroli, quoted in *La Nazione*, 11 December 1997.
35. A. Stille, *Excellent Cadavers* (London: Vintage, 1996) p. 329.
36. Interview in *L'Ora*, (Palermo) 4 April 1991, reproduced in *Mafia o Sviluppo Un dibattito con Libero Grassi*, (Palermo: Osservatorio Libero Grassi, 1992).
37. *Ibid.*
38. L. Violante, *Non è la Piovra*, (Turin: Einaudi, 1994) p. 207.
39. L. Violante (ed.) *I Soldi della Mafia, Rapporto '98* (Bari: Laterza, 1998) p. 266.
40. *La Repubblica*, 23–24 February 1992.
41. *Il Mondo*, 9–16 March 1992.
42. *Corriere della Sera*, 1 April 1992.
43. G. Sinisi, Presentation of book, "Giovanni Falcone: Interventi e Proposte 1982–1992" in *I Collaboratori di Giustizia* conference papers published by the Fonadzione Giovanni e Francesca Falcone, Palermo 21–22 May 1994.

3 The political response

1. *Corriere della Sera*, 8 April 1992.
2. Cited in *Corriere della Sera*, 25 May 1998 (anniversary of Scalfaro's presidential election).
3. For interpretation of the antimafia legislation the author has drawn on G. Nanula, *La Lotta alla Mafia*, (Milan: Giuffrè Editore, 1996). The analysis given here is substantially the same as that contained in: A. Jamieson, 'Antimafia Efforts in Italy 1992-1997', *Studies in Conflict and Terrorism*, Vol. 21, July–Sept 1998 No. 3, Taylor & Francis, London/Philadelphia, pp. 233–60. The author is grateful to Taylor & Francis for permission to reproduce.
4. *L'Unità*, 5 August 1992.
5. G. Neppi Modona, 'Garanzie per gli Accusati e per gli Accusatori: USA e Italia, due Sistemi a Confronto', published in papers of the conference *'I collaboratori di Giustizia, Legislazioni e Esperienze a Confronto*, (Palermo: Fondazione Giovanni e Francesca Falcone, 1995) p. 97.
6. *La Repubblica*, 10 June 1992.
7. Palermo public prosecutor Gioacchino Natoli, in conversation with the author, Palermo 6 June 1998.
8. *Corriere della Sera*, 10 June 1992.
9. L. Violante in *L'Unità*, 21 July 1992.
10. Address to the Italian Senate, 23 July 1997.
11. *Corriere della Sera*, 21 July 1992.
12. *La Repubblica*, 1 October 1992.
13. Commissione Parlamentare Antimafia, *Relazioni della XI legislatura* (9 marzo 1993–18 febbraio 1994), Camera dei Deputati, Roma, 1995, p. 24. Henceforth called Antimafia Commission, XI legislature.
14. *Ibid.*, p. 29.
15. *Ibid.*, p. 44.
16. *Ibid.*, p. 59.
17. *Ibid.*, p. 65.

18. *Ibid.*, p. 69.
19. Gaspare Mutolo before the Antimafia Commission, 10 February 1993.
20. Leonardo Messina before the Antimafia Commission, 4 December 1992.
21. *L'Unità*, 7 April 1993.
22. Antimafia Commission, XI legislature, p. 849.
23. *Ibid.*, p. 1176.
24. *Ibid.*, p. 761.
25. *Ibid.*, p. 1161 note 11.
26. *Ibid.*, pp. 1416–17.
27. *Ibid.*, p. 1160.
28. *Ibid.*, p. 1036.
29. *Ibid.*, p. 1157.
30. *Corriere della Sera*, 16 February 1994.
31. Panorama, 11 February 1994.
32. *Corriere della Sera*, 28 March 1994.
33. For example, court deposition of collaborator Francesco La Marca, cited in *La Repubblica*, 2 June 1998.
34. *Narcomafie*, Turin, March 1996, p. 36.
35. *L'Espresso*, 27 May 1994, quoted in P. McCarthy, *The Crisis of the Italian State*, (Basingstoke: Macmillan Press, 1997) p. 152.
36. M. Brutti, 'Cosa Nostra nella Crisi del Sistema Politico Italiano, in L. Violante (ed.) *Mafie e Antimafia Rapporto '96*, (Bari: Laterza, 1996) p. 64.
37. *Corriere della Sera*, 14 December 1995, 6 January 1995.
38. *L'Espresso,* 4 December 1997.
39. *L'Espresso*, 2 October 1997.
40. Official communication by the Prime Minister, Silvio Berlusconi, to the Parliamentary Antimafia Commission, Rome, 21 October 1994.
41. *Corriere della Sera*, 15 May 1998.
42. L. Violante, *Non E' La Piovra*, (Turin: Einaudi, 1994) p. 286.
43. McCarthy, *op. cit.* p. 207.
44. *Corriere della Sera*, 13 December 1995.
45. In conversation with the author, Palermo, 5 June 1998.
46. Ottaviano Del Turco, Chairman of the Antimafia Commission (XIII legislature) in conversation with the author, Rome, 4 November 1998.
47. Interview with the author, Palermo, 5 June 1998.
48. *Corriere della Sera*, 14 January 1994.

4 The law-enforcement response

1. *La Repubblica*, 4 August 1992.
2. *La Repubblica*, 26 July 1992.
3. *Corriere della Sera*, 28 August 1992.
4. Ministero dell'Interno, *Rapporto sul Fenomeno della Criminalità Organizzata* (1993), Rome, April 1994.
5. Colonel G. Cornacchione, Italian Army, in presentation to Nato Defence College, Rome, 29 September 1995.
6. Judge Gian Carlo Caselli to the author on 5 June 1998, Palermo; judge Giovanni Tinebra to the author on 11 June 1998, Rome.

7. In conversation with the author, Palermo, 5 June 1998.
8. *L'Unità*, 25 July 1992.
9. *L'Unità*, 28 August 1992.
10. *L'Unità*, 16 January 1993.
11. Fondazione Rosselli, 'Reparti e strutture specializzate di polizia investigativa' (chapter) in *Secondo Rapporto sulle Priorità Nazionali. La Criminalità Organizzata*, (Milan: Arnaldo Mondadori Editore, S.p.A., 1995) pp. 198–209.
12. Antimafia Commission, XI legislature, p. 765.
13. Ministero dell'Interno, 1994 *op. cit.*, p. 134.
14. For more details see A. Jamieson, 'Mafia and Institutional Power in Italy', *International Relations*, Vol. XII No.1, April 1994.
15. Ministero dell'Interno *Rapporto Annuale sul Fenomeno della Criminalità Organizzata* (1997) Rome, December, 1998.
16. *Direzione Investigativa Antimafia*, semi-annual report, December 1993, p. 79.
17. Interior Minister Giorgio Napolitano to the Antimafia Commission, session of 18 April 1997.
18. Antimafia Commission, XIII legislature, annual report, 7 July 1998, p. 28.
19. Information supplied by Home Office Minister Alan Michael, cited in *Guardian Weekly*, 24 August 1997.
20. *Corriere della Sera*, 5 January 1993.
21. General M. Nunzella, talk given at conference 'I Collaboratori di Giustizia', Fondazione Giovanni e Francesco Falcone, Palermo, 21 May 1994.
22. Author's interview with Antonio Manganelli, Questor of Palermo, Palermo, 28 May 1998.
23. Assistant chief prosecutor of Palermo Luigi Croce, in round table discussion organized by *La Repubblica*, 15 July 1993.
24. Fernando Masone, Chief of Police, to the Parliamentary Antimafia Commission, 1 July 1997.
25. L. Violante (ed.), *I Soldi della Mafia, Rapporto 1998*. (Bari: Laterza, 1998) pp. 264–5.
26. J. Benyon, S. Morris, M. Toye, A. Willis, A. Beck, *Police Forces in the New European Union: A Conspectus*. Centre for the Study of Public Order, University of Leicester, April 1995.
27. 'Per aspera ad veritatem' *Rivista di intelligence e di Cultura professionale*. Conference papers of European Seminar 'Falcon one' on organized crime, Rome 26–28 April 1995, p. 227.
28. SISMI Director Cesare Pucci and SISDE director Angelo Finocchiaro to the Parliamentary Antimafia Commission, 12 January 1993.
29. *Per aspera ad veritatem, op. cit.* pp. 249–55.
30. *Ibid.*, pp. 257–71.
31. *Panorama*, 10 March 1995.
32. *La Repubblica*, 24 July 1992.
33. *Il Sole 24 Ore*, 26 June 1992.
34. *Corriere della Sera*, 14 August 1992.
35. *La Repubblica*, 27 August 1992.
36. *La Repubblica*, 3–4 October 1993.
37. In conversation with the author, 8 July 1998, Rome.
38. Intervention at an 'Institutional Forum' on the occasion of the entering into force of the Europol Convention, Rome, 1 October 1998.

39. Pier Luigi Vigna in conversation with the author, Rome 8 July 1998.
40. Ilda Boccassini interviewed by Enzo Biagi on the programme 'Il Fatto', RAI Uno, 20 February 1998.
41. Giovanni Tinebra in conversation with the author, Rome, 11 June 1998.
42. Ilda Boccassini interviewed in *Panorama*, 3 March 1995.
43. I. Boccassini, 'Le Valutazioni sull'Attendibilità delle dichiarazioni dei collaboratori di giustizia e il tema dei riscontri', conference papers from *I collaboratori di giustizia: Legislazioni ed esperienze a confronto,* Fondazione Giovanni e Francesca Falcone, Palermo 21–22 May 1994.
44. For information concerning the forensic and scientific investigations I am indebted to technical director and chief chemist, Dr Giovanni Vadalà, and to his colleagues Franceso Saveria Romolo and Paolo Egidi, respectively technical director and chief explosives analyst, all of the Scientific Police department of the State Police in Rome.
45. This information comes from collaborator Giovanni Brusca, who personally detonated the bomb at Capaci. His account is given in S. Lodato, *Ho Ucciso Giovanni Falcone, La Confessione di Giovanni Brusca,* (Milan: Mondadori, 1999, p. 103).
46. Interview by the author with Giovanni Falcone, Rome, 28 February 1989.
47. Judge Gioacchino Natoli, in conversation with the author, Palermo, 6 June 1998.
48. A. Jamieson, *Collaboration. New legal and judicial procedures for countering terrorism*, Conflict Studies 257, Research Institute for the Study of Conflict and Terrorism, London, January 1993, and A. Jamieson, 'Le Organizzazioni Mafiose' (chapter) in L. Violante (ed.) *Storia d'Italia. Annale Criminalità*, (Milan: Einaudi, 1997) pp. 461–92.
49. *Direzione Investigativa Antimafia*, semi-annual report, June 1996, p. 22.
50. Information taken from *Procura della Repubblica presso il Tribunale di Palermo, Direzione Distrettuale Antimafia, Richiesta di autorizzazione a procedere nei confront di ANDREOTTI Giulio, Senatore della Repubblica*, Palermo, 27 March 1993.
51. Author's interview with Questor of Palermo, Antonio Manganelli (formerly director of the Central Protection Committee), Palermo, 28 May 1998.
52. Former Prefect of Palermo, former deputy national police chief, Senator Achille Serra, quoted in *Panorama,* 16 January 1997.
53. *Panorama*, 16 January 1997.
54. L. Violante (ed.) *Mafia e Società Italiana, Rapporto '97* (Bari: Laterza, 1997) p. 218.
55. *Panorama*, 30 October 1997.
56. M. Centorrino, 'Il Giro d'Affari delle Oganizzazioni Criminali', in L. Violante (ed.) *I Soldi della Mafia, Rapporto '98*, (Bari: Laterza, 1998) p. 14.
57. *Ibid.*, p. 17.
58. M. Centorrino and A. Giorgianni, 'L'Illegalità nel Sistema Finanziario: il Caso del Riciclaggio', in M. Centorrino and G. Signorino (eds) , *Macroeconmia della Mafia*, (Rome: La Nuova Italia Scientifica, 1997) p. 67.
59. G. Turone, 'La Lotta contro il Riciclaggio' in L. Violante (ed.) *Mafie e Antimafia, Rapporto '96*, (Bari: Laterza, 1996) p. 155.
60. Centorrino and Giorgianni in Centorrino and Signorino, *op. cit.* p. 58.
61. *Ibid.*

62. Ministero dell'Interno, *Rapporto sul Fenomeno della Criminalità organizzata (1996)*, September 1997.
63. Centorrino and Signorino, *op. cit.* p. 61.
64. *La Gazzetta del Sud*, 4 March 1995, cited in Centorrino and Signorino, *op. cit.* p. 60.
65. D. Masciandaro, 'Criminalità ed Attività Finanziarie Illegali nel Mezzogiorno', in Centorrino and Signorino, *op. cit.* p. 108.
66. Communication to the author from national antimafia prosecutor Pier Luigi Vigna, Rome, 19 November 1997.
67. Fondazione Rosselli, *Secondo Rapporto sulle Priorità Nazionali: La Criminalità Organizzata*, (various authors, individual chapters not attributed), (Milan: Arnaldo Mondadori, 1995) p. 173.
68. Council Act of 27 September 1996 drawing up the Convention relating to extradition between the Member States of the European Union. Official Journal C313, 23/10/96 p. 0011–0011.
69. R. Righetti, 'Techniche di Occultamento della Ricchezza da parte delle Organizzazioni Criminali, in L. Violante (ed.) 1998, *op. cit*, p. 82.
70. A. Pansa, Il Riciclaggio in Italia, in *ibid.*, pp. 90–135.
71. D. Masciandaro in Centorrino and Signorino, *op. cit.* p. 112.
72. *Ibid.*, p. 123.
73. *Corriere della Sera*, 10 January 1996.
74. D. Masciandaro, 'Criminalità ed Attività Finanziarie illegali nel Mezzogiorno: Riciclaggio ed Usura', in Centorino and Signorino, *op. cit.* pp. 112–14.
75. Oliver Galea, partner in Coopers Deloitte (Italy), in conversation with the author, Palermo, 2 June 1998.
76. Undersecretary of State at the Justice Ministry Giuseppe Ayala, quoted in *Corriere della Sera*, 20 February 1998.
77. Judge Gioacchino Natoli in conversation with the author, Palermo, 6 June 1998.
78. E. Ciconte, *Processo alla 'Ndrangheta*, (Bari: Laterza, 1996) pp. 140 and 143.
79. Condensation of statements made to the Parliamentary Antimafia Commission by: the deputy chairman of the CSM, Carlo Federico Grosso on 11 March 1997, by the judges of the Palermo prosecution service to the Commission on 5 February 1997, by Justice Minister Giovanni Maria Flick on 4 March 1997; also chief prosecutor Gian Carlo Caselli in conversation with the author, Palermo, 5 June 1998.
80. Assistant chief prosecutor of Palermo Guido Lo Forte to the Antimafia Commission, 5 February 1997.
81. Dr Emanuele Marotta, deputy director, Europol, the Hague, personal communication to the author, September 1998.

5 The grassroots antimafia

1. P. Borsellino, paper given at conference, '1992: In Europa senza Mafia' reproduced in *Secolo d'Italia*, 18 January 1989.
2. A. Puglisi, *Sole Contro la Mafia* (Palermo: La Luna, 1990).
3. Reproduced in *Narcomafie*, Turin, April 1996.

4. M. De Luca (ed.) *Nonostante Donna*. Storie Civili al Femminile, (Turin: Edizioni Gruppo Abele, 1996).
5. *Narcomafie*, Turin, June 1996.
6. De Luca, *op. cit.* p. 56.
7. Speech reproduced in *Narcomafie*, Turin, June 1996.
8. Father C. Scordato, 'Chiesa e Mafia' in *Mafia e Società Italiana, Rapporto '97*, (Bari: Laterza, 1997) p. 69.
9. N. MacKenzie, *Secret Societies*, (London: Aldus Books, 1967) p. 261, quoted in D. Gambetta, *La Mafia Siciliana*, (Turin: Einaudi Tascabili, 1994) p. 59.
10. Gambetta 1994, *op. cit.* p. 60.
11. Cited in F.M. Stabile, 'Chiesa e Mafia', in *L'Antimafia Difficile*, (ed. U. Santino), (Palermo: Centro Siciliano di Documentazione Giuseppe Impastato, 1989) p. 110.
12. *Ibid.*, p. 115.
13. Cited in S. Lodato, *Dieci Anni di Mafia*, (Milan: Rizzoli, 1990) p. 102.
14. F.M. Stabile, in Santino 1989, *op. cit.* p. 119.
15. G. Brunelli, 'I Silenzi e le Grida', in *Narcomafie*, Turin, June 1993.
16. Entire document reproduced in *La Repubblica*, 29 September 1992.
17. *Corriere della Sera*, 9 October 1992.
18. Final communiqué of Sicilian episcopal conference, CESI, 3 October 1992, quoted in G. Brunelli 'I Silenzi e le Grida' in *Narcomafie*, Turin, June 1993 p. 25.
19. *L'Unità*, 10 May 1993.
20. Padre Scordato and associates of the San Saverio Centre in conversation with the author, 29 May 1998, Palermo.
21. *Sunday Telegraph*, London, 11 October 1998.
22. In conversation with the author, February 1993.
23. *La Mafia Restituisce il Maltolto, Guida all'Applicazione della Legge 109/96 sull'Uso Sociale dei Beni Confiscati ai Mafiosi*, (Turin: Edizioni Gruppo Abele, 1998).
24. *La Repubblica*, 27 April 1993.
25. G. Chinnici, U. Santino *La Violenza Programmata*, (Milan: Franco Angeli, 1989); U. Santino, G. La Fiura, *L'Impresa Mafiosa* (Milan: Franco Angeli, 1990); G. Chinnici, U. Santino, G. La Fiura, U. Adragna, *Gabbie Vuote* (Milan: Franco Angeli, 1992).
26. E. Villa, *Narcomafie*, Turin, May 1994, pp. 6–7.
27. P. Giannino, *Narcomafie*, Turin, July–August 1994, p. 15.
28. A. Grimaldi, *Narcomafie*, Turin, February 1993, p. 36.
29. L. Sommella, 'Napoli: Ragazzi a Rischio', in M. Cavallo (ed.) *Le Nuove Criminalità, Ragazzi Vittime e Protagonisti* (Milan: Franco Angeli, 1995) p. 76.
30. Census carried out by *Libera*, 1994–98.
31. In L. Violante (ed.) *Mafia e Società Italiana, Rapporto '97*, (Bari, Laterza, 1997) p. 272.
32. *Ibid.*, p. 276.
33. F. Ramella, C. Triglia, 'Associazionismo e mobilitazione contro la criminalità organizzata nel Mezzogiorno' in Violante 1997, *op. cit.* p. 33.
34. *Ibid.*, p. 287.
35. *Ibid.*, pp. 270–1.
36. *Ibid.*, p. 288.
37. L. Violante, (ed.) Introduction to *Mafie e Antimafia Rapporto '96*, (Bari: Laterza, 1996) p. xiv.

38. S. Lupo, 'Di Fronte alla Mafia: Consenso, Passività, Resistenza', in L. Violante 1997, *op. cit.* p. 20.
39. Ramella and Triglia in Violante 1997, *op. cit.* p. 26.
40. F. Ramella, C. Triglia in Violante 1997, *op. cit.* pp. 24–46.
41. http://www.itdf.pa.cnr.it/web/praesidium/falcone.html
42. *Corriere della Sera*, 15 July 1997.
43. *Corriere della Sera*, 17 February 1998.
44. Author's interview with Giovanni Falcone, Rome, 28 February 1989.
45. *Corriere della Sera*, 21 February 1999.
46. *Narcomafie*, Turin, July–August 1997, p. 34.
47. Author's interview with Antonio Manganelli, Palermo Chief of Police, Palermo, 28 May 1998.
48. Noted in Chronology prepared by the Centro Siciliano di Documentazione, in *Narcomafie*, Turin, June 1996 p. 33.
49. *Avvenimenti,* 28 January 1998.
50. U. Santino, *Oltre la Legalità* (Palermo: CSD Appunti 6, 1997) p. 47.
51. Ugo Pastore, judge of Juvenile Criminal Court, Naples, intervention at the International Seminar 'Criminal Organization and Exploitation of Minors' organized by the International Association of Juvenile and Family Court Magistrates, Naples, 4–6 April 1997.
52. Judge Piero Gaeta, *Ibid.*
53. Santino 1997, *op. cit.* p. 53.
54. G. Falcone, *Interventi e Proposte (1982–1992)* (Milan: Sansoni Editore, 1994) pp. 343–4.

6 The international response

1. Jan Ruml, interviewed by news agency ANSA, cited in *La Repubblica*, 26 June 1991.
2. *Le Monde*, 22 July 1992.
3. *Ibid.*
4. Antonio Manganelli, Police Chief of Palermo, interviewed by the author, Palermo, 28 May 1998.
5. Conference 'Drugs, the New Evil Empire' organized by RISCT (London) and news agency adn kronos (Rome) to launch the publication of A. Jamieson, *Drug Trafficking after 1992*, Conflict Studies 250, RISCT May 1992.
6. *La Repubblica*, 12 June 1992.
7. *Der Spiegel* 35/1992.
8. *La Repubblica*, 27 August 1992.
9. *Corriere della Sera*, 13 September 1992.
10. See in particular, 'Appropriate Modalities and Guidelines for the Prevention and Control of Organized Transnational Crime at the Regional and International Levels' a working paper prepared for the World Ministerial Conference against Transnational Organized Crime, reproduced in The United Nations and Transnational Organized Crime, *Transnational Organized Crime* Special Issue, Vol. 1, No. 3, Autumn 1995, (eds) P. Williams and E.U. Savona, Frank Cass, London.

11. E/CONF.88/7 12 July 1994. Conclusions and Recommendations of the International Conference on Preventing and Controlling Money Laundering and the Use of the Proceeds of Crime: A Global Approach. 18–20 June 1994.

12. E/CN.15/1997/7 'Implementation of the Naples Political Declaration and Global Action Plan against Organized Transnational Crime', Commission on Crime Prevention and Criminal Justice.

13. E/CN.15/1997/7/Add.2 16 April 1997. Presented to the Commission on Crime Prevention and Criminal Justice, 28 April–9 May 1997.

14. E/CN.15/1998/5 18 February 1998. Presented to the Commission on Crime Prevention and Criminal Justice, 21–30 April 1998.

15. E/CN.15/1997/7/Add.1.

16. E/CN.15/1997/6 Report on the Intergovernmental Expert Group Meeting on Extradition, held at Siracusa, Italy from 10–13 December 1996.

17. *International Herald Tribune*, 17 August 1995.

18. *Direzione Investigativa Antimafia*, semi-annual report, June 1996, p. 74.

19. The Birmingham Summit, 17 May 1998 on http://birmingham.g8summit.gov.uk.

20. Doc 12247/1/94 ENFOPOL 161 REV 1.

21. Cited in Home Affairs Committee *Third Report. Organized Crime* (London: HMSO, July 1995), para. 73.

22. *Ibid.*, para. 72.

23. Personal communication from Dr Emanuele Marotta, deputy director Europol, The Hague on 18 November 1998.

24. *Direzione Investigativa Antimafia*, semi-annual report, December 1995, p. 77.

25. *Ibid.*, p. 73.

26. *Direzione Investigativa Antimafia* semi-annual report, December 1994 p. 103.

27. *Direzione Investigativa Antimafia*, semi-annual report, June 1996, p. 77.

28. *Direzione Investigativa Antimafia*, semi-annual report, December 1993, p. 110.

29. *Direzione Investigativa Antimafia*, semi-annual report, December 1994, p. 103.

30. *Direzione Investigativa Antimafia*, semi-annual report, December 1995, p. 79.

31. *Direzione Investigativa Antimafia*, semi-annual report January 1998, p. 71.

32. *Direzione Investigativa Antimafia*, semi-annual report, December 1995, p. 79.

33. *Ibid.*, p. 80.

34. *Direzione Investigativa Antimafia*, semi-annual report , June 1996, p. 77.

35. *Direzione Investigativa Antimafia*, semi-annual report, December 1995, p. 80.

36. *Direzione Investigativa Antimafia*, semi-annual report, December 1993, p. 112–3.

37. *Direzione Investigativa Antimafia*, semi-annual report, January 1998, pp. 69–70.

38. *Direzione Investigativa Antimafia*, semi-annual report, December 1994, p. 109.

39. Home Affairs Committee *op. cit.* para. 21.

40. EDU/Europol, Situation Report on Organized Crime in the European Union 1996.

41. *Direzione Investigativa Antimafia*, semi-annual report, June 1996, p. 78–9.

42. *Direzione Investigativa Antimafia*, semi-annual report, December 1995, p. 82.

43. *Direzione Investigativa Antimafia*, semi-annual report, June 1996, p. 85–6.

44. C. Sterling, *Crime Without Frontiers* (London: Little, Brown, 1994), p. 119.

45. *Direzione Investigativa Antimafia*, semi-annual report, December 1994, p. 108.

46. *Rapport de la Commission D'Enquête' sur les moyens de lutter contre les tentatives de pénétration de la Mafia en France', publié au Journal Officiel*, 28 January 1993.

47. *Direzione Investigativa Antimafia*, semi-annual report, June 1996, p. 82.

48. *Direzione Investigativa Antimafia*, semi-annual report, December 1995, p. 85.
49. *Ibid.*, p. 84.
50. Home Affairs Committee, *op. cit.* para. 2.
51. *Ibid.*, para. 46.
52. *Ibid.*, para. 75.
53. *Ibid.*, para. 63.
54. *Ibid.*, para. 170.
55. Home Office Working Group on Confiscation. Third Report: Criminal Assets, November 1998.
56. NCIS Annual Report, 1993/94.
57. *Direzione Investigativa Antimafia*, semi-annual report, June 1996, p. 80.
58. M. Smith (author *of New Cloak, Old Dagger: How Britain's Spies Came in from the Cold*, Gollanz, London 1997) in the *Weekend Telegraph*, 26 October 1996.
59. Home Office Circular 46/96 14 October 1996.
60. National Crime Squad, 1 April 1998.
61. Home Affairs Committee, *op. cit.* para. 77.
62. M. Galeotti, 'Mafiya: Organized Crime in Russia', *Jane's Intelligence Review, Special Report No. 10*, June 1996 and L. Fituni (Director, Center for Strategic and Global Studies, Russian Academy of Sciences) in conference paper, *CIS: Organized Crime and its International Activities,* Hanns Seidel Foundation, Wildbad Kreuth, 22–24 September 1993.
63. Detective Inspector G. Saltmarsh, in conference paper, 'The Expansion of Transnational Organised Crime into the Upperworld Business Community', Unisys International Management Centre, St Paul de Vence, France, 21–21 September 1998.
64. R. Tjalkens, Europol Drugs Unit, 'The Effectivenss of the Anti-Money-Laundering Measures within the E.U.', paper given at conference 'Anti-Money-Laundering and Economic Crime', Jurys Hotel and Towers, Dublin, 30 March 1998.
65. E.U. Savona, 'Problemi e Strumenti dell'Azione Internazionale di Contrasto al Riciclaggio', in L. Violante (ed.) *I Soldi della Mafia. Rapporto '98* (Bari: Laterza, 1998) p. 239.
66. Tjalkens, *op. cit.*
67. M. Cassard, *The Role of Offshore Centres in International Financial Intermediation*, IMF Working paper (WP/94/107), September 1994.
68. Gian Carlo Caselli, chief prosecutor of Palermo, interviewed by the author, Palermo, 5 June 1998.
69. Personal communication from Dr Emanuele Marotta, deputy director, Europol, the Hague.
70. Jack A. Blum, *Enterprise Crime: Financial Fraud in International Interspace*, Working Group on Organized Crime, National Strategy Information Center, Washington DC, June 1997.
71. *The Politics of Corruption and the Corruption of Politics*, Report on Corruption, NACLA Report on the Americas Vol. XXVII, No. 3, November/December 1993.

7 War ... and peace?

1. *Ministero degli Interni, Rapporto Annuale sulla Criminalità Organizzata in Italia (1993)* Rome, April 1994, p. 367.

2. *L'Unità*, 28 April 1993.
3. A. Jamieson, 'Mafia and Institutional Power in Italy', *International Relations* Vol. XII, No. 1, April 1994.
4. DIA report cited in *Panorama*, 5 September 1993.
5. G. De Gennaro, vice-capo della Polizia, Direttore Centrale della Polizia Criminale, in *Per Aspera ad Veritatem*, Atti del 1° Seminario Europeo 'Falcone One' sulla Criminalità Organizzata, Roma, (conference organized by SISDE) 26–27–28 April, 1995 pp. 293–306.
6. The testimonies of state's witnesses concerning the 1993 attacks were first illustrated by Pier Luigi Vigna, then chief prosecutor of Florence, in a paper entitled 'Strategia terroristico-mafiosa connessa con gli attentati del 1993 in Italia: una riconstruzione completa' at the SISDE conference cited above, *Per Aspera ad Veritam*, 1995, pp. 273–91.
7. Filippo Malvagna to the prosecution offices in Catania and Rome, 8 April 1994.
8. Salvatore Annacondia to the Rome prosecution office, 11 August 1993.
9. Salvatore Cancemi to the Caltanissetta prosecution office, 16 February 1994.
10. Maurizio Avola to the Catania prosecution office, 17 March 1994.
11. *Corriere della Sera*, 13 September 1997.
12. *La Repubblica*, 14 January 1998.
13. *Corriere della Sera*, 5 August 1996.
14. Vigna/SISDE 1995, *op. cit.*
15. P.L.Vigna, 'Le Tracce di chi Ordinò le Stragi', in *Mafia e Antimafia, Rapporto 1996*, (ed.) L. Violante, (Bari: Laterza, 1996) pp. 100–15.
16. Antimafia Commission. XI Legislature, Report on the links between Mafia and Politics, Rome, 1995, p. 61.
17. *Ibid.*, p. 63.
18. Liana Milella in *Panorama*, 5 September 1993.
19. Salvatore Cancemi to the Florence prosecution office, 8 March 1994.
20. *Corriere della Sera*, 27 March 1997.
21. *La Repubblica*, 14 January 1998.
22. Pier Luigi Vigna to the Parliamentary Antimafia Commission, Rome, 27 January 1998.
23. *La Repubblica*, 6 October 1997.
24. Pier Luigi Vigna in conversation with the author, Rome, 8 July 1998.
25. Testimony by Giovanni Brusca to Caltanissetta court, 23 January 1999, cited in *Corrierre della Sera*, 11 February 1999.
26. *Corriere della Sera*, 24 July 1993.
27. *Corriere della Sera*, 25 September 1997.
28. Statement made in Florence court by Giovanni Brusca, cited in *Corriere della Sera*, 22 May 1997.
29. Statement made in Florence court by Giovanni Brusca, cited in *Corriere della Sera*, 28 March 1997.
30. T. De Zulueta, 'How Sindona Swindled the World', *Sunday Times*, 6 January 1980.
31. Quoted in S. Turone, *Partiti e Mafia dalla P2 alla Droga*, (Bari: Laterza, 1985) p. 258.

32. *Procura della Repubblica presso il Tribunale di Palermo, Direzione Distrettuale Antimafia, Richiesta di autorizzazione a procedere nei confronti di Andreotti Giulio, Senatore della Repubblica,* 27 March 1993.

33. The information for the summary comes from the official request by the Palermo prosecution service to the Senate to proceed against Senator Andreotti, as per note 32 above. There were two supplements to the request, dated 13 April 1993, and 19 April 1993. See also: A. Bolzoni and G. D'Avanzo, 'I processi a Giulio Andreotti: Palermo' in Violante, 1996, *op. cit,* pp. 72–87.

34. *Ibid.,* p. 79.

35. *Ibid.*

36. Interrogation of T. Buscetta by G. Falcone on 1 February 1988. Contained in *Richiesta di autorizzazione,* 23 March 1993.

37. *Osservatorio Milanese sulla Criminalità Organizzata al Nord* (Omicron) No. 6, Settembre/Ottobre 1997.

38. Ministero dell'Interno, *Rapporto sulla Criminalità Organizzata in Italia (1995),* Rome June 1996.

39. U. Marchetti, G. Ganzer, A. Pansa, 'Impegno Investigativo e strategie inquirenti in Italia', in *The Waste Industry: Italy–America Achieving a Crime-Free Market,* New York, 5–6 June 1997, conference papers published by New York University School of Law and Eurispes, Rome, December 1997, pp. 62–81.

40. Ministero dell'Interno, *Rapporto sulla Criminalità organizzata in Italia (1996),* Rome, September 1997, p. 264.

41. *Corriere della Sera,* 21 March 1998.

42. R. Siebert, 'La Mafia e le Donne' in L. Violante (ed.) *Mafia e Società Italiana, Rapporto 1997,* (Bari: Laterza, 1997), pp. 108–30.

43. *Giornale di Sicilia,* 28 June 1995, cited in Siebert, *op. cit.*

44. A. Block, *East Side–West Side, Organizing Crime in New York 1930–1950,* (New Brunswick, N.J: Transaction Press, 1982).

45. A. Bolzoni, S. Lodato, *C'era Una Volta la Lotta alla Mafia,* (Milan: Garzanti, 1998).

46. Interview by Liana Milella, *La Repubblica,* 5 November 1997.

47. *La Stampa,* 25 January 1988.

48. U. Santino, *Sicilia 102, Caduti nella lotta contro la Mafia e per la democrazia dal 1893 al 1994,* (Palermo: Centro Siciliano di documentazione Giuseppe Impastato, 1994).

Index

(heavy type means the pages are particularly devoted to the subject)